MW00620473

"Occasionally we encounter a book that t̩ touches upon a deeper level of personal exp(living with music. They help us reconnect w̩ ....ure, with its inspiring, comforting, and reconciling presence."

Jan Baars, Extraordinary Professor of Aging,
University of Humanistic Studies, Netherlands

"This book is a joy to read. In clear, compelling language, the authors explain the pathways by which music brings coherence, joy, healing, and growth to our lives. Packed with evidence and personal stories, the volume is a fabulous achievement and a significant addition to the field."

Andrea Creech, Professor of Music Pedagogy, McGill University, Canada

"This is an extraordinary treatise on the impact of music and aging on our lives. The authors achieve a beautiful balance between humanism, science, and spirituality in a writing style that is universally accessible. The book is an inspiring guide to achieving balance and wellness in oneself and society."

J. Todd Frazier, Director of the System Center for Performing
Arts Medicine, Houston Methodist Hospital, USA

"The authors have masterfully examined complex topics, presenting insightful research and demonstrating music's unique ability to positively influence wellness throughout the aging process. Professional and recreational musicians seeking a broader understanding of music's transformative characteristics will benefit from this impactful resource."

Susan Hochmiller, Assistant Professor of Voice, Gettysburg College, USA

"This clever book explains music and music therapy through a scientific lens and personal stories. It provides intriguing insights and an optimistic view on aging and personal growth. What a gift!"

Hanne Mette Ridder, Professor of Music Therapy, Aalborg University, Denmark

"Warning: This book may inspire you to dust off an old musical instrument, join a choir, or unearth your vinyl collection...."

Katie Overy, Reid School of Music, University of Edinburgh, Scotland

"This is a major study which develops a compelling argument for the importance of music in promoting health and wellbeing. The authors provide a stimulating and original argument about the transformative power of music. It is an important reference for academics and practitioners alike."

Chris Phillipson, Professor of Sociology and Sociology Gerontology,
University of Manchester, UK

"The authors have managed to weave current social issues and scientific, philosophical, spiritual, and psychological literature together into one magnificent symphony. It is a beautiful homage to the power of music. This is a truly wonderful source for both scholars and music lovers!"

Toru Sato, Professor of Psychology, Shippensburg University, USA

Music, Wellness, and Aging

Music is a metaphor that connects people to a profound sense of life. In this book, music intersects with wellness and aging as humans adapt to life changes, stay engaged, remain creative, and achieve self-actualization. Along with discussion of cutting-edge research, the book presents stories and interviews from everyday people as well as professional and nonprofessional musicians. It discusses individual and social wellness, age-related and pathological changes in health, music therapies, personal resilience and growth, interpersonal and community relationships, work and retirement, spirituality, and the psychology of aging. The case studies show how music, wellness, and aging connect to define, direct, and celebrate life, as these three concepts allow people to connect with others, break down barriers, and find common ground.

Scott F. Madey is Emeritus Professor of Psychology at Shippensburg University, Pennsylvania.

Dean D. VonDras is Professor of Psychology at the University of Wisconsin–Green Bay, Wisconsin.

Music, Wellness, and Aging

Defining, Directing, and Celebrating Life

Scott F. Madey

Shippensburg University, Pennsylvania

Dean D. VonDras

University of Wisconsin–Green Bay

CAMBRIDGE
UNIVERSITY PRESS

CAMBRIDGE
UNIVERSITY PRESS

University Printing House, Cambridge CB2 8BS, United Kingdom

One Liberty Plaza, 20th Floor, New York, NY 10006, USA

477 Williamstown Road, Port Melbourne, VIC 3207, Australia

314–321, 3rd Floor, Plot 3, Splendor Forum, Jasola District Centre, New Delhi – 110025, India

79 Anson Road, #06–04/06, Singapore 079906

Cambridge University Press is part of the University of Cambridge.

It furthers the University's mission by disseminating knowledge in the pursuit of education, learning, and research at the highest international levels of excellence.

www.cambridge.org
Information on this title: www.cambridge.org/9781108844697
DOI: 10.1017/9781108953290

© Scott F. Madey and Dean D. VonDras 2021

This publication is in copyright. Subject to statutory exception and to the provisions of relevant collective licensing agreements, no reproduction of any part may take place without the written permission of Cambridge University Press.

First published 2021

A catalogue record for this publication is available from the British Library.

Library of Congress Cataloging-in-Publication Data
Names: Madey, Scott F., 1956– author. | VonDras, Dean D., author.
Title: Music, wellness, and aging : defining, directing, and celebrating life / Scott F. Madey, Dean D. VonDras.
Description: New York, NY : Cambridge University Press, 2021. | Includes bibliographical references and index.
Identifiers: LCCN 2020046976 (print) | LCCN 2020046977 (ebook) | ISBN 9781108844697 (hardback) | ISBN 9781108953290 (ebook)
Subjects: LCSH: Aging – Social aspects. | Well-being – Age factors. | Music and older people.
Classification: LCC HQ1061 .M3223 2021 (print) | LCC HQ1061 (ebook) | DDC 305.26–dc23
LC record available at https://lccn.loc.gov/2020046976
LC ebook record available at https://lccn.loc.gov/2020046977

ISBN 978-1-108-84469-7 Hardback
ISBN 978-1-108-94873-9 Paperback

Cambridge University Press has no responsibility for the persistence or accuracy of URLs for external or third-party internet websites referred to in this publication and does not guarantee that any content on such websites is, or will remain, accurate or appropriate.

Contents

Program Notes
Music, Wellness, and Aging

I am very surprised to find out how much I enjoy aging ... Nobody ever believes me when I say it, but I get more fun out of being 78 than I ever did at being 58 and certainly 38. Now it is true that one can't see so well ... and I can't concentrate as long, but I can hear music ... I find I have more to do now that is fun.

– Rollo May[1]

At the beginning of a concert, we often receive the program with its attending "preface" that lists information about the musical pieces to be performed, the composer, and the ensemble members and key players. This information often announces various essential features of the music and what to listen for, as well as historical or personal events that inspired the composer. The musical work often intends to tell a story that metaphorically portrays and provides interpretation of our living experiences. As we begin our discussion of *Music, Wellness, and Aging,* we also provide "program notes" that detail what the reader may expect and what to "listen" for, and a little background about what inspires our work.

As the existential therapist Rollo May alludes to in the epigraph, in this book we hope to describe how music may be a key feature of enjoyment in later life, and how music may benefit our well-being. In doing so, we invite the reader to also explore how music is part of their everyday life, and how it may serve as a resource that aids and enhances their living.

In writing this book, we wrestled with how to approach the weighty topics of music, wellness, and aging – topics large enough in their own right, but we also had to consider the challenges in integrating these concepts into a coherent discussion. For us, we had to find a balance between our effort to express the transcendent quality of these concepts and to maintain scientific integrity. Thus, in our discussion we describe relevant scientific research, and present stories about everyday people, as well as professional and nonprofessional musicians who enjoy music. Each chapter of the book describes the intersection of music with wellness and aging, and includes topics such as the well-being of the individual and

society, longevity and age-related physical changes, age-associated neurological illnesses and everyday functioning, the rehabilitative and therapeutic potential of music, the effect of music on work routines and
adjustment in retirement, and how music may serve as an orienting aspect
of one's spirituality and way of understanding end-of-life issues. In discussing these topics and others, we embrace the phenomenological–
humanistic approach of Carl Rogers, Abraham Maslow, Carl Jung, and
others.[2] In doing so, we emphasize the importance of understanding the
whole person, their unique characteristics and insights, and the key
concerns they address throughout their developmental journey and in
later life. Further, we recognize how one's unique life experiences inform
and define how we look at the processes of development and adaptation,
and how music may play an important role in our personal growth and
wellness as we age. In this book, we emphasize personal stories that
express ways of adapting and coping and in finding new understanding
and moments of celebration in later life.

Charting of the Chapters

Chapter 1 is titled "Overture." An overture is the introduction to an
extended orchestral work or opera. This first chapter introduces the
connection of music to wellness as we age. It underscores that music is
a pervasive influence, found in all cultures, and embodies the heart and
soul of a people. We discuss how music may be beneficial to both the
person and society. Further, we establish the phenomenological–humanistic orientation of music, wellness, and aging. This approach recognizes
social connection as a basic need, and self-actualization as an essential
human motivation. Self-actualization refers to a need for personal
growth, where there is the expression and fulfillment of the upper limits
of one's abilities, talents, and greatest possibilities, and the essence of who
we are that is reflected in creative activities such as music. We further note
that the process of self-actualization is a central aspect of our well-being
throughout the life course.[3]

In Chapter 2, "In Search of a Perfect Harmony: Music and Wellness in
Later Life," we discuss physical changes that are encountered in aging
and how music may optimize health outcomes and wellness. A harmony is
a combination of simultaneously sounded musical notes that may express
emotional tensions as well as relieving and pleasing effects. Thus, this
discussion underscores how music may influence exercise patterns, contribute to a healthy lifestyle, and be used as a coordinating element in the
structuring of our everyday living.

In Chapter 3, "Hearing the Muse's Message: Changes in Sensory–Perceptual and Cognitive Processes," the existential concerns of the great Maestro Ludwig van Beethoven are noted; how he was able to compose musical masterpieces while confronting severe hearing loss is discussed. In this chapter, we also describe age-related changes in sensory–perceptual and memory systems that underlie one's musical experiences. There is also discussion of how musical activities may affect the neurological processes involved in learning and memory, their use in coping with pain, and, despite chronic illness, still may provide the person a source of enjoyment and emotional connection with others.

In Chapter 4, "Sing a New Song! Therapeutic Interventions with Music," we continue our discussion of how music may provide therapeutic benefit. This chapter broadens our discussion of music as a therapy, and describes the beneficial use of music in the areas of depression, recovery from stroke, and other neurological impairments such as Alzheimer's disease. In accord with our humanistic tack, we emphasize the whole-person approach as we consider neurological impairments and the promise of music therapy to facilitate cognitive–behavioral function and to cope with disability. Therefore, we describe pathological changes in neurocognitive performance and how music may afford opportunities for regaining behavioral function, self-expression, and enhanced quality of life.

In Chapter 5, "Trio: Resilience, Recovery, and Growth," we discuss how music may play a role in confronting age-associated health and wellness concerns. A trio refers to a group of three musicians, such as a jazz trio, but also refers to a composition written for three instruments or with three chapters. Correspondingly, the central focus of this chapter is on resiliency, the capacity to recuperate quickly; recovery, the return to wellness; and personal growth, the process of gaining new insight, understanding, and adapting. Again, embracing a humanistic orientation, we explore how music may give vital meaning to life, aid in the recovery from surgery, and provide assistance in managing illnesses. Scientific as well as personal descriptions of how musical activities may bolster well-being and provide a path to illness management and recovery are offered.

How music may be connected with broader social and interpersonal concerns is taken up in Chapter 6, "Tutti: Music in Relationships and Communities." The musical term "tutti" connotes that a passage is to be performed with all voices or instruments together. Therefore, in this chapter we expand our discussion to consider social experiences and involvements, and how music may facilitate social attachment and affiliations in later life. We also consider systems of community and social support, mentoring, and how music may offer a bridge between age and cultural groups. This discussion importantly acknowledges that through music we can practice social justice.

The rhythmic patterns of careers and what happens when we retire are taken up in Chapter 7, "Rhythm and Blues: Work and Retirement." Rhythm and blues is a style of music that combines the deeply felt and soulful concerns of life with very accented and shifting rhythms. The rhythm and blues influence can be found in the musical styles of funk, hip-hop, and rock. Thus, this chapter describes how music might be used motivationally in the workplace and how it may be a central activity in our retirement. Beyond music's ability to direct and positively affect our work and retirement, we discuss career choices and the vicissitudes of workplace and career changes. We also note stages of retirement and concerns for equity in the workplace and the economics of retirement. We also discuss ways of making a musical "comeback."

In Chapter 8, "Requiem: Spirituality and End of Life," we again discuss music as a reflection of our deepest and most important existential concerns. Indeed, music connects us with the transcendent and is used to express our spirituality. The term "requiem" refers to music that honors those who have died. Thus in this chapter, we discuss death and dying, and our approach to living that gives us comfort, hope, and a sense of finality. We also explore Buddhist thought (e.g., right view, right livelihood) as a metaphor and method to apply to our attitude toward music and music as a profession. This chapter recognizes how music may be involved in spiritual expressions and in the celebration of the end of life.

In Chapter 9, "Coda: Defining, Directing, and Celebrating Life," a final discussion emphasizes the unique experience of each person as they continue into later life. The term "Coda" refers to the concluding passage of a musical piece or movement. Therefore, in this discussion we again recognize how music may make available new ways to understand the existential challenges of aging, and to direct us in the enterprise of self-actualization and wellness. As Rollo May notes, in the process of aging we seek to bring together and integrate our understandings of all the earlier times of our life, and find new ways of adapting to and enjoying life.[4] We point out entrapments of aging (e.g., the belief that aging is all about decline) and how to overcome them. Moreover, we suggest that music may help older adults look at the world in a fresh, new way and to make positive adjustments to life's challenges. As a universal phenomenon, we note that music breaks down barriers that separate us from others, allowing us to see that which is common to all of us, and to celebrate living.

Reasons for Writing This Book

The reader may ask how we have come to write about music, wellness, and aging in the first place. This is easy to answer, we think, for the following reasons: We believe that music reflects our deepest existential concerns and connects us to a richer sense of the life we hold and the transcendental experience we live out. Indeed, whether it is composing, performing, or simply listening to music, we become involved in the "transformative practice of self-actualization."[5] Thus, we realize that music provides a novel avenue for understanding the processes of wellness and aging. Further, as we recognize how music is often reflective of who we are and where we are headed in life, we realize too that music connects us to ways of staying healthy and happy throughout adulthood.

Music is suggested to be a holistic experience that "draws on body, space, time and relationships to offer a sacred experience."[6] Therefore a second reason to write this book is to provide insight into the interdependencies that we recognize when we consider central life activities such as the enjoyment of music and its involvement with and influence on health and development through the adult years. We acknowledge interdependencies and connections exist among many areas and aspects of our living. Much like Carl Jung's distinction of and relationship between individualistic and collective viewpoints in his psychological writings, we too note the connectedness of all of our areas of living and the interdependencies of life forces. Thus, much like the dynamic contextualism suggested in the Talmudic understanding that "We don't see things the way they are, we see things the way *we* are," we propose that to best understand wellness in later life is to explore this interest through a phenomenon such as music – a phenomenon that is noted for its ability to dynamically shape and influence our thought and action, activate and entrain neurological processes, and stir our emotions and artistic motivations. So much like the oneness that comes forth from the duality expressed by the concept of Yin and Yang in Daoist philosophy, we hope to understand in a deeper way all the different aspects of the person in development, recognizing the interchange and influences of music with wellness and aging.

A third reason to write this book is with the layperson in mind. A large body of literature on the topics of psychology of music, aging, and wellness has been the purview of a specialized readership. However, as the psychologist Daryl Bem[7] advised, it is best to always write in a way that everyone can understand. Thus, we take his advice in writing this book and hope that it invites both the lay reader and the specialist to discover and enliven new interests in the music they have enjoyed throughout their life. Indeed, we hope that our focus on research, personal narratives, and stories of others will assist the reader in considering and coming to a greater understanding of the importance of music in their own process of growth and development in later life, and to realize how music defines, directs, and leads them into a celebration of living.

About the Authors

This book is a natural outgrowth of both authors' musical backgrounds, their scholarly focus, and professional collaboration of more than 25 years. Dean holds a BA in music and a PhD in psychology. He plays piano, and has been a member of bands and ensemble groups since elementary school. He is currently professor of psychology at the University of Wisconsin–Green Bay, where his research and teaching focus on adult development, health, and aging. As Dean describes, "As a young child, I remember hearing at nap-times my Mom singing songs that she liked best and felt comforting to children. My Mom and Dad loved music – it was always a part of our family life. Both Mom and Dad, wanting to give their children something more than they had growing up, enrolled all my brothers and sisters in music classes, where we each learned to play a musical instrument and became members of school bands. We all acquired a love for music. And, beyond our early schooling, some of us went on to learn other instruments and continue our involvement in music. Perhaps in a way that is most basic, I learned that music is an expression of the deepest concerns of the person – and a universal language. I learned too that music often describes and reflects our development, from early childhood to old age; the essential aspects of ethnic and cultural communities; and characteristics of sociohistorical eras. Thus, whether expressing feelings of deep intimacy in a love song, or life struggles reflected in the blues, or the transcendent and pastoral characteristics of nature heralded in symphonies and folk songs, in many ways music characterizes our inner world of experience and connection with the universe around us. I believe that music depicts the most essential aspects of our psychology because it fundamentally depicts how we are and who we are. Moreover, it portrays, and in some ways may even direct, our movement across the life course. Therefore, I feel music affords us a window through which we can look to understand both our psychology and our development in later life."

Scott is an emeritus professor and holds a PhD in psychology. He has taught at Cornell University, University of Toledo, and Washington University in St. Louis; since 1998 he has taught at Shippensburg University. He has taught courses such as the history of psychology, multicultural health psychology, and the social psychology of aging. During his last year of teaching, he developed a course on the psychology of music. He is also a musician who plays the French horn, alto horn, and guitar. He has played professionally and semiprofessionally all over the United States and is currently involved in the community concert band, swing band, and German band; he also plays in a jazz duo. As Scott describes the influence of music in his life, he notes, "I started in middle school playing trumpet that my dad rented and then moved to French horn (that I still play to this day). Early on, I became interested in guitar (around age 14). Mom and Dad scraped together enough money to get me a guitar and amplifier. Throughout high school and beyond, I played in music groups. I later found out that my mom sang in a big band when she was younger. One of my grandfathers, a coal miner, also played bass fiddle in a band on weekends and at weddings. I was fortunate to live in many places in the United States and to play music with folks from a variety of cultures and musical expressions, ranging from Tennessee, Texas, Virginia, Ohio, New York, and Pennsylvania, where I presently live. Although I primarily focus on playing jazz these days, I am eclectic in my listening and playing, appreciating all styles. The people I met and the places I lived are part of my character and make up who I am and how I conduct myself toward others."

So in many ways, apart from our training in psychology and background as university professors, both authors are also lovers of music, involved musicians, and musicologists. However, we do not feel we are exceptional in our love of music. Our appreciation and enjoyment of music is something we share with most everyone else! In fact, a recent in-depth study of consumer interaction with music in the United States conducted by the Nielsen Company indicated that 90 percent of the population listens to music every day and on average does so about 32.1 hours a week.[8]

In Our Time of Living

At the time of this writing, the coronavirus (Covid-19) pandemic has triggered quarantines across the globe, and music is being used to cope and maintain hope, as well as to sustain a connection between and with people at this difficult time. This is also a time where there is dire and profound need for humanitarian relief and societal reforms to address the evils of racism, extreme economic disparity, and armed conflicts that restrict equal access to health care and medicines, proper nutrition, a safe place to live, educational and occupational opportunity, and protection from environmental and man-made hazards. Indeed, as we look throughout our local and global communities, we see a world with many ills. Yet, we also see and hear the voices of many who seek to protect those who are most vulnerable, to provide care and refuge for those displaced, and to offer hope and love. For example, the stage and screen celebrities Rita Wilson and Idris Elba, who both tested positive for the coronavirus, electronically sent their favorite playlist of songs to others to enjoy, as well as offered songs to convey their feelings and connection to others.[9] Similarly, in the lockdown quarantines that have occurred across the globe, people of all ages have sung songs and given impromptu performances from their apartment balconies and throughout their communities, lifting spirits and reflecting the expression of hope that music provides.[10] Moreover, as the coronavirus spread, the musical artists Lin-Manuel Miranda and Yo-Yo Ma launched a Web page that included personal concerts and the sharing of songs for people throughout the world to use as they adjusted to staying at home and continuing to connect with one another.[11] In a similar action, *El Sistema*, the comprehensive Venezuelan music education program, has broadcasted prerecorded concert programs by the Simon Bolivar Symphony Orchestra via YouTube to extol hope.[12] There has also been response to the pandemic of racism via the release of anti-racist songs and musical recordings by both amateur and professional musicians throughout the world.[13] Further, music initiatives and concerts have been undertaken to offer hope and garner humanitarian relief for those displaced because of war in Syria, for the Rohingya forced to flee their Myanmar homeland because of ethnic persecution, and for asylum seekers fleeing from violence in Central and South America.[14] As all these examples suggest, music reflects and expresses our deepest human concerns, needs, and yearnings and serves as an important vehicle to convey calls for action and movement toward social justice.

Societal ills such as these in many ways compel us to consider how we find meaning in our lives, how we connect to others, and how we continue to embrace our highest values and live with purpose. As we seek to understand how music is linked with wellness at this time, we understand, as arts therapist Natalie Rogers notes, that "The expressive arts are profound in helping people become aware of all their feelings and particularly help them accept their dark or shadow side. The arts are a way to channel that energy constructively. You can dance your rage, paint your fear, or despair. Then several things happen: you discover how to find inner balance, inner peace ... to have more compassion."[15] We also realize that there are many paths to defining, directing, and celebrating our later life and many ways of embracing wellness. Fundamentally, however, as Natalie Rogers further relates, we recognize that as we involve ourselves in the creative process, whether it is through composing a song, playing an instrument, singing with others, immersion in reflective listening, or dancing to music, we discover a variety of ways of responding to the challenges of the day and world that we confront. Indeed in our creativity we move deeper into a process that connects us with the most essential aspects of what it means to be human, become refreshed and revitalized through this spiritual and psychological centering, find new resources that inspire us to come to the aid of others, and build a society that is "well" as we take the next steps in our own becoming.[16] Thus we believe music is a major factor that may promote and foster our wellness at this difficult time and as we age. In the chapters that follow, we hope to demonstrate the various paths and ways music influences wellness in later life as presented both in research and the stories of people involved with music.

Acknowledgments

We wish to thank Janka Romero and Ilaria Tassistro, Commissioning Editors, Psychology, and Emily Watton, Senior Editorial Assistant, Psychology, at Cambridge University Press for their assistance in making this book possible. We also thank five anonymous reviewers of earlier chapters for their helpful comments and suggestions.

A very special thanks goes to Jim Weatherhead for allowing us to use excerpts from his story and Cookie Hopper who maintains the website "The Faces of Ankylosing Spondylitis."

Our sincerest thanks go to the following: Heather Gateau McEndree, Paula Hepfer, Carl Sponenberg, New Horizons, The Shippensburg Town Band, Keith Davis, Brian Helman, Mac Randall, *JazzTimes*, John Mulholland, *The Guardian*, and Richard Rejino.

We also thank our music teachers, professors, colleagues, and most importantly our students whose influence continue to direct and inspire us and have made this work possible. We also express great gratitude to our parents, brothers and sisters, nieces and nephews, and our entire family, whose symphony of love and support continue to resound through our writing of this book.

Last, very special thanks go to Paula Madey, and Mary Elizabeth and Jack VonDras, for their sustaining love and encouragement throughout this project, and in our journey in life together.

1   Overture

Music is healing; it's coping, and it's a story. Music is the connecting bridge between the ones that I love and me .... Music is my center, my common ground, my healing place.

"Kalie: Music Is My Healing Place"[1]

In many ways, music is essential to our psychological wellness as individuals and to the wellness of a society. Music pervades all aspects of society and human thought. The creation of musical sound indeed involves a transformation that is set "by the art of the musician."[2] But music also involves a listener who perceives music in a personal way. Music is a paradox of unity and diversity. Music follows structure and, paradoxically, at the same time, is resistant to theory[3] Music is universal, giving emphasis and meaning to the human experience.

We stay authentic through music, but music too has to be authentic. To be authentic is to see life in a realistic way, to be self-reflective and to understand one's motivations, to be able to freely express emotions and to laugh at ourselves, and to care about and accept others.[4] Thus, to be authentic, music has to come from a place that conveys the hopes, experiences, and struggles of a people and society. Authentic music is universal. It embraces all cultures, views, and walks of life. Authentic music embodies the heart and soul of a people and society. Simply, it is the music of what people listen to and make. It is an outlet for healing and connects us to others. Conversely, a society where the expression of music is prohibited or restrained is unwell. Wellness not only relates then to wellness of the individual but also to the wellness of a society. What determines individual wellness? What defines a well society? In this chapter, we discuss concepts of wellness of the individual and wellness of a society, and begin to sketch out the intersection of music, health, and aging.

To begin, we must first consider what it means to be healthy. The World Health Organization (WHO) defines health as a "state of complete

1

physical, mental, and social well-being and not merely the absence of disease or infirmity."[5] This definition moves beyond the biomedical definition of health, which is the absence of illness. Health from a biomedical perspective is somewhat circular and implies that if you are not sick, then you are healthy. However, a drawback of the WHO definition is that it is difficult to characterize the fixed or the relative qualities of being in "a state of complete physical, mental, and social wellbeing" and, thus, if or when a veritable "state of wellbeing" is satisfied. How do we understand someone with a physical, mental, or emotional disability? Are they by definition unhealthy? What is the role of a person's spiritual outlook with regard to health? To be considered healthy, then, is a process that takes a certain level of self-management.[6] Key in this process is resilience, adaptation to change, the capacity to cope, and the ability to reach one's full potential. As we take up these concerns, we recognize that health involves a holistic process and thus requires an approach that looks at the wellness of the person and at the wellness of society. We further discuss our investigative approach and expand on our conceptions of the wellness of the individual and wellness of a society in the following pages.

Wellness of the Individual

Individual wellness is grounded in a psychology that emphasizes wholeness of the individual, a connectedness to others, a sense of belonging, and authenticity. These are not new concepts or views of psychology of the individual. They are founded in earlier theories put forth by Alfred Adler, Gordon Allport, Abraham Maslow, Carl Jung, and Carl Rogers.[7] They reflect an existentialist, phenomenological perspective. For example, Rogers proposed that living in the here and now and living an authentic life are essential to psychological wellness. Concepts such as phenomenological, existential, person-centered, self-actualization, becoming, and growth were terms used to describe the process of moving toward and becoming an authentic person. Disruptions, or incongruences between one's real and ideal self, result in being unwell. Other symptoms of being psychologically unwell are anxiety, worry, frustration, and anger. Psychological wellness is intertwined with an individual's process of becoming who they were meant to be and a life review that accentuates positive psychological, emotional, and spiritual growth.[8]

A person can be unwell vis-a-vis music when one's orientation to music changes in that it creates inauthenticity and existential crisis in the person. For example, one could still attempt to belong to a music scene (e.g., punk) but can no longer maintain that lifestyle or has "aged" out of the scene. Changes in technology and changes in medium (e.g., vinyl, cassette, 8-track, CDs – the potential demise of CDs – iPods) can affect how one incorporates music into one's sense of self. Physical and health changes can affect one's music orientation. For the musician, not being where you are meant to be, struggling to stay young, physical changes in health, and not playing what feels right to you but instead playing for the sole approval of others can negatively affect one's orientation toward music and well-being. Hearing loss for many musicians and nonmusicians can change one's orientation toward music that was once enjoyed but now is less enjoyable. These changes in orientation toward music may impact how we find meaning in our lives.

The Grand Avenue of Music

Musicologists such as Harris Berger[9] and Kenneth LeFave[10] have designated music as a phenomenology. That is, music may be described as an entity that we understand through our conscious experience of listening and interpreting, composing and playing, acting out and dancing to, and through our deeper psychological interpretations and meaning given to various musical experiences. This deeper individual experience and the broader cultural connection of music as a phenomenology provide the nexus to metaphysical and psychological aspects of the person. When we consider these connections, we thus embrace a phenomenological psychology.[11] This definition of psychology that we will espouse in this book will be one that is also universal, depicting the deepest and most central aspects of the person.

We recognize that taking a universal, phenomenological approach to understanding the connection between music, wellness, and aging can be challenging. Within modern psychology, at the present time, a diffusion of definitions, theories, and approaches exists, leading the outside reader to conclude that there is no unifying principle to the field. Indeed, as the psychoanalytic theorist Carl Jung remarked many years ago,[12] much of modern experimental psychology falls well short of being a universal explanation of human experience, of life processes, the person's deepest concerns, and inclusive of the innermost and culturally common motives that direct our behavior. Thus, we will define psychology in universal and metaphysical terms, leaving consideration of technical and methodological approaches and schools of thought such as neuroscience, cognitive science, behaviorism, and behavioral management as secondary concerns in our presentation of the phenomenology of music as it relates to wellness and aging.

Embracing a phenomenological orientation, we recognize psychology to express the deepest aspects of the person, involving conscious and unconscious processes that invoke and express a psychology imbued with faith and spirituality that arises from the organic neurobiological platform of the human brain and peripheral sensory mechanisms. In a sense, this is a type of psychology that encompasses all human experience and that includes and is connected with the traditions found throughout all world cultures.

We can further understand a psychology that connects and encompasses all human experience from the perspective of Eastern philosophies, where opposites such as male-female, inner-outer, and subjective-objective are connected and represent a whole, or oneness. This oneness of opposites is also understood to reflect a balance, a complementarity, and a harmony. It is exemplified in the Daoist symbol of Yin and Yang. Thus while forming a whole, Yin and Yang are considered opposites. For example, Yin represents female qualities. Additional qualities are black, dark, and passive. Yang represents male qualities. Other qualities include white, light, and active. Although they are opposites, each one contains aspects of the other. This symbol also connects to a larger cosmological order. Yin and Yang were formed out of Chaos and eventually created a balance in the cosmos. When these two components are out of balance, adversity and ill health occur.[13]

With regard to aging and health, we also find a similar connection of opposites and oneness in our inner psychological and outer social experiences. That is, in adult development and aging we experience ascent and descent in biophysical systems, a psychological turning inward at midlife as we shift and reposition ourselves from an outer-looking orientation from time since birth to an inner-looking orientation of the time left to live and a sloughing off of social contacts. Illness and death may limit one's interaction and exchange with family and friends from levels experienced earlier in adulthood. In all these moments of development and change, we have an opportunity to come to new understanding of what maturing and growing older really means. We similarly recognize a union between opposites when we consider wellness and illness. A contemplation of these two states may lead us to novel insights regarding life changes, awareness of new strengths, and a fuller realization of life's bliss.

This type of connection between opposites, especially in the union of the outer physical and social environments with our inner psychological experiences, has also been noted in the way music innervates emotion, perception, movement, learning, and memory and may provide a beneficial therapy for a variety of neurological impairments. As we consider wellness and healing, we recognize the intersecting influence and role that music therapy has in the prevention, management, and recovery from illness. As noted by Andrea Creech and colleagues,[14] to be able to listen to music, to be with others in a social activity involving music, to be involved in playing an instrument, singing, composing – all are suggested to enhance well-being in later life. Thus, we realize how music therapy has great potential in the treatment of both physical and psychological illnesses, such as depression, pain, and neurological disorders.

Moreover, like the symbol of Yin and Yang found in Daoism, this is a type of psychology that can be described as metaphysical, suggesting and portraying a theoretical model of human nature that is inclusive and descriptive of all peoples, and sees relationships and connections between all phases and facets of life and living experiences. Accordingly, our discussion hopes to give emphasis to the universal characterization of human experience as portrayed and reflected in music and musical experiences. Thus, although we present that music is connected to wellness and aging, we also propose that various elements of music are metaphors of a broader human experience. For example, rhythm connects us to life's movement as we progress from infancy to older age. Harmony is to be found in the relationships we establish with others and in society. Melody is our individual experience in the world. Thus, wellness through music for the individual is finding meaning and one's place with one's self, with others, and with one's community.

Wellness of Society

Indications of a well society can be found in its moral values and social justice. Social justice involves fairness and justice toward its individuals. A fair and just society provides safety and security for all its members. It has embodied mechanisms to redress wrongs and seeks to truly represent the will of a people. It has the moral obligation to provide safety nets for at-risk individuals, such as health care, retirement, and maintaining the dignity of the individual through the life course. A well society is one where grievances are identified, and individuals engage in a strong social advocacy. It reflects one's connectedness to and sense of community and allows for personal and community growth to the benefit of its citizens.

Health Care and a Well or Unwell Society

In a speech given in March 1966 to the Convention of the Medical Committee for Human Rights held in Chicago, Dr. Martin Luther King Jr., hoping to raise social consciousness about the immorality of institutional racism as noted in the inferior and segregated medical care provided to African Americans in United States, stated that "of all the forms of inequality, injustice in health care is the most shocking and inhumane because it often results in physical death."[15] As Dr. King noted, particularly egregious in its provision of care is the United States, which holds the dubious distinction of being the only industrialized country in the world that does not provide some form of universal health care for its citizens.[16] Equal access to excellent and exemplary health care, regardless of the person's gender, socioeconomic status, race, ethnic background, country of origin, or immigration status, is crucial to defining a well society. Equal access to excellent and exemplary health care is grounded in the principles of fairness and justice. A society that provides access to the best health care possible for all its citizens can be characterized as good and fair.

The World Health Organization (WHO) has proposed key elements that make up a good and fair health-care system. The concept of goodness is identified as the best attainable average level of health care of all of its citizens. Fairness is measured by the smallest feasible difference or disparity among individuals and groups. According to the WHO, characteristics of a good and fair health-care system are *good health, responsiveness,* and *fairness in financing.* Good health refers to making the health status of the entire population as optimal as possible across the life course. Some indicators of good health are a low infant mortality rate and high disability-adjusted life expectancy. Responsiveness refers to making adjustments and accommodating peoples' expectations of respectful treatment and client orientation by health-care providers. It also implies that there is a fair distribution of responsiveness across individuals and groups. Fairness in financing refers to ensuring economic support and protection for everyone, with costs distributed according to one's ability to pay and equal protection from the financial risks associated with an illness.[17]

Although the United States is ranked as one of the most responsive nations when it comes to technological advances and understanding the needs of its citizens, according to the WHO, for North American countries it is ranked as one of the least fair for health finance protection with Canada and Cuba, adjacent countries, ranked higher than the United States. The US health-care system with regard to responsiveness knows what its citizens want and need, but it is also one of the most expensive health-care systems in the world, spending 17.9 percent of its GDP on health care, amounting roughly to $10,739 per person.[18] As a result, many US citizens still face bankruptcy when confronted with a devastating illness or need long-term medical care.[19]

Implications of Health Care for Musicians

The implications for musicians who live in an unwell society with regard to health care is that many are unprepared financially to address the costs of medical care. This becomes particularly crucial for the aging musician. Financial ups and downs are an inherent part of the "gig economy" (i.e., short-term contracts and freelance work) of the music profession. Although musicians' unions have provisions to provide pension plans for working musicians, these plans may not necessarily provide health-care insurance.[20] In addition, many musicians only play part-time, do not belong to a union, or play professionally but have a sporadic schedule. The costs of medical care can be prohibitive. Thus, many musicians are at risk and unprepared financially to cover health changes as they age. Too often, musicians are compelled to set up a crowdfunding platform such as a "GoFundMe" Internet page to pay for costly medical bills. Some musical groups have formed LLCs, which can then purchase group health insurance. Fortunately, many countries provide universal health care to its citizens. With the enactment of the Affordable Care Act (ACA) in the United States, people can access affordable health insurance if otherwise not eligible for Medicaid or Medicare, or do not have their own private or employer-provided plans.[21] But the ACA (along with Medicaid and Medicare) has come under political attack and has an unclear future at the time of this writing. Along with many others, musicians are now at the forefront of fighting to keep the ACA.[22]

Wellness and Music Community

Music is essential to the wellness of society. Wellness through music at a societal level is exemplified in grants for the continuation and development of music through incentives such as the endowment for the arts and other grants. A well society provides music education programs and music camps for aspiring and accomplished musicians of all ages. A musically well society appreciates the spiritual and community role that music plays. It can be in religious services and meditative music, in communal healing rituals, or in protest of social unwellness and the exhortation of societal reforms. It can also be an enjoyable enterprise that brings together families and community such as in town bands, community concerts, kinfolk reunions, and music festivals. Importantly all arts, whether performing, visual, literary, cultural, digital, and electronic, have been linked to health. The arts play a key role in promoting community health through their ability to provide the individual a sense of enhanced self-efficacy, positive ways of coping, and emotional regulation. Indeed, involvement with the arts is noted to lower stress and enhance immune function, reduce loneliness and isolation, and increase adoption of healthy behaviors.[23]

A Society That Is Unwell and Political Oppression

A sickness of a society is exhibited when music is prohibited, limited, or when musicians are persecuted. The thwarting of the natural expression of music leads to a sickness not only of the person, but also of the society at large. In societies that are unwell, artists and musicians live in fear and as condemned individuals at the whim of the prevailing social winds and at the mercy of despotic autocrats with populist and nationalistic views. During the Stalin regime in the Soviet Union, musicians lived in an uneasy fear and at times outright condemnation by the Soviet dictator. Many disappeared or were murdered because they fell out of favor with Stalin or did not compose according to the ideology of socialist realism.[24] Party sympathizers would patrol bars and clubs to report on compliance with new regime policies. For example, the valve trumpet was considered a perverse instrument, and use of mutes to make a "wah wah" sound was prohibited. Jazz percussionists could be accused of creating "extreme rhythms."[25] The famous classical composer, Shostakovich, received both reward and condemnation by Stalin and always kept a suitcase packed waiting for that midnight knock at the door. As an advocate, Shostakovich later wrote and signed petitions for the release of musicians condemned to labor camps under Stalin's regime and helped survivors find work.[26]

Music enriches a culture and is a context in which one evaluates the wellness of a culture. Traditional folk music provides identity to a culture. To fully know that traditional music is the lifeblood of a culture is to witness the lengths that autocratic and dictatorial regimes go to ban it. Stalin, for example, banned folk music, and any "folk" melodies composed at that time had to be state approved.[27] Regions within the old Soviet Union were targeted. The traditional music of Mongolia and Tuva was banned. Here, traditional musical instruments were confiscated, and folk and religious festivals were prohibited. Azerbaijani musicians also suffered under Soviet rule. For example, the actress and singer Panfiliya Tanailidi was arrested for allegedly spying for Iran and was shot. Jazz saxophonist, Parvis Rustambeyov died in a KGB-run prison.[28]

Under other oppressive regimes such as the Taliban, the rubab, the national instrument of Afghanistan and considered "the lion" of instruments, was silenced. The rubab is a stringed, lute-like instrument that has its own unique sound.[29] The Taliban destroyed all musical instruments and imprisoned musicians. All musical expression, unless it comported with Islamic law, was banned. The result was that many Afghani musicians such as rubab master Ustad Mohammad Rahim and singer Usted Mawash fled the country to live in exile.[30]

US Discrimination

Music has always been a form of protest against discrimination and injustice. Every generation has witnessed the rise of musicians advocating civil rights, calling out injustice, and fighting poverty. Musicians and singers such as Pete Seeger, Joan Baez, Woody Guthrie, Miles Davis, Nina Simone, Moby, Bono, Nataanii Means, Inez Jasper, Frank Waln, and countless others have stood as the vanguard to call out, to raise awareness of, and to fight social injustice.[31]

Historic and extant examples of racism and tactics of disenfranchisement of African Americans have been white-voting-only primaries in the South, voter suppression, terror tactics (such as lynchings, shootings, and maimings), poll taxes, literacy tests, segregation, and the Jim Crow anti-black racist laws. The rise of Black Lives Matter and other human rights organizations highlights present discriminatory policies of the United States that involve incarceration rates, police brutality, the death penalty, and racially biased drug policies, to name a few. Likewise, hate crimes and violence against LGBTQ+ individuals have been well documented. Although hate crimes based on the victim's sexual identity are believed to be underreported, sexual orientation is ranked as the third highest motivator for hate crimes.[32] One move toward rectifying civil rights injustice toward LGBTQ+ individuals is the recent 6–3 ruling by the US Supreme Court that extends the rights of LGBTQ+ individuals under Title 7 of the Civil Rights Act of 1964 from discrimination in employment.[33]

At present, the world is facing one of its most devastating pandemics in history – Covid-19. Although this pandemic is affecting us all, in the United States the number of cases and number of deaths have been disproportionally found in racial and ethnic minority groups.[34] This disparity has important implications for how we respond morally. A well society ensures that no group suffers disproportionally to another group. A well society responds by recognizing utmost the dignity of the person and strives to maintain basic ethical values. To live a human and humane existence is challenged full-force by the Covid-19 pandemic and will serve as our testament or our condemnation to how we responded to those most in need.

Immigration

Another form of discrimination is immigration laws. The year 1907 witnessed the largest number of immigrants coming to the United States. Through Ellis Island alone, 1.3 million people entered the United States that year.[35] During the ensuing years, anti-immigration and eugenic ideologies became more accepted, and these ideologies were used to limit immigration from areas that were deemed morally and physiologically "unfit." One of the most restrictive immigration laws in the United States was enacted in 1924. This law restricted immigration to quotas based on the 1890 census and limited to certain countries. Those who entered the country in 1890 were primarily from Northern European countries. Excluded from entering the United States because of the immigration act of 1924 were immigrants from Eastern Europe, Asia, Russia, and Italy.[36] Sadly, at the time of this writing the US administration has been implementing immigration policies that restrict or ban entry into the United States because of religion or geographic origin.[37]

Music, Wellness, and Aging

One of the fastest growing populations in the world is the number of people 65 years of age and older. The top 5 countries with the highest percentage of its population age 65 and older are Japan (28.2 percent), Italy (22.8 percent), Finland (21.9 percent), Portugal (21.8 percent), and Greece (21.8 percent). The top 5 states in the United States with the highest percentage of its population age 65 and older are Maine (20.6 percent), Florida (20.5 percent), West Virginia (19.9 percent), Vermont (19.4 percent), and Delaware (18.7 percent).[38] We are indeed an aging population. This change in demographics comes with important concerns to people as they age. For example, how do we begin to understand what defines health as we get older? How do we address health concerns of older individuals? How do we as a society create the conditions that allow all, regardless of age, to reach their unique potential, to become a self-actualized individual? To begin to address these questions, we sketch out and offer a way to begin to understand aging as a possible path to self-transcendence, as well as how we might transcend the life–death duality.

Seeing children grow up and leave home and witnessing parents retire, decline, and die have profound effects on the individual. Erik Erikson,[39] a psychosocial developmental theorist, suggested the central crisis of midlife is generativity versus stagnation. Generativity refers to the care taking and concern we provide and express to children, older family members, and friends, as well as institutions and organizations in our communities. Stagnation reflects a regression to an earlier status of isolation and lack of intimate connection. Thus, in many ways there is a dynamic expression of psychosocial concerns and development at midlife. Does personality change as well? This is an important question to ask, and the answer is, it depends. It depends on what facets of personality you are measuring in an empirical sense and, as Jung suggested, whether you will embrace the possibility of widening consciousness and psychic growth.[40] Generally, with regard to empirical assessments, core aspects or central trait measures seem to remain relatively stable, although there may be a slight increase in agreeableness and decline in neuroticism, and a shifting balance in the expression of masculine–feminine traits.[41] Other research, such as those from the Berkeley Longitudinal Study,[42] which explores more malleable aspects of personality like autonomy or self-control, suggest greater expression in these aspects as one moves from young adulthood to midlife. Similarly, from midlife to old age there are also noted gender shifts in the expression of femininity and dominance.[43] Allied research has suggested that from midlife to old age there is an increase in the expression of positive and decrease of negative emotional behaviors.[44] It is important to recognize that these changes in personality and emotional behavior should be considered within the broader context of midlife and old age, where we see marriages and family life from a more mature perspective. Also to be recognized are cultural influences and different social roles, such as being a grandparent, that influence self-concept and what we might consider as possible ways of being.

Erikson proposes the central crisis in old age is integrity versus despair. In this stage we ask ourselves how my life has been purposeful and meaningful. Can I look back upon my life with a sense of integrity? At this stage there also exist continued changes in social processes, such as disengagement, changes in self-esteem and possible ways of being or possible selves, and how we compensate for change as well as how to live our lives effectively and to achieve our goals. Society's reaction has not always been kind to the older person. Indeed, ageism and age discrimination are still very much present in our society. But truly, we should recognize that in old age there are no limits to the kinds of interests or activities one may pursue.

Risk for disease and declines in health become more a part of our everyday experience and concern as we age. For biologists the key question is what causes aging? Several theories of why we age exist and certainly how we age reflect genetic inheritance (e.g., if grandparents and parents were long lived, we will be more likely to live to a ripe old age, too) and lifestyle factors that influence health (e.g., smoking, diet rich in fats, and high-stress jobs are associated with earlier mortality). Exercise, proper diet, and enriched environments help to slow declines in brain and cognitive abilities. In general, declines in sensory–perceptual processes and cognitive function occur with advancing age. But there is considerable individual variability in the extent to which these declines may imperil the older person in their finding happiness and in their everyday living. That is to say, some older adults show significant declines in vision, hearing, and cognitive function, while others seem to have vision as keen as an eagle's, are still sharp as a tack, and are very much involved in living. How do we maintain a vital involvement in life? The answer to that question often involves fitness routines, proper diet, and ways of being, or things like anti-aging creams, cosmetic surgeries, and hip or knee replacements. Perhaps reflecting our uneasiness with aging, we might even search for the "right" vitamins or herbal remedies to take or even seek out an anti-aging drug that would extend life and enhance our living. Certainly, how we answer the question that "aging" poses to us seems to turn on our personal approach to life and how we view our own development. As implied here, individuals who stay vitally involved are also more likely to exercise, follow healthy nutritional guidelines, and stay intellectually active.

What Kinds of Changes Occur in Later Life?

Aging is a natural, intrinsic, universal, and inevitable process. We are all getting older. But by midlife, most of us are likely to experience physical changes such as graying and thinning of hair, if not baldness. Thinning and wrinkling of skin and changes in muscle and bone also occur. In our joints there is a gradual thinning and loss of cartilage for most of us, and by midlife the first stages of arthritis occur for many. Changes in sensory–perceptual systems also occur. For example, decline in hearing sensitivity, especially for higher pitched sounds, and changes in visual acuity, especially for focusing on objects near to us, happen. All of these changes are due to the natural decline and wear-and-tear on the biological mechanisms that underlie these systems. Any or all of these physical changes may impact upon our everyday functioning and social routines, and ultimately our quality of life.

If you have been physically active or involved in an exercise routine, you may have maintained your muscle strength or slowed its loss somewhat. You may have also lowered your risk for age-related diseases such as cardiovascular disease and diabetes, which increase in risk and occurrence with advancing age. At midlife, we note an increase in risk and diagnosis of early signs of chronic disorders, such as arthritis and lung disease. As we have become a more health-conscious society, there has been a growing awareness that poor lifestyle choices in adolescence and in early adulthood, such as smoking tobacco, making poor nutritional choices, eating a high-fat diet, and avoiding aerobic exercise, have powerful influences on health later in adulthood. With advancing age, there is an increase in risk for a variety of diseases. Indeed, as reported in the Global Burden of Disease Study, worldwide the leading causes of death include heart disease, cancers, pulmonary disorders, and infectious diseases.[45]

For women, menopause occurs in midlife. But for men, too, by midlife there is a decline in testosterone production, an andropause, that mimics the loss of estrogen production that occurs at menopause for women. These changes may influence sexual activity. However, just as physical contact and romance have been a part of one's life in young adulthood, it still is an area of important interest at mid- and later life as well.

In the area of cognition, declines in our ability to think and process information as fast as we did earlier in life and to take on complex and abstract problems like we did when we were younger are often noted. These changes in our thinking and intellectual function reflect the shifting status and neurological integrity of brain systems as we age. Yet there is maintenance and even perhaps a modest increase in our knowledge of the world and established intellectual routines that we use in our work and in our everyday problem solving with advancing age. This "knowing about the world" and "how to do things" is an aspect of intellectual function that reflects educational background and other learning experiences, such as continued learning on the job and the gathering of information through various media sources, that continues in the course of our living. Thus, though at midlife and in old age we are slower in our information processing and may experience greater difficulty in working with novel problems, we may also be at the pinnacle of our career trajectory and work-life, and the knowledge we have gained through the years can be put to good use.

At midlife and in old age, we also become more aware of our own finite existence. With regard to personality, both Carl Jung and gerontologist Bernice Neugarten proposed that midlife is a time of turning inward, where we seek a deeper understanding of life's meaning and purpose.[46] Thus, spirituality and religious activities, or a deeper clarification and refinement of one's orienting life philosophy devoid of nonsecular beliefs, are noted as important concerns of some adults at midlife and in old age, and these activities provide a source by which to answer these critical questions. Indeed, there seems to be an increase in spirituality and self-reflection about life's meaning as one moves from early adult-hood to midlife and then into later life.

Similar to other phases of development in the life cycle, aging is a process of continued growth and change. As we mature, we grow, and we often change our perspective on important topics such as life and death, questions of who we are, and what our relationship is toward others. Consequently, as Swedish sociologist Lars Tornstam proposes in his theory of gerotranscendence, as we age and grow into later life there is a redefinition of the self, our relationships to others, and a new under-standing of "fundamental existential questions."[47] These existential questions address how we approach life and death. We become less fearful of death as we age. As Tornstam suggests, we transcend the life–death duality. We also come to appreciate, existentially, that life is a mystery. We become less self-centered and we rejoice that we are more connected to the universe. We redefine what is important in our relationships toward others. We shrug off those things that weigh us down, and we transcend the duality of right and wrong. We become more tolerant of others.[48]

How can we come to grips with what may seem to be profound changes, disruptions, and challenges as we move through our life? Tornstam further proposed that reaching an existential transcendence is not achieved by everyone. One reason is that we may hold the expectation that we should be the same person as we were when younger. We are unwilling or cannot let go of the same values, inter-ests, or activities we found important earlier in life.[49] Our thesis is that music intersects with wellness and aging and aids us in moving past these unproductive expectations. Music provides us a source of mean-ing, definition, and identity to the self, our connection to others, and to our perception of the transcendent. One's connection with music con-tinues throughout one's life. As we age we see the world in a new way. Thus, we also suggest that through music there is opportunity to gain different perspectives and insights as we get older regarding our rela-tionships with others, how we cope with changes, our relationships with our own aging parents, and with our children as we age. Others propose that over time, we gain more autonomy and environmental mastery and are able to regulate emotions.[50] These insights can take a long time to happen. Yet, music can play a role in finding new insights. As we age it becomes important in some aspects of our lives to move from external motives to internal motives. Over time, positive self-expression and identity of self may be driven less by external forces but instead more by internal, self-defined goals. One example, for a listener of music, is a change from one type of music in part driven by peer acceptance to one of listening to music that internally feels good. For the musician, a shift from playing one genre of music (e.g., rock) to another (e.g., jazz) over time may be driven by many considerations but does reflect and become part of one's identity and sense of continuity of self.

Indeed, in later life the person may be most poised to express the wisdom acquired through work and living experiences to gain insight into one's intra- and interpersonal dynamics and qualities, and to come to a new and deeper understanding of life's purpose and meaning. An insight-filled expression from verse 41 of the *Tao Te Ching* informs us that "Great Talents Ripen Late."[51] One way these great talents ripen, we propose, is through musical expression such as writing a song, singing in the choir or shower, playing an instrument by oneself or with others, just listening to music, or through other ways that the person becomes involved with music.

A Funny Thing Happened on the Way to Band Practice

Continuing to consider how music intersects with and is related to wellness in later life, we might start by saying, "A funny thing happened on the way to the band practice." That is, as we began thinking about our experiences in music and psychology, we recognized many connections and complexities that needed to be approached in a new way. It is true – life is like a novel, with the story becoming more complex in later chapters. But there is a basic plot to describe, too – much like the protagonist in Jacob Needleman's story of a student, seeking the meaning of things, who enrolls in a philosophy course only to be disappointed because the deeper meaning he hopes to discover is obscured by the current theories and approaches.[52] We too have found disappointment in various approaches to understanding processes of wellness and later life development that had become ensnared in the medicalization of aging and notions of successful aging that limit and quash understanding and exploration of human nature and the individual's experience.[53] In our reckoning, it seemed that it was through music where we had access to and recognized deeper aspects of human nature and the nascent concerns of living and social relations. Further, it was in our musical experiences with others that we observed an intersection with personal wellness and concerns for life-span development. Indeed, through our encounter with other musicians and music lovers who communicated humanistic principles that emphasized finding deeper personal meaning in our living, who relayed information about their own life discoveries, and who gave insight into how one might continue to grow and become, we recognized an orientation that seemed to be much more attuned to and descriptive of a universal human experience.

Finding Deeper Meaning in Our Personal Experience with Music

From a humanistic perspective, it is noted that we develop and strive toward self-actualization throughout our life. From the earliest times in development to the very last moment before death, we explore and seek to discover new insights into living, all acquired through a life of reflection and experience. Music is a vital property of our life that intersects with and relays information about the many dimensions and concerns of our development. Indeed, through music we are able to express wisdom acquired through life experiences, to convey insight into intra- and inter-personal dynamics and qualities, and to realize a new and deeper under-standing of life's purpose and meaning.

Thus, the connection of music to wellness and aging is a personal experience. The meaning one derives from music as it relates to wellness and one's experience of aging is dependent upon the listener. Music is integrated into life, conjuring up in the listener memories, images, and feelings. It also connects with one's identity, sorrows, hopes, and dreams. The essence of music is deeply linked to our essence as humans. We believe this linkage goes beyond the philosophical debates around form and idea to something even more transcendent but real. The emotions, thoughts, and images we experience when we listen to music are not mere illusions. Music only has meaning and attains reality in the context of the listener, and that listened experience may be different for different people.[54]

When we experience a deeper meaning from the musical experiences we encounter, we often describe them as expressions of joy, our passion, wisdom, a method to healing and wellness, a way to motivate us, and a place of solace and sanctuary. In a way, we are transformed by music, leading us to ask and seek answers to the questions: How might I become? How might I live? In what will I find comfort, happiness, relaxation, meaning, and fulfillment?

In our writing we hope to use music as a central avenue to explore and provide some notion of prescriptive activities that interface with and direct the phenomenology of well-being in later life. This is not an unfamiliar type of activity. From the very earliest music offerings to the most contemporary compositions, instrumental music and song have offered another doorway for us to enter to seek ways of addressing these types of questions. People have used music as a platform to prescribe, develop, and express a deeper personal and social consciousness. So we recognize there are many central questions to consider as we travel along in our journey. Three central and related questions we hope to address include "What defines me in later life?" "What might direct me onto the wellness pathway?" And, "What can be celebrated?" Our view is that self-actualization, becoming who you were meant to be, is a process of defining, directing, and celebrating life. But to grow as a person involves reflecting on one's experience and interactions with others. It also involves doing. As you read this book, we hope you will reflect on what defines and what directs your life, what can be celebrated, and where does music fit in. Perhaps it is through the pleasurable musical experiences you currently enjoy. You may find that you want to again pick up an instrument you played when younger but have neglected or take up a new instrument altogether. You may decide to join a choir or sing in a group. You may find ways to experience music you currently love in a new way or decide to listen to new artists or music genres. Music, indeed, can become the common ground and a place of healing. Through music there are many paths to defining, directing, and celebrating our later life and many ways of embracing wellness. We describe these paths and ways to wellness in the following chapters.

2   In Search of a Perfect Harmony: Music and Wellness in Later Life

Music . . . takes us out of the actual and whispers to us dim secrets that startle our wonder as to who we are, and for what, whence, and whereto.
– Ralph Waldo Emerson

As Emerson intimates, music is a special conduit to explore the transcendent questions of who we are and where we will travel in the latter half of the life course.[1] As the renowned existential philosopher and theologian Paul Tillich notes, concerns about our personhood, and our path in development, reflect universal and essential processes of meaning-making and are of central importance of people within all cultures, and across all historic settings.[2] Therefore, recognizing the importance of interpreting and understanding one's personal experiences of development and aging, in this chapter we discuss aspects of physical change, longevity, and wellness in later life. We also describe how various musical involvements may reveal as well as direct these processes and interpretations.

But before we go any further, we should ask how, as Emerson alludes, can music tell us about who and how we are? More broadly, how does music serve as a special conduit for exploring these aspects of living in later life? The first way of addressing these questions is to recognize music as a phenomenological expression of conscious and unconscious experiences that mirrors the deepest aspects, feelings, and concerns of the person. In that way, then, as philosopher Lewis Rowell notes, music is realized as a reflection of the archetypal myths that Jung suggests embody our deepest psychology and that are manifested in our behavior.[3] Thus, music lays open to us an "indirect testimony . . . a gestalt . . . of related ideas, beliefs, and images" of the inner person and the world in which they live.[4] In a similar manner, philosophers have proposed music to be "a secret language of the soul,"[5] where, "aspiring to disclose the ineffable," music offers insight into and a critique of the person and society.[6] Thus, another way to resolve these questions is to recognize music as a universal expression, describing what words cannot. Indeed, as noted by the writer and amateur musician Ward Cannel and the composer and pianist Fred

Marx, "every human society has a variety of musical compositions and instruments, and people from one part of the planet can learn to sing and play the music from another part. Thus, the ability to *make* music is part of human nature."[7] Therefore, whether as method of artistic or self-expression, a system of communication or social critique, an entertainment or hobby, therapy or vocation, music characterizes and points us toward the innermost dimensions of who we are and the dynamic world in which we live. For these reasons, then, as musicologist Michael Gallope has described, we understand music to be a semiotic expression of the person and their socio-cultural-environmental surround.[8] That is, music symbolically portrays the person's quest for and interpretations of life's meaning and purpose, processes of challenge and adaptation, and of one's relationship to others, the natural environment, and the cosmos. Therefore, in accordance with Emerson's understanding, and as we will proclaim throughout this book, music represents a very unique lens of analysis, providing us insight into and understanding of various psychological aspects of the person, one's development and aging, and one's quest for adaptation and wellness in later life. How music may affect us and provide greater insight into the human condition, attracting universal appeal and an international audience of researchers, is discussed next.

The Power of Music to Affect Thinking, Feeling, and Acting

Music has long been identified in the areas of advertisement and marketing to powerfully influence consumer behavior.[9] Indeed, music is used in media advertisements to manipulate the hedonic value and referential meaning associated with branded products, to evoke emotions that will set in motion consumer purchasing behavior, and has even been shown to influence older adults' generosity when tipping.[10] These powerful effects of music to alter our thinking, feeling, and acting lead us to consider how music may innervate mind–body relations and affect behavior. In later chapters, we will delve more deeply into how music may therapeutically aid older adults, but we should first recognize that there is rather credible evidence suggesting that music has a healing power, offering very positive benefits as an element of recovery and rehabilitative interventions.[11] For instance, music listening and music making have both been found to aid older adults in recovery from neurological injuries caused by stroke.[12] Similarly, other beneficial biophysiological effects are also suggested. For example, research from lab studies with rodents suggests that listening to music may optimize immunological responses against cancerous cells, as well as survival after heart transplantation.[13] Further, considering psychiatric illnesses, music making has been indicated to improve and relieve depressive symptoms, as well as the maintenance of well-being in individuals with dementia.[14] So how is it that music has a positive effect on our thinking, feeling, and action?

A review by British health researcher Daisy Fancourt and colleagues provides us some insight into this question. As noted by Fancourt and colleagues, listening to relaxing, slow tempo music, beyond the psychological effect of enhancing positive affect, may produce a switch from the "flight-or-fight" sympathetic nervous system response to the "rest-digest-recover" parasympathetic nervous system response.[15] This switching to the "recovery mode" facilitates a lowering of blood pressure, heart rate, respiration, and galvanic skin conductance levels. These biophysiological changes denote the lowering of stress response and a more "relaxed" state, which aids healing. Beyond the modulation of sympathetic and parasympathetic response, however, there is also evidence that music listening and music making may also moderate a variety of neuro-endocrine and immunological responses. For example, listening to calming music is reported to lower beta-endorphin levels, an endogenous morphine-like chemical that is produced in response to stress or pain, thereby producing an overall more relaxed physical state.[16] Similarly, other research also suggests music to modulate neuro-hormonal release. For example, research by Fancourt's team involving cancer patients and their caregivers in an hour-long singing intervention noted reduction in cortisol, beta-endorphin, oxytocin production, and a general activation of cytokine molecules that mediate and regulate immunological function, inflammation, and blood cell production as a result of the singing intervention.[17] Relatedly, a study by Japanese researcher Kaoru Okado and colleagues involving older adults with advanced dementia in a music therapy intervention reported that involvement in music therapy lowered adrenaline and noradrenaline levels, catecholamines that are produced when under stress.[18] In addition to the music and catecholamine relationship, Okado's team also found lower incidence of congestive heart failure events among those who received music therapy, suggesting that musical therapy may enhance parasympathetic tone and thereby improve coronary status in older individuals with congestive heart failure.

Allied research has indicated moderation of blood flow as well as activation of and response in limbic and paralimbic brain structures (neurological areas intimately involved with emotionality) when listening to joyful or sad music, as well as consonant and dissonant music.[19] Adding to our understanding, a Canadian research team led by Valorie Salimpoor reports peak emotional responses while listening to music to also accompany enhanced dopamine release, a "feel good" hormone.[20]

Salimpoor and colleagues propose that it is this dopamine effect of music that makes it so universally valued. Similarly focusing on the universal effect music has on our emotions, cross-cultural research by American researcher Alan Cowen and colleagues suggests several distinct types of subjective feelings associated with various music samples across cultures.[21] These feelings included conceptualizations such as amusing, angry, beautiful, dreamy, energizing, indignant, joyful, relaxing, sad, scary, and triumphant – thus again underscoring that music has a universal emotional appeal, stirring a broad spectrum of psychological processes, and evoking feelings within the person.

Other research has indicated that musical rhythms may coordinate and thus become synchronized with and drive electrical processes of the brain, producing an "entrainment" effect. Entrainment is noted to occur when changes in baseline alpha waves occur as a function of variations in musical pulse or tempo, which concomitantly also evoke and trigger social–emotive expression.[22] These entrainment effects provide illumination into what it means when a person remarks, "The music makes me come 'alive'!" or "I am really 'feeling' the music!" Indeed, research by Swiss investigators Patrick Gomez and Brigitta Danuser has indicated fast music tempo to be associated with higher physiological arousal (i.e., faster heart rate, respiration, skin conductance) and the expression of positive affect.[23] Further, in examining various features of music, these same researchers note that greater emotionally positive arousal is produced by musical excerpts in the major mode and for downward melodic movement, while emotionally negative arousal is more often associated with musical excerpts in the minor mode and with increased harmonic complexity. Fittingly then, these entrainment and arousal effects suggest a whole new interpretive meaning to songs such as "I've Got the Music In Me," composed by Bias Boshel and recorded by The Kiki Dee Band.[24]

Looking more closely at neurochemical production and hormonal secretions, some research has suggested dynamic gender and situational variation in their release while listening to music. For example, research by Hajime Fukui suggests that in certain situations music listening may inhibit secretion of testosterone in male college students while enhancing testosterone production in female college students.[25] Other research has suggested that the relationship between music and testosterone production found in men may be enhanced if there is a dance partner present.[26] It should be noted, however, that the association reported between music and neuro-hormonal chemical production is inconsistent from one study to the next.[27] Therefore, as we seek to understand how music may make us feel happy or sad, excited or relaxed, it is not correct to just understand that music produces benign mind–health relationships and effects. We also need to understand the qualities of the musical sounds and their interactive relationship with various features of the person and the environment (e.g., gender characteristics of social actors, dynamic features of the social situation, high- versus low-stress environments). For example, experimental research exploring the effects of music exposure versus no music exposure while playing a violent video game indicated that exposure to music elevated subjects' production of cortisol, suggesting that music may add to and further exacerbate stress levels in thrilling or exciting performance arenas.[28]

The Problem of Noise

Many of us have experienced discomfort from hearing loud music blare from an audio speaker. Indeed, the loudness of sounds can be painful and damaging to the cells of the inner ear.[29] The sound threshold at which one feels discomfort is about 120 dB (e.g., the loudness level of being at a rock concert or near a chainsaw when operating), and the threshold at which pain is reported is about 140 dB (e.g., the loudness level of a nearby gunshot or standing close to the runway when a jet takes off).[30] Similarly, like the unpleasant sounds produced by fingernails scratching a chalkboard, very low- or very high-frequency sound exposure may produce harmful effects. The human range of detectable sound extends from 20 to 20,000 Hertz (Hz) for young people, and, as we will discuss in Chapter 3, there is decline in the upper limit with advancing age.[31] Yet, exposure to low-frequency sounds (20 to 100 Hz) and infrasound (i.e., very low-frequency sounds below 20 Hz) present in the roar and hum of boilers, railroad diesel engines, and natural sources such as windstorms and earthquakes, beyond just being annoying, may result in ear pain, balance disturbance, headache, and nausea; affect heart rate and breathing; and produce changes in the endocrine and central nervous systems.[32] Exposure to ultrasound (i.e., inaudible very high-frequency sound about 20,000 Hz or higher) is suggested to produce similar ill effects, such as nausea and headache, as well as neurological injury.[33] Thus, there are many deleterious effects of noise on hearing.[34] Notwithstanding these immediate effects, however, it is also important to mention other ill-health effects due to chronic noise exposure.[35] Research in this area suggests long-term exposure to noise increases blood pressure and release of stress hormones, and thereby also the elevation of risks for cancer,[36] diabetes,[37] and heart disease.[38] Further, recognizing the potential ill effects of sound exposure, we should also be aware that loud and monotonous music has been used as a form of psychological warfare as well as torture.[39]

Understanding Aging and Development into Later Life

Before we go too much further, we should ask how we might explain aging and continued development into later life. In the next sections we discuss shifting perceptions of aging, how we might consider our story of development into the last chapters of life, and discuss biological processes that underlie physical changes that occur throughout the adult years.

Shifting Perceptions of Aging

Becoming an adult and maturing into later adulthood, in both a biological and psychological sense, are both affirmative experiences and a realization of our evolutionary potential.[40] Yet, for most younger people, personal knowledge of these processes and the concerns of later life are not yet fathomable and thus perhaps not well understood. This lack of insight and understanding is not necessarily avoidable, either. As the philosopher and phenomenologist Maurice Merleau-Ponty posits, the body is our first point of reference and understanding.[41] Thus, we perceive and construct knowledge about ourselves and the surrounding world from the point of view of our sensory–perceptual and emotional–cognitive experiences. Moreover, there is both a logical and valid truth expressed when we say, "I'm seeing it with my own eyes" or "I'm hearing it with my own ears." This egocentric orientation has in many ways contributed to the tension, and at times discontent, expressed in the understanding of and relationship between younger and older generations.[42] Further, conflict in generational points-of-view and parent–child detachment is recognized as a normative process in the young person's identity development and process of becoming.[43] Thus, as reflected in the rock song "My Generation" composed by Pete Townshend and recorded by the rock band The WHO in their same-named 1965 debut album, in our youth we seek out our own identity, free from the criticism of parents and authority.[44]

Indeed, the song "My Generation" celebrates a newly found sense of self-autonomy while also expressing the angst and insecurity of youth.[45] However, as Pete Townshend has continued his career into his seventies, it might also be regarded as an anthem about finding your place in the world, as well as the younger person's uncertainty about the next steps in development that lie beyond adolescence and the time of youth.[46] Indeed, in his music and throughout his career, Townshend has characterized the struggles of forming and maintaining a mature identity, as well as other life challenges that occur throughout the life cycle.[47] Thus, the song "My Generation" might, as the sociologist Lars Tornstam posits in his gerotranscendence theory, reflect the analytical lens of young adulthood, which often portrays aging merely as a pathological process.[48] This "young" lens omits the recognition of aging and later life development as a natural and holistic process. Yet as Tornstam proposes, as we encounter physical changes and health challenges in later adulthood, we are likely to revise our understanding of the ups and downs we experienced at earlier times in development, what we consider as our most important accomplishments, and what living a "fulfilled life" means in old age.[49] Thus, aging should not be thought of as simply a time of decline and decrement, but rather as a continuation of discovery and new awareness of life's mysteries. Optimistically then, old age may best be understood as a time of fresh possibilities as life experiences unfold and new horizons come into view.

To help us see that aging is a natural and holistic process, we might characterize our development to be much like a literary work. That is, the process of aging is like a great novel, with many chapters that relate our life story – stories that have become interwoven and more elaborate as the person continues in their developmental journey into old age.[50] Indeed, despite the various changes in physical and intellectual capacities that may occur, many older adults express a shift in how they perceive and understand their aging, which is revealed in statements like, "I am doing so much more now, and understanding things so much clearer than I did than when I was younger – even with the physical changes and unwelcomed health problems that make me feel like my hands are tied behind my back!" As a result, many older adults describe their life story, their hopes and goals, and their ability in overcoming life's next challenges in a generative and empowered way.[51] They convey a sense, irrespective of what they may have conceived old age to be like earlier in life, that they have more to contribute and more to do as they continue in their development.

Physical Changes in Later Life

Each person's life story, undoubtedly, contains discussion of the physical changes that occur as we mature and the health concerns that arise as we age. Indeed, most of us will become keenly familiar with these changes and concerns as we mature and age. Key to our understanding, then, is recognition of the biological processes that underlie the physical changes that occur throughout the adult years. From the expression of growth hormones that innervate development throughout the earliest times in life, to the release of sex hormones and maturation of secondary sexual characteristics at the onset of puberty, to the time of menopause and andropause at midlife, we note a close rhythmic relationship between biological processes and physical changes that occur across the life span. These changes, however, especially as we move into the second half of the life span, are not necessarily embraced or accepted. Indeed, since ancient times there has been an interest in finding, as the Spanish explorer Ponce de Leon ventured, a "fountain of youth" that would extend life and prevent the declines of aging.[52] Moreover, a noted and frequent topic of sacred music is the seeking and finding of "an elixir of new life." Thus, both in Western and Eastern traditions, we also find reference to and a hope for a "fountain of life" that would resolve the existential crises associated with our physical decline and death, and provide us a life that would never end.[53]

To enlighten our understanding beyond the ancient yearning for "a life everlasting," as biomedical scientist Kunlin Jin describes, biologists have offered theories of aging that point to genetic programming, as well as to damage or programming errors that may occur in the natural decline and degradation of the body's physical systems.[54] These programming theories suggest that aging follows a biological schedule of sorts. For example, the programmed longevity theory suggests that there is a predetermined switching on or off of genes that controls early pediatric growth, the onset of puberty and menopause, as well as when age-associated deficits and death of cells occur. Thus, from this theoretical perspective, processes of maturation, aging, and death are suggested to be an execution of our genetic programming. Another programming theory suggests that the neuro–endocrine system serves as an aging clock. The endocrine theory proposes that aging is hormonally regulated and that factors such as a healthy coping style and traumatic life stressors may respectively slow or speed up rates of aging. The physical changes (e.g., graying of hair, wrinkling of skin, increased risk for hypertension, stroke) we often observe when a person becomes President of the United States, with all the extreme mental stress of this job, provide some visual evidence suggesting the endocrine system as a moderator of biological aging.[55] A third programming theory, immunological theory, suggests that there is a biologically planned immunological response, which invariably becomes less efficient and thereby increases our susceptibility to infections and disease as we mature through adulthood, and as a result causes aging and the occurrence of death.

In contrast, other biological accounts of aging include theories that highlight the accumulated wear and tear to biological systems over time.

These theories emphasize damage and programming error, and the idea here is that like a piano, in due course and with continuous use, hammers and mechanical action parts become worn, strings corrode, and the soundboard cracks. Indeed, with advancing age, biological systems just wear down or go awry. One early theory of this type, put forth near the height of industrialization in 1882 by German biologist August Weisman, was aptly called the wear-and-tear theory.[56] This theory suggests that the cells and structures of the body, much like other mechanical systems, as a result of the strain and stress of continued use, simply become exhausted and wear out. More recent wear-and-tear theories include cross-linking, free radical, and DNA damage theories. Cross-linking theory suggests that over time a gradual accumulation of cross-linked proteins within the cell occurs and that this cross-linking results in cellular changes and tissue damage, which slow bodily processes and cause aging. Free-radical theory also suggests modification of cellular processes, positing that unstable oxygen atoms are created through normal metabolic processes and are thrown off, causing oxidative stress or damage to the cell's DNA and other structures. This oxidative damage accumulates over time, producing a decline of cell and organ function that causes aging. The DNA damage theory also focuses on the occurrence of damage to DNA within the cell and the inability of cellular repair mechanisms to keep up with the damage that occurs. This theory highlights the variation in the RNA-DNA transcription that results in genetic mutations. Over time, the accumulation of genetic mutations and associated damage causes cellular deterioration and malfunction that represents biological aging.

All of these theories provide scientific accounts for aging, whether it is the shortening of the telomeres during DNA replication that impacts the cells' response to stress and continued growth, a cross-linking of proteins within cells that makes the cells of the body stiffer, free-radical production that causes damages to inner structures of the body's cells, or a programmed cell death that implies that a self-destruct command may be part of the genetic program that controls cellular processes. As we look beyond the cell, then, and consider other systems of the body (musculo-skeletal, endocrine, limbic, pulmonary, etc.), we realize that each of these systems also shows the basic effects of genetic programming and the wear and tear of aging. Thus, as we consider these various theories, both genetic and nongenetic processes can be recognized as causal factors influencing aging processes. Further, as we again think about how we understand aging, we realize that many of the physical changes we encounter often produce an associated psychological effect. For example, as we have grown from childhood into adulthood, we have experienced different feelings about our new "adult" physical characteristics and abilities. The thoughts and feelings we had about our development have often been positive, but at times we might have also felt a bit awkward about how we looked or the ways we felt about our bodies. Similarly, with development into midlife and old age, we continue to take notice of and consider other physical changes. For example, we experience wrinkling of skin and change in hair color and texture, as well as other physical capacities such as strength and stamina. In response, we may have undertaken a sort of psychological zero-sum calculation to understand how our physical abilities and limitations may impact upon ideal images of self, as well as our interpersonal and environmental interactions. The result of these calculations at midlife or in old age may be positive in that we believe we "still have it!" despite some apparent declines in physical abilities over the years or negative in that we feel we are "over the hill" a bit and headed toward more decline.

Longevity and Health

Living to a ripe old age is something many of us hope to do. But the question of how long one might live is often qualified by the choices we make and the ways in which we live. In casual conversation, many of us, with some unease, may remark that we do not hope to end up living and dying in a nursing home. In fact, having to live in a nursing home is a rather uncommon occurrence for most older adults. The US Bureau of the Census suggests that around 3 to 4 percent of adults age 65 or older lived in nursing homes in recent census counts.[57] However, there is a caveat to recognize here, and it is that the rate of nursing home use increases with age: The number of older adults living in skilled nursing homes ranges from about 1 percent of adults 65 to 74 years of age, to 3.2 percent of those 75 to 84 years of age, to around 10 percent of those 85 to 94 years of age, and to nearly 25 percent of those ages 95 and older. Nonetheless, it is still unlikely that most of us will breathe our last breath in a nursing home. In fact, in western societies, most people die at home or in hospice care.[58]

As we consider the physical challenges and existential concerns of later life, it is important to note that with advancing age comes an increased risk for illness and death. Thus, as a matter of fact and without illusion, we recognize that illnesses will occur throughout the adult years, and each ailment and sickness represents an increase in risk of death. Indeed, as suggested in Tornstam's gerotranscendence theory, like the shadow we cast as we walk along in the afternoon sunlight, illness and death are part of an increasing personal awareness of the physical limitations that we experience in later life.[59] These limitations both inform and offer us a new awareness of our relation to life processes and the joining of our personal sense of being with the perils of illness and disease. Thus, at midlife, there is an existential resetting of our "life clock" from the early reference point of youth and "all the physical ways I've grown up and all the things I've accomplished and experienced since I was born or my last birthday" to a time of a mature awareness and a consideration of "all the things I still might hope to do before I die."[60]

Uneasily, some of us might be asking now, "But what types of illnesses and causes of death are we talking about?" In research that considered the top 5 causes of death of men and women in the United States, it is reported that about 20 percent, or 1 in 5 people, die of ischemic heart disease (or coronary artery/heart disease), followed by dementia of the Alzheimer's type (8.3 percent and 12.7 percent for men and women, respectively), lung cancer (7.4 percent and 6.7 percent for men and women, respectively), chronic obstructive pulmonary disease (almost 6 percent for both men and women), and cerebrovascular diseases (5 percent and 7.3 percent for men and women, respectively).[61] Rounding out the top 10 causes, this same research notes various forms of cancers (prostate, 2.8 percent; breast, 3.4 percent; colorectal, 2.6 percent for men and 2.5 percent for women), lower respiratory infections (roughly 3 percent for both men and women), diabetes (almost 3 percent for both men and women), and chronic kidney disease (almost 3 percent for both men and women) as causing death. Collectively, these causes of death are also suggested to be linked to a wide range of risk factors that go beyond genetic predisposition and include lifestyle factors such as poor dietary habits (high-fat and high-calorie foods), use of or exposure to tobacco smoke, use of alcohol and drugs, obesity, low physical activity, and working in hazardous environments.

So, what are the secrets to a long life? We often hear the health-associated exhortations to exercise, eat right, refrain from tobacco products, or drink in moderation. Is that enough? Our risk for disease and the causes for our death strongly relate to the lifestyle choices we make and our ability to eat healthy foods, exercise, limit our use of alcohol and tobacco products, and practice safe sex and healthy mental hygiene. Further, physical activity is recognized as an essential healthy lifestyle practice that prevents risk of disease and aids the management of chronic illness. Indeed, as reported in research by mobility and balance scientist Stephanie Studenski and colleagues, physical activity is an important dimension of health. They note that at age 75, walking-gait speed predicts 10-year survival for both men and women.[62] Moreover, these researchers suggest that walking speed is as important a predictor of mortality risk as are age, chronic health conditions, use of mobility aids, and other predictive factors such as smoking history, blood pressure, body mass index, and hospitalization history.

Should we join a marching band then? Well, maybe – if that is a way for you to find fulfillment in your living. Indeed, in reviewing a longitudinal study ongoing since 1921 that followed children into later life, health psychologists Howard Friedman and Leslie Martin report that all of the commonly prescribed health practices, such as getting more exercise, improving dietary habits, a moderate use of alcohol, and abstaining from tobacco, are secondary to living a fulfilled life.[63] What these researchers indicate is that the "real" secret to a long life is to have a sense of living a purposeful and meaningful life!

Music and Mind–Body Interaction in Later Life

When we consider the ways in which we may live in later life, we are reminded of the older adults we have observed. For example, one author relates a concert he attended in the 1980s by the Spanish classical guitarist Andres Segovia, who performed well into his nineties.[64] Then at eighty-eight years of age, Maestro Segovia, with careful and slow steps, was escorted to his chair on the stage and once seated performed in a way that was wonderfully animated and full of passion. In that hour or so of his performance, he was again youthful and agile, alive with the energy and effervescent spirit of the music he performed. In this example there is something of importance to recognize – something much deeper than just the activity of playing music to acknowledge. It is that in our playing of a musical instrument, singing, attending a concert, or just listening to a recording, we are involved in a ritual of sorts – a musical ritual that activates our memory and connects with our emotions that lends new insight into our current living and life experiences. Thus, whether performing or just listening to music, we become immersed in a mind–body interaction, one that reflects an ancient practice calling us to life.[65] Moreover, like many other creative activities, music may connect us to the deepest moments and points of reference in our life journey. So the benefit of music is not just in the physical activity, but also in the way music may psychologically buoy us and be a navigational guide as we quest for deeper meaning in our living.

As Candace Pert, neuroscientist and leader in the discovery of the opioid receptor, has proposed, wellness and illness have a psychosomatic component.[66] According to Pert, every system of the body is coordinated and run via the "molecules of emotion" (e.g., acetylcholine, dopamine, norepinephrine, testosterone, estrogen, oxytocin). Our thoughts and actions affect the production and uptake of neurotransmitters and vice versa. Thus, our emotional experiences and expressions affect the balance of the neuropeptide–receptor relationship throughout our body and, resultantly, our immunological system response and healing.[67] These neurochemical processes underlie cognitive-to-physiological relationships and the mind–body interaction.[68] Further, there is a wide array of cognitive and behavioral therapies that both induce and demonstrate mind–body interactions such as the relaxation response and that serve as alternate therapies or adjutants for traditional medical therapies.[69]

Therefore, in accord with the mind–body interactions of playing or listening to music, other health-associated benefits (psychological, emotional, social, and spiritual) are to be recognized. Research exploring the connection of music to the quality of life in older adults reports that musical activities such as listening to and making music influence how older adults may characterize and express enjoyment about their lives.[70] Further, research by music psychologist Stefan Koelsch and neuropsychologist Lutz Jäncke reports that in contrast to listening to tranquilizing music, listening to exciting music increases heart and respiration rates and affects regional activity of the heart as measured by electrocardiogram.[71] Moreover, these same researchers suggest that in contrast to silence, listening to pleasant, unpleasant, or simple isochronous sound pulses (i.e., sounds without melody, rhythm, or harmonies) was found to increase heart and respiration rates as well as reduce heart rate variability, again suggesting the powerful effect of the "musical beat" to play an important role in the autonomic nervous system responses to music. Other research has indicated that musical activities such as playing the piano may boost the level of general bodily activity (e.g., increases in blood flow and heart rate, and blood pressure proportional to exercise intensity) similar to that of taking a brisk walk.[72]

With regard to the health benefits of singing, research by the health and music research team of Stephen Clift and Grenville Hancox reports that members of a university choir self-reported that their participation enhanced mood and reduced stress, as well as improved lung function, breathing and posture, and feeling of being more energized.[73] Other longitudinal research following almost 13,000 adults in Sweden suggested that, after controlling for other risk and confounding variables, attendance at cultural events, reading, and singing in a choir were associated with lower mortality risk.[74] Furthermore, as geriatric psychiatrist Gene Cohen noted, involvement in music has a beneficial general health effect.[75] For example, in a 30-week intervention study where ambulatory and healthy enough to participate older adults were assigned to sing in a choral group or to a similar social activity control group, at the 12-month follow-up survey, the choral group self-reported higher rates of physical health and lower rates of doctor visits, use of medication, instances of falling, and health problems compared to the control group,[76] thus suggesting that music is more than a mere pastime experience that reflects significant life experiences and our celebration of our living, but also a way of maintaining wellness!

Music and Exercise

Getting started and staying with an exercise routine is problematic for many older adults, especially during rehabilitation following an injury. Research using music therapy as part of a rehabilitation program, however, suggests that listening to instrumental and vocal music spurred older adults' compliance to the physical exercise program.[77] Thus, special aspects of music may play a key role in motivating and directing individuals in their exercise routine. For example, a particular piece of music's rhythm, its melodiousness, and its cultural impact and association all have been noted to affect psychophysiological processes, with rhythm being the most important.[78] Further, exercising to music that highlights its vibrant rhythmic flow is suggested to increase participants' fun and enjoyment and thus their intrinsic motivation to exercise.[79] Moreover, similar to what is noted in young athletes, for older adults who are athletes or exercise regularly, music may serve to enhance mood and allow for dissociation from unpleasant feelings such as pain or fatigue, affect pre-event activation or relaxation, reduce perceptions of exertion during aerobic training and increase attainment of flow states, and extend work output and the acquisition of motor skills via the synchronizing of movement with music.[80]

When reduced strength or disability prevents individuals from participating in traditional aerobic types of exercise programs, activity programming that incorporates the movements of the orchestra conductor may provide another opportunity for physical exertion and benefit. For example, Conductorcise, a program that is oriented around listening to music and conducting the orchestra, created by conductor, clarinetist, and educator David Dworkin, pairs the physical movements of the conductor with the expressive themes of recorded orchestral music. Research examining the benefits of Conductorcise suggests it to be a viable technique to enhance mental and physical activity levels, and thus improve healthfulness, even for frail older adults.[81] Hence, as the research suggests, we see a rather substantial and wide influence of music as a component of physical exercise routines. In the next section and throughout the book, we will continue to explore ways musical activities may define and direct our everyday living and what we may do to improve our health and well-being, and age in a celebratory way.

Music as a Condition for Utopian Living: Environment–Behavior Relationships

As we found in the area of exercise, music may serve as a guide and motivator for physical activity and optimal athletic performance. Indeed, music transports us to a "different place." In many ways, then, as Sir Thomas More's *Utopia* describes,[82] we recognize music as an essential aspect of the "ideal" living conditions for older adults. What is more, music has been recognized as a key element of the idyllic environment *throughout* the Utopian literature. For example, from the *Epic of Gilgamesh*,[83] where there is no illness, no old age, and no mourning, to the place of Elysium noted in Homer's *Odyssey*,[84] with its "permanent background music provided by nightingales,"[85] to Edward Bellamy's *Looking Backward: 2000–1887*,[86] where having orchestral music piped into every home effectively creates a paradise in which the limits of human felicity are realized, we find music distinguished as one of life's great tonics and essential dimensions of the ideal environment.

In More's story of *Utopia*, he envisions a society where respect for and the privileges of old age are celebrated, and living is pleasurable. Focusing on pleasurable living, More posits that "we're impelled by reason as well as an instinct to enjoy ourselves in any natural way which does not hurt other people, interfere with greater pleasures, or cause unpleasant after-effects."[87] In his description of "pleasure," More further suggests it to be characterized in various physical–sensory experiences, as well as the deeper mental processes of learning and understanding, and via our reflective contemplation and seeking of "truth."

There is, however, a distinction of how physical–sensory pleasures may be characterized. As More discerns, we should distinguish physical–sensory pleasures directed by organic needs, such as the quenching of our thirst, in the satisfaction of eating food, relief of bowel or bladder tensions, or the discharge of sexual energies, from other sensory pleasures that are not directed by organic needs. This latter type of pleasure, experienced via the sating of bodily requirements, powerfully occupies our senses and emotions and "is the pleasure of music."[88] Thus, similar to what we find in the area of physical performance, music, from deeply cerebral orchestral works to foot-tapping folk songs, occupies our thinking and feeling, and compels our behaviors through its affordance of pleasure. Further, in our enjoyment of music and what it reveals about us, we again become aware of deeper aspects of our human nature.

Each of the utopian stories briefly noted, those of Gilgamesh, Homer, Bellamy, and More, focus on human happiness and how we might better arrange physical and social environments so that everyone experiences acceptance, honor, and joy in their living. However, when we look closely at the lives of older adults throughout the world, we recognize the very difficult and challenging conditions many endure, and the hardship and suffering they experience. Yet, we can imagine a place like Utopia and hope of its discovery. We can also realize it is yet within our ability to create such an environment. But how might we go about creating a "utopian-like" environment, where we can experience the best living conditions and fulfill our life potentials? This is a concern that seemingly interests and involves us all, not only as a desire that everyone may live in a place that provides safety and security, but also as a hope of how we can help each other be healthy and find remedy for life challenges.

The utopian notion of an ideal environment that, when created acts to bring forth the superior nature of the person and community, in many ways is reflective of the mind–body, yin–yang dialecticism found in Eastern philosophy. That is, much like the harmonic consonance and dissonance of tonal relations found within music, there is a wholeness and harmony revealed in the unity and interdependence among opposing elements. This philosophical perspective is one that has been appreciated and expressed in the psychological writings offered by Carl Jung and Carl Rogers,[89] has had a growing influence within Western and global psychology,[90] and is thus signified by the notion of "dynamic equilibrium,"[91] the "yin-yang of wellbeing,"[92] and the "mind-body monism" of alternative medicines.[93] Eminent in describing this dialecticism between life forces is the *Tao Te Ching*,[94] which inspires axiomatic expressions such as "the bass and the treble complement one another," "the subjective experience and the aural surround share the same moment," and "music's melodic form and its emotional content arise from one another."

With regard to factors that influence processes of aging, similar reciprocal relations involving social–environmental, psychological, and biological systems have been proposed as interacting forces that dynamically mediate physical changes and declines throughout adulthood.[95] Thus, to move closer to the creation and realization of utopian living, an embrace of contextualism – the perspective that recognizes interdependent relations between behavior and environment – is prescriptive. Indeed, a guiding principle of modern psychology is that to best understand people's needs and their behaviors and to improve their emotional and physical wellness, we must also understand and have knowledge of the sociocultural and physical context in which they live.[96]

Music as an Aspect of Utopia: Reprised

If music is a source of pleasure, how might we use it to enhance the living environment for older adults, including those who are still very independently living within the broader community? One way, as Bellamy alludes, is to arrange for music to be available during certain times of the day in retirement centers, assisted-living residences, nursing homes, as well as homes of community-dwelling older adults, so as to offer opportunity to find enjoyment and enhancement of human felicity.[97] Indeed, having the choice of participating in musical activities (e.g., attending a concert, background listening, performing) is one way for older adults to maintain feelings of competency and personal control.[98] In this regard we find a rich use of musical activities by older adults to discover and find deeper meaning and joyfulness in living. For example, interviews conducted by music educator Terrence Hays with adults in Australia ranging from sixty to seventy years of age who were casual music listeners as well as amateur and professional musicians documented the importance of music in the lives of older adults.[99] As participants noted in Hays' research, music affords an opportunity to express one's individuality and inner self, and to enjoy psychologically elevating experiences. Indeed, participants reported that music affects their whole being – physical, mental, and spiritual. Further, in support of the utopian positions offered earlier that music is a source of pleasure and a way to enhance and to find the highest boundary of our "human felicity," many participants noted that music provides a source of pleasure that is psychologically uplifting.[100] Other research participants interviewed by Hays emphasized how music impacted their general well-being and alluded that much like a massage, music produces a soothing and calming effect.[101] In addition, similar to what we noted in the area of exercise and athletic performance, listening to music was also reported to help in structuring the daily routines, in feeling competent and in control, in completing mundane chores such as housework, or in making going for a walk more enjoyable.[102] Perhaps most remarkable were reports that, like the background music of "nightingales singing" suggested in Homer's utopian world, music filled an "emptiness" in their life after work or careers have ended or spouses and friends have passed on.[103]

Furthermore, the influences of music on the lives of older adults are widespread and reported within many different cultural communities. For example, qualitative research by Darina Petrovsky and colleagues, exploring how older adults from predominantly African American community choirs perceive their involvement, report that participants' characterize their singing as doing something they love, where they benefit from having a joyful time together and the exhilaration of performing for others.[104] In a related manner, recognizing community singing as a potential intervention to enhance quality of life, experimental research by Julene Johnson and collaborators involving community-dwelling older adults from diverse backgrounds reports involvement in the community choir to reduce loneliness and increase interest in life.[105] Similarly, research by Jane Southcott and Rohan Nethsinghe, exploring the phenomenological experiences of elderly Russian immigrant members of a community choir in Australia, suggests that singing may enhance the individual's sense of autonomy and resiliency, communal connection, and access to inner resources that aid in meeting life's challenges.[106] Other research by Southcott and Sicong Li, exploring older Chinese adults' involvement in a weekly singing class, suggested community singing provides a way to enhance emotional, physical, and psychological well-being.[107] As these studies collectively suggest, music helps to coordinate and in a positive way accentuate the lives of many older adults. Moreover, considering deeper psychological influences, music may broaden access to engaging social and communal experiences, and make aware psychological resources that gird up and improve the quality of life.

At the Center of Life's Celebration

We will take up more specific discussion of quality of life and how music may enhance well-being and produce healing in later chapters. But let us end this chapter by describing a few places where music serves as a catalyst for the celebration of living. One place of special note is Casa di Riposo per Musicisti, a retirement home for musicians in Milan, Italy.[108] Founded in 1896 by the composer Giuseppe Verdi, and thus simply known as Casa Verdi, is a residence where both young and older retired musicians live. It is a place where music is always heard and performed, and where older musicians continue to teach and learn from younger musicians. Much like the operatic masterpieces *Otello*, and *Falstaff*, which Verdi composed during his seventies and respectively premiered at ages seventy-four and seventy-nine,[109] Casa Verdi is a place of vibrant living. It offers an abundance of care, respect, and support, and where, for both young and old, there is opportunity to discover deeper meaning and purpose in living. Thus, Casa Verdi is one example of a "utopia"– a place where we find younger and older generations living in harmony and working together, with music at the center of life's celebration.

Another reflection of the utopian ideal is the Triangel Partnerschaften, or Triangle Partnership, in Braunschweig, Germany.[110] This project brings together gifted high school and university students with nursing home residents to sing and play music together. Like Casa Verdi, this partnership hopes to provide benefits for everyone involved: For older adults it is the opportunity to continue to be involved with younger people, to remain intellectually stimulated, and to be active in the expression of their musical talents, as well as to explore and find new meaning in their living. For high school students, it is the opportunity to perform their music outside the school and to learn from their social interaction with the older adults. For university students, it is the opportunity to learn about the critical application of music therapy with older adults. Thus, as it is aptly named, this collaborative partnership offers and promotes intellectual, social, and personal enrichment for both younger and older musicians.

A similar intergenerational program is offered at The George Center,[111] an American music therapy center near Atlanta, Georgia. Incorporating music throughout all its care programs, The George Center brings preschoolers and assisted-living residents together to sing, dance, and play, and combines high school and college students with older adults in an intergenerational rock band. The George Center also offers a wide array of music therapy programs that include interventions to improve memory and neurocognitive functioning, and to promote a healing experience in end-of-life care. The reported positive outcomes of The George Center's hospice, hospital, and neonatal care music therapy programming has been reduction in the length of stay and use of certain types of drugs, along with lower overall cost of treatments.[112] Thus, like the aim of Casa Verdi and the Triangle Partnership, the programs at The George Center are intended to be educational and inspirational for all involved, and to herald a celebration of living.

As Ralph Waldo Emerson alludes, music innervates connections between mind-body-spirit, stirring our emotions and influencing the expression of our living. Indeed, music inspires our most complex feelings, thoughts, and actions – and as an essential aspect of our experience, provides us comfort and a place where we can feel we belong and celebrate our living. In Chapter 3 we will further consider how music may be a source of enjoyment and connection with others, as well as its effects in sensory and neuro–cognitive processes.

3   Hearing the Muse's Message: Changes in Sensory–Perceptual and Cognitive Processes

> Music from my fourth year has ever been my favorite pursuit. Thus early introduced to the sweet Muse, who attuned my soul to pure harmony, I loved her, and sometimes ventured to think that I was beloved by her in return ... and my Muse often whispered to me in hours of inspiration, – Try to write down the harmonies in your soul ... so I obeyed, and wrote.
>
> – Ludwig van Beethoven, "Letter to the Elector of Cologne, Frederick Maximilian"

Our encounter with music involves us in a broad range of psychological processes, from very basic sensory perceptions, and as Ludwig van Beethoven notes, to the deepest aspects of our being.[1] Moreover, each person is recognized to have a unique capacity to experience and to understand music.[2] As music therapist Mary Priestley has noted, music connects us with the emotions and expressions of life themes that reflect a common and shared deeper psychology, the collective unconscious.[3] Thus in many ways, music can be regarded as a language system involving the identification, classification, and contextual structuring of the basic elements of sound that produce melodic form, harmony, and expression of emotion. These basic elements are rhythm (e.g., beat, tempo, syncopation), dynamics (e.g., loud or soft), melody (e.g., pitch, theme, continuity), harmony (e.g., major or minor key, chord, consonant or dissonant), tonal color (e.g., register, range, instrumentation), texture (e.g., monophonic, homophonic, polyphonic), and form (e.g., binary, ternary, through-composed).[4] These different parts of music allow us to represent and communicate our deepest concerns and strongest desires, most powerful inspirations, and lasting hopes – a system of expression and understanding that once installed and active may continue to involve the person throughout life. So, that even in the case of profound hearing loss, the individual may still "hear" music.

An example of how music may still be experienced and understood, despite deafness and isolation from the external auditory environment is depicted in the life of the great classical composer Ludwig van Beethoven.

In a letter to his physician Dr. Franz Gerhard Wegeler in 1880, Beethoven describes his condition at thirty years of age:

> ... my ears are buzzing and ringing perpetually, day and night. I can with truth say that my life is very wretched; for nearly two years past I have avoided all society, because I find it impossible to say to people, *I am deaf!* In any other profession this might be more tolerable, but in mine such a condition is truly frightful ... To give you some idea of my extraordinary deafness, I must tell you that in the theatre I am obliged to lean close up against the orchestra in order to understand the actors, and when a little way off I hear none of the high notes of instruments or singers. It is most astonishing that in conversation some people never seem to observe this; being subject to fits of absence, they attribute it to that cause. I often can scarcely hear a person if speaking low; I can distinguish the tones, but not the words, and yet I feel it intolerable if anyone shouts to me.[5]

Hearing impairment occurs for many reasons. Beethoven's deafness has been attributed to many causes that, notwithstanding chronic exposure to acoustic stimuli, include the effects of rheumatic fever, cirrhosis of the liver, exposure to and ingestion of lead in the wine he consumed, syphilis, as well as other diseases.[6] Nevertheless, well after recognizing his hearing impairment, Beethoven composed perhaps two of his greatest works, "The Emperor," *Piano Concerto No. 5 in E♭ Major, Opus 73*, composed in 1809–1810, and "The Choral Symphony," *Symphony 9 in D Minor, Opus 125*, composed in 1817–1824.[7] Thus as various music historians have described, Beethoven's deafness perhaps aided his composing, "by shutting out extraneous noise and focusing his mind even more intensely on the melodies within"[8] and by allowing him access to a vastly deeper and more passionate inner life.[9] But beyond a more ardent and sagacious artistic expression realized through his deafness, how did Beethoven compose music if he could not hear it? We will take up this question at the end of the chapter. Immediately, however, let us consider age-related changes in sensory–perceptual and cognitive processes. As we do, much as Beethoven alludes in his letter to Dr. Wegeler concerning the social stigma of hearing impairment, we will also consider how sensory and cognitive deficits may broadly influence quality of life and provide opportunity for deeper insight into our living.

Age-Related Changes in Sensory–Perceptual Processes

Age-related changes in sensory–perceptual processes are common and often manifest themselves in how we interpret quality of life in our later years. But what does it mean to have "quality of life" or "to live the good life" in old age? In Chapter 2 we noted that living in a utopian-like milieu would certainly make life easier. The environmental design expert Derek

Clements-Croomes suggests, "We live through our senses."[10] So part of the answer to our questions involves the working efficiencies of our sensory systems, as well as other functional capacities (e.g., healthfulness of body, mind, and spirit) and the degree of challenge from the surrounding physical and social–cultural environments. Certainly the functional status of sensory systems (vision, hearing, balance, etc.) and how these may affect our physical and mental health, physical activity, and social functioning are key components of how we define "quality of life."[11] To address the other question, what does it mean "to live the good life" in old age, is perhaps more complex. Everyone will "normally" experience declines in sensory function of one sort or another as they age, and thus everyone will have their own answer to this question – their own expression of the "art of living." Thus, questions about the deeper meaning of life and how we might live are central to our sense of identity, autonomy, and relation to community. To begin to cast greater light on these topics, in the following sections we will briefly discuss the sensory–perceptual systems involving vision and hearing, as well as smell and taste, balance and movement, and touch and pain. We will also include discussion of how various accommodations and interventions may provide benefit and aid us in our "art of living."

Peripheral and Central Aspects of Sensory–Perceptual Functioning

One way to think about sensory–perceptual systems and processes is to consider what is peripheral, or closer to the "outside" of the body, and what is central, or more toward the "middle" of the body. Using this distinction, we recognize that the sensory receptors located in our nose, skin, ears, eyes, and on our tongue represent the peripheral aspects of the biophysical platform that supports our sensing and perceiving, while the processing centers in our brain represent more central aspects involved in the psychological coordination of our sensory–perceptual experiences. As we conceptualize how we hear music, then, we might think of the ear as a microphone, a peripheral feature, where the structures of the ear (e.g., the ear drum, the three small bones of the middle ear, and the small hair-like receptors of the cochlea located in the inner ear) convert physical sound energy into a neurological code that is then sent on to the innermost auditory areas of the brain for processing. The auditory centers of the brain, the central feature, may be thought of as a mixing console that allows the sound information to be reengineered and orchestrated into the moving melodic themes and harmonies that we recognize as music. In a similar way, we might consider the eye much like a camera, with the pupil and lens focusing light onto the photo-receptor cells of the retina, which send along neurological signals to higher-order visual centers in the brain. Other sensory–perceptual systems might also be conceptualized in a similar fashion. Taste and smell, senses of the tongue and nose, respectively, may be thought of much like peripheral electronic sensors that detect the chemical fingerprints of flavors and odors, and that send information on to the brain's olfactory center where processes of pattern recognition and a richer assay of our aromatic experiences are appreciated. The proprioception (i.e., awareness of physical movement and orientation) and equilibrium senses, respectively, involve peripheral motion sensors and carpenter-type bubble levels that detect movement, spatial positioning of the body and balance, and relay this information onto higher-order brain centers. The skin senses might be thought of as force, thermostatic, and damage detectors, relaying the peripheral information from pressure, temperature, and pain sensors on to higher-order regulatory centers in the brain.

Age-Related Changes in Vision and Hearing

Both peripheral and central mechanisms may change and affect our sensory–perceptual processing in many ways. For example, the development of cataracts cloud and blur vision, and with the basic wear and tear of the mechanical systems of outer, middle, and inner ear come changes in hearing sensitivity. Similarly, a stroke may affect vision or hearing centers of the brain, resulting in visual neglect, a syndrome where stimuli in the visual area opposite the area of the brain where the stroke has caused damage is not acknowledged, or Wernicke's aphasia, the inability to process and comprehend the sounds of language. Thus, there are noted declines in sight and sound perceptions that occur to most people as they age, and with the hope of providing therapy via corrective lenses and hearing aids, the areas of vision and hearing have historically garnered special research attention. Investigation of visual acuity and hearing sensitivity throughout the adult years has indicated normal declines in structures of the eye and the ear, respectively, termed presbyopia (i.e., old vision) and presbycusis (i.e., old hearing).[12] Beyond these changes that normally occur with aging are visual and auditory pathologies such as cataracts of the eye, illness-related injury to the inner ear, or injury to processing centers of the brain.

As we also recognize in the general population of older adults, decline in visual acuity presents problems for older musicians, and increased illumination, increasing size of musical notation, and adjustment of the lens line on bifocal glasses are helpful accommodations.[13] But certainly age-associated diseases of the eye (e.g., cataracts, diabetic retinopathy, glaucoma, macular degeneration) are also of critical concern, affecting one's ability to function and effectively interact with the environmental surround. In terms of quality of life, visual impairment affects contrast sensitivity and depth perception, and as a result increases risk for falling as well as injury from falling.[14] Further, severe visual impairments in later life, as reported by researcher Linda Moore and colleagues, are likely to disrupt the person's ability to perform regular routines and activities of everyday living.[15] In addition, as one encounters severe visual impairment, they may feel a loss of independence and autonomy. Further, later-life visual impairments may not occur in isolation, but rather are coupled with other sensory deficits that in combination further adversely affect physical and emotional health and social functioning.[16] Thus, the limitations caused by visual and other sensory deficits in old age are likely to disrupt social interactions with family and friends in some ways.[17]

Similar to what we find in the area of vision, with advancing age there is decline in the sensitivity to tones and pitches, especially higher pitches. As a result speech detection, a process that involves analyzing all the different pitches and sounds of language, becomes more difficult.[18] Hearing loss also results from chronic exposure to environmental noise, such as the very loud sounds of the industrial workplace or the constant and jarring cacophony in crowded or traffic-congested neighborhoods. Further, as noted in the case of Beethoven described earlier, hearing loss may result from infections that cause damage to the middle and inner ear, as noted in Meniere's disease and rheumatic fever. Hearing loss may also occur due to injury of the ear drum, middle ear, or inner ear, as well as brain areas involved in auditory processing.[19] Furthermore, akin to the disruptions caused by visual impairments, loss of hearing sensitivity may also affect how one may live and their quality of life,[20] especially with regard to how one may effectively interact with the surrounding environment, feel safe, and take part in social activities.

Certainly noise and the chronic loud blare of sound have detrimental effects that can damage hearing at any age. As noted by audiologists Frank Lin and colleagues,[21] and by Mark Ordy and colleagues,[22] damage to hearing accumulates with each episode of noise exposure, and thus nearly two-thirds of adults in the United States age 70 years and older show some degree of hearing loss. Further, within their study, these researchers indicated that the loss in hearing is greater for higher pitched tones (3000 to 8000 Hz) than for lower pitched tones (1000 to 2000 Hz). Cochlear hearing loss, where the small hair cells within the cochlea responsible for transforming the physical sound wave energy into neural code are damaged, represents the primary form of hearing impairment.[23]

This age-associated hearing loss affects pitch detection, and because the sounds of speech (i.e., the perceptually unique sounds produced when vowels and consonants are enunciated) are respectively a mixture of low and high pitched frequencies, also speech perception. There is, however, significant individual variability in the degree to which hearing loss occurs, and this variation is related to factors such as environmental exposure, gender, race, and socioeconomic status.[24] For example, a pioneering study by world famous ear surgeon Samuel Rosen and colleagues reports that older members of the Mabaans, a Sudan tribe of desert nomads living in a relatively noise-free environment, had rather exceptional hearing sensitivity across the 2000 to 8000 Hz range.[25] Comparatively, in a number of similar investigations involving groups of men and women in the United States, none report hearing sensitivity trends similar to that of the Mabaans.[26] The collective research does suggest, however, that individuals in the United States who report low noise exposure have better hearing sensitivity throughout the adult years than those with average or high noise exposure. Other research suggests effects of noise exposure and hearing impairment to be a global concern, noting that in contrast to high-income countries, there is a greater prevalence of hearing impairment in middle- and low-income countries where there is greater exposure to excessive noise and infectious diseases that can damage hearing.[27]

As we consider hearing damage caused by noise and the amplitude of sound volume, as a scale of comparison, it is noted that the loudness of normal conversation is about 65 decibels (dB), and generally exposure to sounds below 75 dB is considered safe. With concern then for musicians, it is noted that exposure to loudness levels beyond 85 dB (i.e., greater than the sound experienced as you stand about 15 meters from the road when a diesel truck traveling at 65 kph passes by) during rehearsals or performances is a rather commonplace occurrence. Thus decline in hearing sensitivity is noted as an occupational hazard for musicians, even for classical music players. For example, occupational health researcher Heli Laitinen in a survey of classical musicians in Finland found that 37 percent reported experiencing temporary tinnitus (i.e., ringing or buzzing in ears), 15 percent of women and18 percent of men reported permanent tinnitus, and 43 percent of the musicians reported hyperacusis (i.e., a hearing disorder that affects the perception and tolerance of sounds at various wave frequencies).[28] An audiometric-focused study of orchestral musicians by Pouryaghoub Gholamreza and colleagues, where loudness and tonal parameters are varied in the assessment of hearing sensitivity, indicated that 42 percent of research subjects had notches in either one or both ears, and this change in hearing sensitivity was more frequently observed in musicians with greater work experience.[29] Notches refer to areas of the hearing spectrum that show reduced sensitivity to sounds and are indicated when greater amplitude of sound, beyond 10 dB, is needed for the frequency range levels of 3000 and/or 4000 Hz and/or 6000 Hz than at the frequency levels of 1000 or 2000 Hz and at 6000 and/or 8000 Hz.[30] In addition, Gholamreza and colleagues report that 56 percent of the classical musicians sampled reported acute complications of noise exposure (e.g., ear pain or tinnitus) during or after a performance, and 11 percent reported chronic complications due to noise exposure.[31] Further, as noted in the research of audiologist Fei Zhao and colleagues, exposure to loud music is a significant source of hearing loss not only for musicians (e.g., members of an orchestra, rock band, pick-up garage band), but also for individuals whose work exposes them to the increased sound levels of music (e.g., sound engineers, lighting technicians) and those involved in other types of passive music listening (e.g., listening to music using headphones).[32]

Despite the concerns, however, the use of hearing protection is uncommon among musicians and also not consistently used by people who work in a wide range of occupational areas where noise is a hazard and hearing protection is required (construction sites, manufacturing centers, etc.).[33] Indeed, in a survey of classical musicians by Laitinen, 94 percent of respondents reported being concerned about their hearing, yet only 6 percent indicated that they always use hearing protection.[34] Similar trends in hearing loss and use of hearing protection are also reported in surveys involving nonprofessional pop and rock musicians.[35] But with rock music, where sound volume levels can range from 100 dB to 125 dB (equivalent to the sound of a chainsaw's horrid squealing and roaring as it cuts through a large log), the amplification can be much greater than for a symphony orchestra. Consequently, even for the occasional rock-concert fan, or persons who like to turn up the volume on their headphones, the sound levels of the music can surpass the 100 dB mark and cause damage to hearing. The after-effects may bring about a temporary tinnitus that persists for several hours and which may contribute to decline in hearing sensitivity or the development of tinnitus later in adulthood. Thus a word of caution is offered to the professional, as well amateur musician and casual music listener: Be aware of the sound levels that you are exposed to and take precautions to reduce noise when playing or listening to music. If necessary turn the volume down and/or use hearing protection devices such as ear plugs, ear muffs, sound shields, amplification of ambient noises to reduce loud sounds, or filters that eliminate high-pitched sounds. Practice "safe-listening"!

Smell and Taste Sensitivity and Aging

With advancing age there is decline in smell and taste sensitivities. Both of these olfactory senses play a key role in our finding pleasure as we consume a meal or beverage. Common examples demonstrating their critical involvement are when you have a cold and your nose is stuffed up or when you burn your tongue with a hot drink. With a stuffed-up nose or a burned tongue, most of us find reduced enjoyment in our favorite foods and drinks. As noted in reviews of the literature by scientists Richard Doty and Vidyulata Kamath, and by Annika Bramerson and colleagues,[36] about half of adults ages 65 to 80 experience a decrease in olfaction function, and beyond age 80 nearly three-quarters of adults experience decreased olfaction. Moreover, one early study by Doty and colleagues reported that in their research sample, nearly 50 percent of individuals 80 years or older were determined to be anosmic.[37] Anosmia is the experience of a loss of the sense of smell. Related research on taste sensitivity reports that most adults over the age of 65 show a general decline in taste sensitivity.[38] Further, taking into account the wide breadth of our flavor palette, past age 50 there is greater difficulty detecting all five primary taste sensations, that is, sweet, bitter, sour, salty, and umami (i.e., the savory or meaty flavor).[39] Therefore, some foods prepared by an older adult may seem extra spicy to a young taster, due to decline in the older adult's taste sensitivity and perhaps the concomitant increased use of salt, pepper, or other spices so that the dish tastes (to the older chef) appropriately seasoned.

Loss of smell and taste sensitivity occur as a result of injury to the chemical receptor systems of the nose and the tongue or the central processing areas of the brain. These injuries may be caused by viral infections, rhinosinusitis or nasal polyposis, and neurodegenerative illnesses such as dementia of the Alzheimer's type or Parkinson's disease.[40] Research examining the relationship between olfaction and quality of life reports that the loss of smell has a negative impact upon the person's appreciation of food, mood, and emotional balance as well as interpersonal and social functioning, which singularly or collectively may increase risk for depression.[41] Other research has suggested that smell is such a basic component of the evolutionary aspect of the brain that decline in smell sensitivity may be a powerful predictor of mortality.[42] Overall, age-associated changes in olfaction are suggested to affect one's daily meal preparation routines and how meals may be enjoyed as well as one's sense of general well-being and everyday safety.[43] Despite changes in smell and taste sensitivity, however, other research has suggested that the pleasure and enjoyment we take from our olfactory experience increases in later life.[44] This alludes to the fact that although we may experience declines in sensory function with advancing age, we may still appreciate the sweet smell of a rose and the enjoyment of a chocolate candy, and accordingly continue to have a rich and full experience as we savor the simple pleasures of life.

Age-Related Changes in Proprioception and Balance

Like vision, hearing, smell, and taste, there are also suggested age-related changes in proprioception and balance. Proprioception refers to the unconscious awareness of movement and spatial orientation arising from sensors in joints and muscles that provide information about the position of limbs and the body in space. Balance refers to the ability to control one's bodily position while stationary or in dynamic movement. Decline in these sensory–perceptual functions constitute increased risk for falling.[45] For example, balance research comparing healthy older and younger adults indicates an increased fall risk for older adults when a secondary task such as a Stroop test (a test of automatic cognitive processing and conscious control) is performed.[46] These findings suggest that activities like walking and text messaging at the same time, a combination that many of us may find full of distraction and difficult to do without tripping over or crashing into something, to present an even greater challenge in later life. In general, with advancing age, we recognize greater risk for balance disorder and falling as various environmental demands increase, and the dynamic capacities of our proprioception and other interacting cognitive systems change or decline.[47] In terms of quality of life, fear of falling is indicated to diminish one's participation in activities of daily living and one's "joie de vivre."[48] Further, empirical research has reported fear of falling to be related to increased risk for depression, as one recognizes the potential loss of independence, sense of dignity, and material possessions if one were injured in a fall and had to move into a rehabilitation or nursing center.[49]

Music, in its characteristic expressions of hope and celebration, can "put a spring in our step." So, can music play some role in helping the older adult improve balance and reduce risk for falling? The answer to this question seems to be, "yes!" Similar to using Tai Chi exercises to improve balance,[50] intervention programs using music have also reported improved balance of older adults. One such music-based exercise program is called Eurhythmics, developed by the composer Emile Jacques-Dalcroze.[51] Eurhythmics is a physical exercise system that directs movement of limbs and other parts of the body to the rhythms of music. A randomized controlled trial using Eurhythmics once a week for 6 months with older community-dwelling adults at risk for falling showed that assignment to this music-based exercise program improved gait performance and balance, and reduced both the rate of falls and the risk of falling.[52] Other research examining the effects of once a week for 15 weeks jazz dance exercise program with a sample of healthy, community-dwelling women ages 50 years or more also reported an increase in participants' balance.[53] A related dance-based program involving healthy women 65 years of age or older and incorporating a 1-hour Turkish folklore dance–based exercise program reported improvements in balance, distance walked in a 6-minute walk, speed it took to rise from a chair, and time to climb 10 stairs up and down, as well as physical functioning, general health, and mental health indices of quality of life.[54] Allied research involving musical accompaniment of dance-based exercise with older women reported participants' improved single-leg balance with eyes closed, functional reach, and walking time around two cones, suggesting that dance-based exercise may improve balance, locomotion/agility, and reduce risk for falling.[55] In addition, research using Argentine tango dance-based exercise reports similar improvements in balance indices, speed of walking, as well as balance confidence.[56] Overall, music-based exercise activities are noted to provide health benefits for the individual and offer a viable intervention to reduce risk for falling and improve quality of life.

Age-Related Changes in Skin Senses

Sensitivity to touch and skin pressure also declines with age. Research in this area indicates that discrimination of distances between skin pricks administered to different skin surface areas, as well as the ability to identify objects through touch alone, declines with age.[57] Vibratory stimuli are also less easily detected with advancing age, particularly in one's lower extremities. With regard to temperature sensitivity, perception and preferences do not differ between young and old adults. However, coping with cold and maintaining body temperature as well as being able to endure in hot environments decline with increasing age. Indeed, as we often read about or hear in the news reports, older adults are less able to endure temperature extremes, and there are more deaths during the coldest months due to hypothermia (i.e., a lowering of normal body temperature) and more deaths during the hottest months due to hyperthermia (i.e., a rising of normal body temperature).[58]

Pain sensitivity is also suggested to decline with advancing age, yet this is a sensory–perceptual modality where personality characteristics are noted to strongly influence detection and judgment of pain severity.[59]

In a meta-analytical review, pain researcher H. El Tumi and colleagues report a decrease in pressure pain thresholds in older adults in comparison to young adults, yet they report no age differences for heat pain thresholds.[60] With regard to chronic pain, as noted by Sylvia Gustin and colleagues, individuals reporting greater nociceptive pain (i.e., sharp, achy, or throbbing pain often associated with tissue damage) as well as individuals reporting greater neuropathic pain (i.e., the discomfort associated with disease or damage affecting the sensory–perceptual system) were found to exhibit a personality assessment profile reflective of greater harm avoidance and lower self-directness.[61] These findings suggest that pain perception is moderated by personality characteristics despite any changes in sensitivity that may occur with aging. Thus, research exploring the effects of chronic pain on everyday living experiences suggests that the quality of life and chronic pain experience relationship is more a function of beliefs about pain than the intensity of the pain.[62]

Regardless of one's personality characteristics or beliefs, pain for most of us is an unpleasant experience. Further, in terms of everyday living, and in a very colloquial sense, pain usually puts "a hitch in our get-along." This casually expressed consequence is born out in the empirical research, suggesting both chronic and acute pain may impair physical functioning, mood, and social functioning, as well as our general sense of well-being.[63] As we grapple with the challenges of living with pain and note the use of music in exercise programming, we are led to ask the question: Might listening to or making music provide relief from pain? The answer here is a qualified, "yes!" That is, perhaps not for everyone, or for all types of pain, but many people do report that listening to or making music provides some relief from pain. Indeed, as noted in studies by clinical researchers Sandra Siedliecki and Marion Good, and by Ruth McCaffrey and Edward Freeman, listening to music has been shown to be an effective intervention in decreasing rheumatoid arthritis and osteoarthritis pain, as well as pain and anxiety related to postoperative, procedural, and cancer pain.[64] Researchers Siedliecki and Good also report that in a randomized controlled trial study involving individuals with back, neck, and/or joint pain for at least 6 months, listening to a self-selected or researcher-provided 60-minute music program that was pleasant, soothing, and upbeat for 7 days effectively decreased pain as well as depression and disability. Case study research has suggested that regular practice on an electronic keyboard for 30 minutes over a 4-week period increased finger range of motion, dexterity, and strength and decreased self-reported discomfort from osteoarthritis.[65] Further, a meta-review of research incorporating music as a pain distractor or in addition to pharmacological treatment suggested listening to music can provide a modest reduction in pain intensity levels as well as reduced need for analgesics.[66] Thus, as noted in these clinical reports, listening to music may offer a stand-alone intervention or serve as an enhancement in conjunction with traditional acute or chronic pain medication management routines.

Changes in Cognition with Advancing Age

We now direct our focus onto centralized cognitive processes so as to begin to understand how these may change with advancing age and how someone like Beethoven may "hear" music despite auditory impairment. In this area we describe attention and speed of information processing, and how these are dynamically interrelated with higher-order cognitive operations such as executive planning and control, learning and memory, and reasoning and decision making. Further, when we consider the flow of information throughout the cognitive system, we recognize attention and speed of processing as critical elements of a basic "operating system" that initiates, directs, and controls other processing such as remembering and deep thinking. Yet, we often take these fundamental aspects of our psychology for granted and only acknowledge their importance when they start to fail. Thus, it should be recognized that like sensory–perceptual functions, our ability to think and process information also changes as we age, and these changes affect our living and quality of life.

Attention and Aging

Attention processes are composed of many dimensions. We have capacity to select, direct, and sustain attention. There are also resource and capacity parameters of our attention that limit the amount of information that may be attended to at any one time and the speed at which this information may be processed. Furthermore, often we are involved in an automatic type of processing that places minimal demands on our attention capacity. But we are still detecting and processing important information, and likely to attend to and perceive information that is high in personal relevance or out of the ordinary. For example we almost immediately notice a variation in a well-known melody or can detect when someone is singing "off-key." This is known as the "pop-out effect," where we automatically detect differences in the type information that is available.[67] A further characteristic of attention is that, for optimal learning to occur, at times we must be effortful in our processing. That is to say we must use all available attention resources to efficiently process the information and acquire new learning. For example, in learning a new musical piece on the guitar we may focus our attention onto specific aspects of our chording, or the fret location, and our finger position along the guitar's neck as we consider a particular melodic phrase, neglecting other information about rhythmic or melodic phrasing until we have a basic understanding of the new fingering. Then, slowly, and with practice, we learn the correct fingering with appropriate nuanced musical expression until it is almost automatic and part of our well-rehearsed musical repertoire.

With advancing age there are recognized declines in attention resources and capacities.[68] For example, empirical studies have suggested age-related impairment in the executive control responsible for the dividing, selecting, switching, and sustaining of attention focus when performing laboratory tasks.[69] This decline with advancing age in executive processes is also suggested to affect other more complex behaviors, such as driving an automobile. For example, the crash rate of older drivers has been found to increase as the useful field of vision (i.e., the visual area from which useful information can be pulled out in a brief glance) decreases.[70] Suggestive of a potential accommodation for age-associated attentional deficit, other research has indicated that providing opportunity for older adults to use multimodal processing (e.g., using auditory information in conjunction with visual information) helps to reduce cognitive processing demands, resulting in fewer driving and response function errors.[71]

If multimodal processing shows advantages in functional performance, then how might musical involvement provide an advantage in attention or other types of information processing? With concern for musical background, research has indicated positive effects of musical training on attentional processing and enhancement of higher-order cognitive functions.[72] For example, research by cognitive scientists Dana Strait and Nina Krause suggests that in comparison to nonmusicians, musicians demonstrated strengthened auditory attention, providing them perceptual and subcortical advantages for hearing and neural encoding of speech against a background of noise.[73] In a related manner, research by Brenda Hanna-Pladdy and Alicia MacKay involving older musicians and nonmusicians who were matched on age, education, and history of physical exercise reported that older high-activity musicians (i.e., those with at least ten years of experience) had better performance on neuropsychological tests of executive processing, nonverbal memory, and naming than matched nonmusicians.[74] Thus, these findings seem to provide some "good news" and suggest that being involved with music may enhance attention and other types of cognitive functioning in later life.

Speed of Processing and Aging

A related concern for executive functioning is the speed at which information is processed. As described in reviews by cognitive aging researchers James Birren and Laurel Fisher, and by Timothy Salthouse, speed of processing slows as we age.[75] Further, as the task becomes more complex, such as when there are many options to be considered before responding, decision analyses and initiation of behavioral response will take more time. In general, age-related slowing of behavior is suggestive of both structural and functional neurophysiological changes (i.e., reduced synaptic connectivity, neuronal loss) in the brain.[76]

Despite the decline in speed of processing with advancing age, other factors such as context and experience may help to compensate for slower processing. For example, an investigation of expert and novice golfers showed that novices performed worse under conditions when they were instructed to putt quickly, while expert golfers instructed to putt quickly performed better. Interpretively, this research suggests that novices perform best when they have more time to attend to and control the aiming and physical movements of putting, while experts perform best when relieved of having the extra time to explicitly attend to and focus on these automatic execution processes, and "over-think" their putting.[77] A related attention speed of performance effect is shown in playing a keyboard passage, where the novice's performance is enhanced when the attentional focus is more distal, that is, on the musical sounds produced, rather than on the actual movements made to strike the keys.[78] Further, experience on a task may allow one to compensate for the extra time it takes to sort through and process the information and then initiate responses that will optimize outcome or performance. For example, expert typists have been shown to maintain performance speed by reading further ahead in the text that they were typing from so as to allow more time for planning of movements, thus compensating for cognitive slowing.[79] Similar effects are noted with skilled pianists where, in relation to beginners, the advanced pianist reads further ahead in the musical score, allowing them to play at a faster tempo and perform with greater consistency and with fewer errors.[80]

The speed of processing effects leads to the question of how music might play a role in facilitating older adults' speed of cognition. Although there are few studies available to review, they are suggestive of both positive and negative effects. For example, background music may enhance attention and speed of processing. That is, similar to the somewhat controversial "Mozart Effect," where cognitive task performance is suggested to be improved after listening to classical music,[81] upbeat background music was found to increase older adults' processing speed. In these investigations, listening to music by Mozart's "Eine Kleine Nachtmusik" (*Serenade No. 13 in G Major*, K 525) or to Vivaldi's "Spring" (*Concerto No. 1 in E major, Opus, 8 RV 269*) was found to enhance performance on the Digit Symbol-Coding test (a task that requires the pairing of a digit with a symbol), as well as performance on memory tests involving word list recall and semantic fluency (a task that assesses the rapid naming of words from a category or that begin with a particular letter of the alphabet).[82] Further, music may also enhance older adults' spatial reasoning (i.e., ability to think and draw conclusions about objects in three dimensions).[83] These cognitive enhancements are suggested to result from the upbeat characteristics of the music spurring neurophysiological arousal and inducing positive emotion. Other research, however, suggests that background music may interfere with or overtax cognitive resources and thus impair performance on cognitive tasks.[84]

Learning and Memory and Age-Related Changes

As we consider learning and memory, we note that this is a very expansive research subject, which generally suggests age-related declines in rates of learning and memory. Thus, our discussion in this area will be brief, noting key concepts and empirical findings that may allow insight into how we learn and how we remember. Like other information systems (e.g., the computer), learning and memory processes are suggested to involve a flow of data through a series of mechanisms, stages, and stores. Further, when we recollect a particular event that has occurred, we reconstruct this event using all the information that is available in our memory stores. Thus, perhaps due to our inability to have correctly inputted information, or to have access to all the information that is stored, or because of intrapsychic influences that act to protect or enhance "self," our recollections are likely not to be a perfect record of the events we witnessed or of the information we have previously stored. This is one reason why old family stories evolve over time, and with each retelling, they are always *reconstructed* somewhat differently.[85] Indeed, our reconstruction may lead us to produce inaccurate or "false" memories (i.e., memory for items or events that did not occur or are inaccurate in some respect). Research has indicated that false memories are more of a problem for older adults than for younger adults.[86] Yet, in a review of laboratory studies that required participants to recognize a brief musical excerpt previously presented from other excerpts that differed in pitch, tonal structure, rhythm, and transposition, in comparison to younger adults, older adults were noted to perform similarly or with slight age deficit when presentations rates were fast. However, the more musically experienced older adults performed at higher levels than less experienced older adults.[87]

Sensory, Primary (Short-Term), and Working Memory: Positive and Negative Age Variation

As we think more specifically about our memory, we recognize that some things we learn are retained for a long time, while other types of information are forgotten almost immediately. We are continuously receiving information from the environment, but a translation is needed to convert this information from the environment into a neural–cognitive code, and this takes time. Sensory buffers are suggested to hold onto this raw information until the translation is completed. Two types of sensory buffers are iconic memory, a sensory buffer for visual information, and echoic memory, a sensory buffer for auditory information. In general, these sensory buffers are very limited in capacity and are thought to hold information for a very brief time (from about one-fifth of a second to one-half a second) before it decays. However, neuro-imaging research has suggested that auditory sensory memory may persist for as long as ten seconds,[88] allowing other cognitive mediating processes to begin to distinguish musical syntax and musical meaning, as well as other features of sound such as emotional significance.[89] Thus, as neuroscientist Stefan Koelsch and colleagues have noted in laboratory research, one positive age variation to recognize is an age-associated enhancement in musical syntax processing. This enhancement is demonstrated by greater neurological activation in the left-hemispheric prefrontal cortex area of the brain of adults in comparison to children, as the regular tonic-chord sequence of C major, F major, G major, and C major is distinguished from a harmonic progression involving the Neapolitan chord.[90] The Neapolitan is an irregular chord ending where a major triad is built on the lowered second degree of the supertonic; in the key of C major this would be a chord built on the notes of D-flat, F, and A-flat. The result is a "surprise" ending that conveys an emotional tension and ambiguity that may suggest a "heavenly," "other-worldly," or "dream-like" feeling. The age-associated increase in music syntax processing noted by Koelsch and colleagues alludes to the common notion that music is "felt more deeply" and "understood in a different way" as the person gets older.[91] Further, laboratory research indicates that although listening to music stimulates emotional regulation, it may also serve an adaptive function as it enhances the sense of well-being. Indeed, older adults report finding greater transcendence and personal growth while listening to music in comparison to young adults.[92]

After information is translated and tagged for more processing, it moves into primary memory, a short-term information store. The capacity of primary memory is about the size of a seven-digit telephone number. Information flowing into primary memory remains there awaiting further processing by other systems but may decay and be lost within a few seconds if not consciously rehearsed. Information in primary memory may also be automatically rehearsed and chunked (i.e., combining information into meaningful units so that it is easier to process and recall) so as to enhance learning and memory. It is clear that the more automatic the rehearsal, and the faster the processing of information in primary memory, the greater the recall of information.

A closely allied construct to primary memory, working memory, is suggested to share many of the attributes of primary memory, but differs in that it incorporates and accesses other previously learned information used in making decisions, solving problems, and learning new information.[93] Other aspects of working memory include visual–spatial and verbal–auditory processing modalities by which information is encoded and manipulated.[94] The resources and capacities of both primary and working memory are suggested to decline in later life[95] and affect the encoding, consolidating, and retrieval of various aspects of a memory representation so that information is more difficult to recall.[96] Thus, age deficits in learning a list of words may be due to an age-related decline in the neurocognitive mechanisms involved in automatic rehearsal and speed of processing aspects of primary memory,[97] as well as spread of activation and inhibition throughout the neurocognitive network.[98] Moreover, age-associated decline in everyday remembering (e.g., remembering to pay bills, follow medication instructions, making an appointment) is also dependent on the integrity of underlying neurocognitive mechanisms.[99] In addition, as we bear in mind the various modalities (e.g., visual–spatial, linguistic–auditory) of information processing, we should also recognize that deficits in visual or auditory sensitivity may also affect learning and memory processes. Indeed, memory researcher Patrick Rabbitt reports that mild hearing loss may be one factor affecting learning and apparent memory failures in later life.[100] However, we will also see that the picture is not so clear as we consider how memory for musical pieces may be remembered and more accessible, despite declines in other aspects of memory.

Secondary (Long-Term) and Other Types of Memory in Later Life: Remembering Who, What, When, Where, and How

Longer-term memory processes are essential for the enjoyment of music.[101] Indeed, to remember when and where we heard our favorite song and who we shared that moment with, or how to play a favorite melodic passage on the flute, all rely on secondary memory. Secondary memory refers to a very durable and long-term store of information memory. It contains information that has received sufficient encoding and processing to pass beyond sensory buffers and primary memory stores. In comparison to primary memory, secondary memory has a much larger capacity and longer duration, but uses similar visual–spatial and verbal–auditory processing modalities. Can you recall the name of your first music teacher, the way they looked, the songs you sang or instrumental pieces that you played? If you are able to recall these things, it is further evidence to suggest the long durability of the information that is stored in memory and various qualities of the information (i.e., pictorial–spatial and phonological–auditory features) that is represented in secondary memory.

Learning and remembering involve processes that are conceptualized as explicit in that they require attention and conscious processing, as well as implicit in that various types of information may be learned and remembered without any keen attentional focus and below our conscious awareness. This explicit and implicit distinction helps to describe two types of long-term memory systems: declarative memory, an aspect of long-term memory that represents a store of accumulated facts and experiences, and nondeclarative memory, an aspect of long-term memory that contains stores for procedural skills and habits, priming and perceptual learning, conditioned responses, and reflexes.[102] As we consider how aging may affect declarative and nondeclarative memory, we note that declarative memory is often noted to reflect age-related decline, while nondeclarative memory appears to be relatively spared or suggested to show only modest age-related decline.[103] Further, when nondeclarative memory is regularly activated, as one may do if they continue playing the piano or work out on the drum kit into old age, other procedural skills and habits are also more likely to be retained.[104] Thus the notion of "use it or lose it" seems an apropos suggestion to help maintain one's general motor skills and functional capabilities in later life.

There are other types of memory as well that involve these processing systems and buffers. For example, we are better at recognizing that we have seen or heard something than we are at recalling and describing exactly what we saw or heard without any contextual or cueing support. Recognition memory is the type of memory that helps us identify songs from the past and be successful in the common game, "Name that Tune!" Further, although recognition memory is thought to be generally preserved into old age,[105] laboratory research involving younger and older adults suggests a general age-associated decline in identifying previously presented musical excerpts, yet older adults show a positivity effect in that in comparison to young adults, they recognize more positive-emotion musical excerpts in relation to negative-emotion musical excerpts.[106]

Episodic memory refers to a store of knowledge about what, when, and where some event occurred. This is usually the kind of memory we test when we ask someone to remember words from a list and then later request that they recall as many words as they remember. However, we should also understand that some characteristics of the information we remember often has a personal relevance to us. Indeed, research has indicated that though there are often noted age deficits in episodic memory (e.g., recalling words from a word list), older adults' autobiographical information remains fairly good in old age.[107] Especially so if the information is a "flashbulb memory," that is, it is connected with highly emotional information of significant life events (a first musical performance, being married, joining the military, etc.).[108]

Semantic memory is an aspect of secondary memory. Semantic memory refers to a long-term information store that consists of general world knowledge and information, as well as word meanings and abstract relationships. For example, if you were asked to recite the notes of the lines and spaces of the treble clef, you might rely on the well-known mnemonics of Every-Good-Boy-Does-Fine for the lines and F-A-C-E for the spaces. Similarly, if you can recall the opening four-note motif of Beethoven's Fifth symphony (dah-dah-dah-duuhhmmm), you are accessing semantic memory. Thus, both general musical knowledge and characteristic auditory features of particular musical pieces are suggested to be held in semantic memory.[109] Further, as we consider age variation in semantic memory, there is suggested decline in language-based knowledge, yet memory for auditory information may be preserved in normal aging and in dementias such as Alzheimer's disease.[110]

A related long-term aspect of memory involves information about *knowing how* to perform various activities and skills. This nonverbal aspect of long-term memory is labeled as procedural memory and is important for learning how to play a musical instrument. The notion here is that once we learn the motor skill, things like the fingering for a musical passage on a piano or other musical instrument, then that "muscle memory" information is available to us, distinct from any other related verbal or auditory information. Thus, procedural memory references a store of psychomotor instructions that allows us to undertake a particular activity or task once it has been learned. For example, playing the G major chord in open position on the guitar – once we learn the fingering and fret position, we just simply *know how* to play the chord. With regard to aging, research suggests *knowing how* to perform a motor task is relatively well maintained into later life.[111] So despite being a little "rusty," our memory for *how* to play a particular piece of music or musical instrument is likely to be retained throughout the life course.

Moreover, research has indicated that despite age-associated impairment of declarative memory (e.g., the conscious recollection of a song's title and its composer), the efficacy of procedural memory (e.g., the unconscious and implicit memory of how to hold or play a musical instrument) seems to be relatively intact in older musicians who develop dementia of the Alzheimer's type.[112] This ability to know how to hold or play a musical instrument suggests that perhaps there is a "selective sparing" of music-associated memory. This finding also suggests that music intervention activities that target procedural memory may constitute a key method for sensorimotor stimulation and a realistic method of improving memory or rehabilitation for those with dementia.[113]

Furthermore, as we consider music improvisation, and especially the concerns for auditory input analysis, improvisational decision making, and output monitoring, we note that age-related declines in general cognitive characteristics may not be limiting to improvisational abilities and inventiveness.[114] Indeed, both the musical syntax and associated physical movements that allow improvisation of instrumental musical performance are suggested to rely on procedural memory.[115] Thus, what seems to be most important for musical improvisation is the long-term memory of rhythmic, tonal, and chordal motifs that can be reimagined and recoordinated in ad lib musical expressions.[116]

Ludwig van Beethoven, the Deaf Composer

We opened this chapter with Beethoven's description of his deafness, and now we consider the question, how did he compose music with such profound hearing loss? We find an answer to this question when we look closer at working memory and recognize a modality within working memory attuned to music.[117] Similar to the phonological loop component within working memory that is suggested to process language, this modality is postulated to accommodate musical syntax, as well as musical imagery.[118] It also accesses musical representations from longer-term stores, such as associated algorithms that direct improvisational playing and musical composition.[119] These integrative processes of working memory operate using visual and orientation information (e.g., memory for clefs and scales, the high or low pitches associated with musical notes) and verbal and/or auditory information (e.g., memory for words, sounds, and interpretations), allowing us to silently conceptualize and "hear" music as we look at the notes of a musical score. Thus, these aspects of the musical modality of working memory allowed Beethoven to imagine and compose musical masterpieces, despite his significant hearing loss. In addition, highly skilled pianists such as Beethoven are suggested to be least disturbed in learning pieces without hearing their own playing.[120] As the great maestro reports in his letter to one of his closest friends, Karl Frederich Amenda:

my affliction is less distressing when playing and composing ... I have also very much perfected my pianoforte playing ... (nevertheless,) I beg you will keep the fact of my deafness a profound secret, and not confide it to any human being. (Ludwig van Beethoven, 1866, "To Pastor Amenda.")[121]

Further, musical imagery, that is, the "replaying" of music in your head, allowed the composer to recollect and imagine musical attributes such as pitch, timber, and rhythm as he created and annotated the musical score, and to explore and express a deeper meaning in his art. Indeed, the notion that music can be "stuck in your head" is further evidence of the operation of musical imagery in working memory and the emotional significance of those memories.[122] Further, as suggested in an essay titled "Remembering My Roots, Interrogating the Present, Envisioning My Future" by Mildred Dacog,[123] the mental replaying of songs from the times of childhood and adolescence allows us to connect with many cherished memories from the past and with our cultural roots. These treasured memories also provide us a source of comfort and joy, as well as opportunity for deeper reflection on our lives and the many ways of becoming. Certainly for Beethoven, as well, those processes of remembering, examining, and imaging were elements of his composing and reflect a deep inner ritual and quest for hope, well-being, and self-actualization. These deeper, more personal and transcending processes stand as equally significant elements that allowed the great Maestro to find inspiration and to "hear" music, despite his deafness. In Chapter 4, we continue discussion of music, memory, and quality of life as we consider how music may be an intervention and a therapeutic aid in later life.

4 Sing a New Song! Therapeutic Interventions with Music

I am growing old and help me stay young. Let the music be played. Let the songs now be sung.

Back in Indiana, we never really did know, there were folks like music therapists, round. Such a thing to learn today.

I had a stroke. Look at me now. I learned to play the music somehow.

Whoever thought we'd see it, in the halls of Congress today there is music playing and songs being sung. It must be the start of something brand new.

So I'm growing old – help me stay forever young.

– Ken Medema, at the US Congressional Hearing "Forever Young: Music and Aging"

As we have noted in previous chapters, music may support us in our healthy living and staying well. These beneficial effects raise the question of how music may promote rehabilitation when neurological impairment is encountered. As the song by Ken Medema suggests,[1] music offers the hope of recovering key abilities following a devastating stroke. But how does this work? In this chapter, we will consider age-associated neurological impairments, including dementia of the Alzheimer's type, Parkinson's disease, and cerebral vascular accident or stroke, and how musical activities may benefit cognitive functioning when these pathologies are encountered. We start by discussing the "whole-person" approach as a way of caregiving and in understanding the existential challenges that occur with illness. Later in this chapter, we will see how music may aid in the rehabilitation and management of various age-associated illnesses.

Recognizing the Whole Person

It is estimated that at any given time, 5 to 8 percent of adults over 60 years of age are diagnosed with some form of dementia.[2] An epidemiological study from the United Kingdom, however, suggests that the rates of prevalence for cognitive impairment rise to 30 to 50 percent for adults 85 years of age or older.[3] Thus, the risk for neurodegenerative disease is a particular worry for many older adults. This is a concern that is also shared by the caregivers of older adults. How the individual may prevail over age-associated neurocognitive changes, and continue to live adaptively, is a key question of later-life development. Indeed, along with the problems presented by various neurological illnesses, other comorbid disorders frequently arise that may increase with disease, such as agitation, anxiety, depression, sleep disorder, and psychosis.[4] These comorbid conditions are often the focus of disease treatment, as they may be more effectively managed via social and behavioral interventions than the unyielding neurodegenerative disorder itself.[5] For any of these problems, the challenge for caregivers is to continue to see the person as still developing, encountering new challenges in living and in seeking a good quality of life, instead of merely a collection of symptoms or a diagnostic label, and thus no longer a "person."

Therefore, as we discuss neurological impairments, we also embrace and hope to promote the whole-person approach to our understanding.[6] This person-centered method moves beyond the mere reductionism of neurobiological structures and processes to acknowledge and honor the individual, their phenomenological sense of self, and their unique life experiences. Moreover, the whole-person approach offers insight into cognitive and emotional experiences occurring with the existential challenges of illness.[7] For example, as Carl Jung proposes, in all of our behavior we express and reflect the contents of our psychic life. That is, at all moments in our living, we express the "feeling-toned" mental representations of both personal, and thus *"private unconscious"* concerns and viewpoints, as well as universal, and thus common or *"collective unconscious"* impulses and beliefs.[8] The private unconscious mind is suggested to hold and reflect underlying beliefs regarding the psychosocial dynamics of personal power, relationship, responsibility, etc.; this area of psychic life Jung regarded as a manifestation of our personal "complexes." The collective unconscious mind is suggested to reflect deeper existential concerns and aspects of our psyche. This deeper unconscious aspect contains instinctual and universal modal representations of important others, and behavioral and personal characteristics such as a mother, caregiver, hero, etc.; this area of psychic life, Jung suggested, reflected and directed prototypical behaviors recognized as "archetypes."[9] Further, these latter collective unconscious representations are suggested to powerfully direct our behavior, so that our actions portray "this purposeful reflection and concentration to moral and physical forces that comes about spontaneously in the psychic space outside consciousness when conscious thought is not yet – or is no longer – possible."[10]

Thus, as the person takes on the existential challenges presented by old age and illness, we also note that they may yet play the role of hero or heroine, innovator and artist, as well as sage and prophet as they continue to seek personal growth, to learn, and to understand throughout all phases and moments of later life,[11] even as they struggle with impairments caused by a neurodegenerative illness like Alzheimer's disease. Indeed, as counseling psychologist Emily LaBarge and colleagues note,[12] individuals in early stages of Alzheimer's disease confront a wide range of psychological issues, including loss of intellectual function and social alienation. Yet, they still express interest in finding out more about the illness, in relaying information about their unique personal experiences, and in describing their love for and encounter in relationships with family and friends. Moreover, as caregiving expert Susan McCurry describes, "Beneath every dementia syndrome is a real person, someone with strengths or weaknesses that are now attenuated or exaggerated by their disease, to be sure, but nevertheless a human being that wants to be treated with respect and dignity."[13] Certainly, then, the person who has dementia and has suffered a stroke or who may struggle with another form of neurological illness is in many ways just like each of us – they too have a rich personal history and possess unique qualities and characteristics that we can still appreciate, respect, and love. Further, with regard to caregiving, this humanistic orientation offers opportunities for each older person to express their deepest personal thoughts and feelings, to feel valued by others, and to know that they continue to belong to the human family. Thus, in assisting individuals with neurodegenerative illness to continue to live with dignity, it will require our persistent seeking of insight and understanding, selfless-caring, enduring patience, and continued love to help them as they grow older.

Normal and Pathological Changes in Memory Systems

With characteristic certainty, we recognize that with advancing age come changes in memory and an increasing concern about forgetting. One term used to describe normal age-related changes in memory is *benign senescent forgetfulness*.[14] This "normal" type of forgetting typifies the "senior moment," where the older adult reports the inability to recall a person's name or a relatively unimportant event that they had missed, without report of other cognitive deficits. Other problems with remembering, of greater concern and reflecting a much more imperiling disruption of intellectual function, are "nonnormative" and include mild-cognitive impairment and various dementias.

Possible "Normative" Accounts for Forgetting

Several accounts have been put forth to understand forgetting. One account is rather benign and suggests forgetting is necessary to prevent our memory systems from becoming overburdened if we were to *remember* everything.[15] Another normative account proposes that normal age deficits occur as a result of subtle changes in underlying brain structures that impose limits upon and restrict memory processes.[16] Cognitive factors that may lead to this "normal" forgetting include changes in the efficacy of information encoding and subsequent search routines, as well as the extent of processing. Another account suggests that forgetting occurs due to cognitive slowing.[17] That is, slowing may occur due to an increase in the size or number of connections in the system, damage to connective pathways (i.e., loss of neurons), or traffic jams at key intersections on connective pathways. This latter cause is the basis for the interference hypothesis.

The interference hypothesis suggests that the information is stored in a network that is active and transmitting information from one point of connection to other points within the network.[18] Analogous with the transmission and reception of radio signals, information in the network may not be easy to access due to signal interference. Two sources of this signal disruption are proactive and retroactive interference. Proactive interference refers to a type of interference where an obstruction in memory access occurs due to activity that had occurred prior to the presentation of new material. For example, if you decide to switch from your regular telephone service and number (old information) to a new cell phone service and number (new information), your old telephone number may obstruct, or interfere with, learning or remembering your new number. This type of interference, proactive interference, has been suggested to intrude in musicians' learning and remembering new melodic or chordal phrases.[19] A different type of disruption, retroactive interference, occurs when new information obstructs the retrieval of old information. For example, if you have moved recently, you may have had to remember a new street address and postal code (new information). Learning this new address information may hinder, or interfere with, the ability to recall your previous address (old information). Subtle age-related neurological changes are indicated to cause deficits in our ability to inhibit and control system interference, and thus both types of obstruction, proactive and retroactive, are suggested as feasible accounts for age deficits in memory performance reported in laboratory tasks.[20]

Another plausible account for forgetting is disuse. The disuse hypothesis suggests that information stored in memory degrades and decays if not used.[21] This is the "use-it-or-lose-it" theory. For example, which notes are flatted in the B-flat major scale? Although this information has been taught to many of us in our early musical training, without recent practice (e.g., playing a piece in B-flat major), we may have forgotten this specific information. The answer to this question about which notes are flatted in a B-flat major scale are B and E (Bb, C, D, Eb, F, G, A). However, as noted at the beginning of this section and taken up in the next, forgetting is very likely to occur due to normative neurobiological changes as well as pathological neurodegenerative processes.

Memory Impairment and Continuation of Self and Life-of-Mind

Though memory is an essential aspect of our phenomenological sense of self, serving to support one's personal identity and continuous life narrative,[22] problems with accurately remembering recent events and activities, or following along with the flow of complex conversation, are often the types of memory complaints noted to occur in later life. Further, whether mild, moderate, or severe, memory impairment is an existential threat to the person, so that as philosopher Mary Margaret McCabe suggests, "When memory fractures, the person and her virtues and vices somehow fractures too."[23] Yet as McCabe notes, our identity and life narrative is not defined strictly by the solipsism of "I think, therefore I am," but also by the rich interpersonal relationships we have with family members and others in our broader social community. Thus, as noted in research by Lisa Caddell and Linda Clare, individuals experiencing dementia and related intellectual impairments simultaneously express both continuity and change in their identity.[24] Indeed, as one older man from Caddell and Clare's research reports, he continues to enjoy life, loving his wife and daughter, and doing things around the house – but what he recognizes to have changed is that now his memory is bad.[25] Similarly, as novelist and scholar Michael Ignatieff relates about his mother, who died of Alzheimer's disease, throughout the illness, and even in later stages when she could not speak or exude dynamic interpersonal expressions, she characteristically remained the same person.[26] Thus, as we consider various cognitive deficits and neurological illnesses that may occur as the person grows older, we hope to also continue to be aware of the whole person, that is, to be aware that despite the functional declines brought on by neurological illness, the person continues to reside in a symbolic world of meaning, to express a phenomenological sense of self derived through social interactions, and thus continues to have a basic existential need for connection with others.[27] Further, to recognize that the human mind – with its great amalgamation of memories coupled with past experiences, social and cultural frames of perceiving, and characteristic ways of understanding – is perhaps the most complex entity in the universe, and that the person with dementia, notwithstanding various cognitive limitations, still continues to be a sentient being, immersed in a life of mind.[28]

Mild Cognitive Impairment, Age-Associated Neurological Illnesses, and Dementias

Mild cognitive impairment (MCI) is defined by subjective memory complaint along with performance on verbal memory tests that is 1 to 1.5 standard deviations below the norm for the individual's age group.[29] Clinical research suggest that 90 percent of individuals who exhibit the amnestic type of MCI (i.e., increased forgetfulness), rather than nonamnestic MCI (i.e., declines in functions not related to memory, such as reduction in attention, language, or visuospatial processes), progress to show signs of dementia of the Alzheimer's type.[30] As noted earlier, memory and cognition show normal declines with advancing aging. In contrast to normal age-related decline, however, dementia of the Alzheimer's type is indicative of irreversible neuropathological changes (i.e., neurofibrillary tangles and amyloid plaques) in the hippocampus, a midbrain structure intimately involved in learning and memory, as well as in the entorhinal cortex located in the medial temporal lobe area involved in memory, orientation, and perception of time.[31] In later stages of Alzheimer's disease, cerebral cortex areas involved in language, decision making, and executive control and interpersonal behaviors suffer greater impairment.[32] Further, it is important to recognize that memory impairment may occur as a result of other pathologies, such as a Lewy bodies and Parkinson's disease, cerebral vascular accident (stroke), and other neurological disease or injury.[33]

Although Alzheimer's disease is the most common type of dementia, other rather common age-associated neurological illnesses are Lewy bodies and Parkinson's disease.[34] Lewy bodies are abnormal deposits of alpha-synuclein protein in the brain, which may disturb other chemical processes throughout the brain involved with a wide range of behaviors (e.g., memory, mood, movement, perception, sleep, thinking) and are a common cause of dementia. Often associated with Lewy bodies disease, Parkinson's disease is a neurodegenerative disorder affecting the dopamine-producing cells of the substantia nigra, a midbrain region involved in balance and movement control. Parkinson's disease early on causes bodily tremors and movement disturbances, and, as noted in the case of the singer Linda Ronstadt, may also affect voice control and musical expression.[35] In its later stages, Parkinson's disease can impact upon other brain areas and cause dementia.[36]

Decline in cognitive function also occurs due to cerebral vascular accident or stroke. Stroke refers to a literal death of portions of the brain due either to ischemic attacks (small strokes) that cut off blood supply in the brain or hemorrhagic strokes (where there is bleeding into the brain that affects a larger area and are more devastating) that damage brain cells. For all types of stroke, however, onset is typically abrupt, with potential impairment of a wide range of cognitive functions, including attention, memory, language, and executive function, and thus comprises a variety of neurocognitive disorders.[37] As a result, stroke increases risk for dementia.[38] Further, there may be differential loss of cognitive–behavioral function as a result of the underlying neurological system most affected by the stroke. For example, there is greater decline in attention, memory, language, and executive function in stroke patients who develop a behavioral variant of frontotemporal dementia (a dementia caused by cell loss in the frontal lobe of the brain), while declines mostly in attention and executive functioning are found in individuals who develop a language variant of frontotemporal dementia.[39]

From a biological perspective it is important to understand that the brain contains the basic hardware for the execution of all cognitive–behavioral programs. Thus, apart from the more advanced functions such as self-awareness, thinking, and decision making located in areas of the cerebrum, fundamental changes in motor cortex and subcortical areas of the basal ganglia and cerebellum are linked to the functional decline of movement control in old age. Indeed, damage to the cerebellum, an area at the base of the brain involved in movement control, inevitably leads to problems with balance and movement coordination. The classic example is that of a professional pugilist, or boxer, who over the course of a match receives many blows that result in destruction of cerebellum tissue,[40] so that after receiving and weathering many punches during the match, the boxer may be referred to as "punch drunk." That is, the boxer may exhibit slurred speech, walk with an unbalanced gait, show disorientation and intellectual impairment, and thus appear as if drunk. Along with the immediate disruption of balance and coordination, there may be long-term cognitive effects resulting in dementia pugilistica, or chronic traumatic encephalopathy (CTE).[41] Dementia pugilistica or CTE refers to a dementia as a result of brain trauma. Although boxers are particularly vulnerable to this type of dementia, other individuals who participate in contact sports such as football, hockey and soccer are also at risk for traumatic brain injury. It should be recognized as well that other types of injury to the brain, such as a concussion from a fall, are also likely to disrupt memory and may cause retroactive amnesia (loss of memories previous to the injury) or anterograde amnesia (inability to create new memories) and lead to early-onset dementia.[42]

Other pathologies may also impair neurological functioning. For example, Wernicke-Korsakoff syndrome refers to a dementia caused by chronic alcohol abuse and thiamine deficiency, where there is marked inability to learn new information or other types of memory deficit.[43] Proper nutrition is important for healthy brain aging and cognitive function.[44] Thus, when there is poor nutritional habit, vitamin B12 deficiency may occur, which mimics the type of memory loss seen in Alzheimer's disease. However, this "pseudodementia" is potentially reversible through restoration of vitamin B12 serum levels.[45] It should also be noted that neurochemical and neuroelectric imbalances of the brain also impair memory processes.[46] For example, the production of stress hormones (e.g., adrenaline, cortisol, norepinephrine) at high levels over a long period of time is noted to have a damaging effect on biological systems throughout the body, including structures in the brain (e.g., amygdala, hippocampus, prefrontal cortex) involved in learning and memory.[47] In a like manner, altered states of consciousness produced by fatigue or hyperarousal may disrupt normal neurological processes underlying the encoding, storing, and retrieving of information.[48] In general, though neurological illness and injury affect memory, it is important to note that lifestyle, health, and genetic predisposition are all suggested to influence memory performance in later adulthood.

A Path to Healing and Recovery

As noted in Chapter 3, music therapy has been suggested as an effective way of helping the individual to cope with the neuropsychiatric symptoms associated with dementia.[49] Noting the many concerns for changes in neurocognitive and behavioral function with age, injury, or illness, we come to the following question: How might music serve as an intervention to enhance normative functioning in later life, as well as to restore functionality after injury or illness is encountered? In the next sections we will consider how a variety of musical activities may be used as an intervention to help manage illness and reestablish cognitive–behavioral functions.

Music as a Therapeutic Intervention

Music is a psychological and social phenomenon that produces behavioral effects in both humans and nonhumans.[50] Whether it is listening to music to "relax" in the rush-hour traffic or having the "right mix" to listen to on a long road trip, music is a dynamic and multifaceted stimulus that innervates cognitive, emotional, sensory, and motor centers of the brain, and offers an adaptive and rehabilitative intervention for a wide array of psychological and neurological concerns.[51] As we consider music as a possible therapeutic intervention, we should be aware of the many goals of music therapy, including its use to promote personal recovery from trauma, to foster adaptation and wellness, as a technique for relaxation and relief from stress, and as an intervention to manage bodily pain.[52] Music therapy is also used to encourage and support physical rehabilitation, as a method of improving speech and language, and as a memory aid. In addition, music is used to facilitate clinically oriented discussion and expression of feelings, as a method to improve interpersonal communication, and as a therapy to heal and sustain social communities.

Further, we should note that there are many techniques and varied forms of intervention. For example, an active form of musical therapy may employ techniques such as singing, drumming, playing a wind or stringed instrument, scripted or improvisational performance, or the composition of a song or musical piece. These techniques provide a means to facilitate personal adaptation and to foster and enrich personal well-being. Another form of intervention is passive, where music listening is used to aid relaxation, to guide mental imagery that evokes an awareness of previous sensory experiences and deep psychological states, and to facilitate reflective discussion. In clinical practice, each technique and form of intervention is directed by an empirical protocol designed to assist people in attaining their intervention goals. Moreover, though it is the intention of the music therapist to involve the individual or group in the therapeutic process, there is substantial leeway in the goals and structure of the therapy, as well as the personal preferences of both therapist and clients in selecting the types of music that might be used.[53] Thus, the activities as well as musical styles of the therapy will likely reflect individual preferences for the approach to and musical style employed in the therapy.

Music's Influence on the Brain

Music has been suggested to influence emotions and, in turn, as noted in our earlier discussion, also compel physical activity. Further, much like the cognitively stimulating effects of natural training regimens such as dance and sports, musical training activities are also suggested to simultaneously activate and involve many neurocognitive systems and resultantly enhance perceptual, motor, and cognitive functioning.[54] Indeed, certain types of music have been suggested to influence cognitive function. For example, the somewhat controversial Mozart effect is one type of consequence, where an enhancement in children's spatial–temporal performance such as completing a puzzle is suggested to occur after listening to the *Sonata for Two Pianos in D (K. 448)* by Mozart.[55] Relatedly, research using electroencephalogram (EEG) techniques indicates changes in brain electrical activity in younger and older adults while listening to this very rich and exciting musical piece.[56] However, there has also been controversy with regard to the reliability and validity of this effect on intellectual function,[57] suggesting that perhaps the resultant cognitive performance benefits are short term and based on the individual's musical aptitude or preference for this particular musical piece.[58] Nevertheless, the potential for music to innervate neurological and cognitive systems is suggested to be rather profound.[59]

For example, neuroimaging research by Teppo Särkämö and colleagues,[60] using positron emission tomography (PET) scans to reveal metabolic changes at the cellular level, indicates that many brain areas become active in processing various characteristic features of music (e.g., harmonic complexity, pitch, rhythm, timbre, tonality). Similarly, as noted in allied research by Vinoo Alluri and colleagues,[61] like the widespread neurological activation found in language processing,[62] music activates a broad network of neurocognitive systems, with specific activation in outer cortical and subcortical sensory brain areas, as well as in the cerebellum, when music timbre information is processed. Furthermore, Alluri and colleagues report that cognitive and emotional regions of the brain are observed to be most active in processing and responding to tonal information, while the limbic system and pleasure center of the brain (midbrain areas involving the amygdala, hippocampus, hypothalamus, nucleus accumbens, substantia nigra) are noted to become active in processing and responding to musical pulse information.[63] This activation of the brain's pleasure center is tied into the production and release of the neurotransmitter dopamine, a chemical that interfaces with our experience of pleasure and pain, and that also mediates mood.[64]

Similarly, music activates other neurocognitive systems as well. For example, the attentional mechanisms involved in the temporal sequencing of the perception of music and the sensorimotor coordination that allows one to keep a syncopated rhythm all become active with musical stimulation.[65] Further, working and long-term memory systems that overlay and directly coordinate and process musical information, as well as the regulatory mood and emotional processes, are also suggested to be dynamically involved with organizing and acting in response to music information.[66]

The widespread activation of neurocognitive systems as well as specific stimulation within areas of the brain when listening to or playing music alludes to the potential benefits of music-based neurological therapies. For example, physical exercise with music has been suggested to protect against loss of brain cells in the frontal cortex of older adults.[67] Further, the benefits of music-based therapies are suggested to be similar to those of implicit learning (i.e., the incidental neurological activation of adjacent or associated cognitive features), such that music listening spurs activation across neurological systems so as to instantiate and enhance new learning (e.g., distinguishing the regularity of western tonal information, recalling information from an advertisement, learning on verbal memory tasks).[68] Moreover, both musical training and music listening set in motion a wide array of neurocognitive processes that enhance executive function and provide other cognitive benefit.[69] Thus, both listening to and making music have been indicated as therapeutic applications for optimal maintenance as well as rehabilitation of brain function.[70] We will consider a few of these therapies next.

Using Music to Improve Cognition and to Evoke Memory

Given the suggestion that listening to or performing music broadly innervates neural networks as well as specialized brain centers, then how might music help memory? What advertisers have known for a long time is that people become very familiar with and thus remember musical "jingles," so that, just as the advertisers hoped, brand-associated jingles influence product preference and subsequently consumers' buying behavior.[71] Allied research has indicated that recall of text information is enhanced when paired with a musical melody.[72] Further, research has also shown that popular songs that connect with critical periods of development, such as graduation, marriage, or the birth of a child, are also noted to become more familiar and better remembered.[73] So what might we find in research that uses music to aid the memory of older adults?

Research exploring the effects of listening to music on older adults' memory by Nicola Mammarella and colleagues used excerpts from Vivaldi's *Spring (Concerto No. 1 in E major, Opus 8 RV 269, "Spring")*.[74] This study involved healthy older adults, 73 to 86 years of age, who resided in the vicinity of Chieti, Italy, about 200 kilometers east by northeast of Rome. Participants were assigned to the condition of listening to the Vivaldi music, or white noise, or no music, and asked to complete simple tests of working memory (i.e., a digit-span task, the number of digits recalled after verbal presentation; and a word-fluency task, the rapid naming of words that begin with a particular letter from the alphabet). Results indicated significantly higher performance by participants exposed to the Vivaldi music, leading these researchers to propose, similar to the Mozart effect noted earlier, a Vivaldi effect.[75] In describing this effect, Mammarella and colleagues suggested the music produces arousal and activation of neurocognitive–emotional systems, resulting in a keener attentional focus and activation of memory processes, as well as a shift of mood (e.g., feeling happy) that also provides cognitive benefit. Thus, as Mammarella's research team speculated, Vivaldi's *Spring* may either arouse attentional and memory processes in such a way so that greater focus is given to auditory stimuli and the connections between digit items presented, resulting in a more vigorous letter-cuing search within the word lexicon, or enhance mood in such a way that cognitive test performance is benefited. It is conceivable, too, that exposure to Vivaldi's music enhances both mood *and* the attentional and memory search processes.

Related research involving older adults and exploring the effects of background music on cognition used excerpts from Mozart's *Eine Kleine Nachtmmusik* (*Serenade No. 13 in G Major*, K 525) and Mahler's *Adagietto* (the fourth movement of *Symphony 5*). This research reported enhancement of speed of processing, word list learning, and word fluency, along with variation of mood as a function of exposure to the musical excerpts.[76] However, other research exploring the effects of music listening on verbal memory of older adults, while showing increases in arousal and relaxation due to music listening, failed to show cognitive benefits.[77] So like the research involving the Mozart effect, the results of music listening to improve older adults' memory test performance suggest a complex picture requiring further research to illuminate the influence of an individual's background, musical taste, preference, and emotion on memory and cognition.

Long- and Short-Term Effects of Musical Training

When we consider the question of an individual's background, we might ask if taking music lessons early in life provides a cognitive benefit in later life. One study by Agnes Chan and colleagues[78] involved college students at the Chinese University of Hong Kong, who were matched for age, grade point average, and years of education. Verbal memory was assessed in a series of word-list learning trials. Results of this study indicated that across all trials, students who had received music training earlier in life remembered significantly more words from the word lists than did students without music training. Chan and her collaborators concluded that musical training may have a long-lasting effect that aids verbal memory and, like other techniques to improve memory, may offer potential for improving verbal memory, especially in individuals with language impairment. Allied research examining the effect of early music training on later life cognitive performance also suggests benefits. For example, research by Travis White-Schwoch and colleagues[79] examining the neural response time to speech sounds assessed via EEG recordings indicated that older adults who had received musical training during childhood and adolescence exhibited the fastest neural timing in response to a simple speech sound. This early training advantage led these researchers to suggest that early musical training is associated with greater efficiency in neural processing in later life, decades after the last music lesson and rehearsal had occurred.

Does current practicing of a musical instrument make a difference in maintaining later life cognitive abilities? As most music students come to realize, and teachers reinforce, it is the consistent rehearsal, from week to week and month to month, even if it is just for a few minutes each day, that pays off in advancing one's technique and musical expression. Research exploring how to maintain cognitive–motor skills in later life suggests that ongoing involvement does make a difference! For example, research by Raif Krampe and K. Anders Ericsson studying young and older amateur and expert pianists[80] reported that while older participants demonstrated the expected age-related declines in general processing speed, older expert pianists did not show the same degree of performance declines on music-related tasks (i.e., the rate of speed, degree of force, and errors in single-hand and bimanual key strikes on a piano keyboard) as did the older amateur pianists. In fact, older expert pianists performed better on the music-related tasks than young amateurs and only slightly below that of the young expert pianists.

Further, research by Jennifer Bugos and colleagues[81] showed that even musically naïve older adults improve in neuropsychological function after receiving individualized piano instruction. In this research, older adult amateur musicians (i.e., individuals with fewer than five years of musical training) were randomly assigned either to an experimental group that received six months of piano lessons or to a nontreatment control group. A battery of neuropsychological assessments including the Trail Making Test (a test that requires drawing a line that connects numeric points or alternates between numeric and alphabetic points) and the Digit Symbol-Coding test from the Wechsler Adult Intelligence Scale III were administered at baseline. Although there were no differences between groups at baseline, at the six-month post-training and three-month post-research delay, however, significant improvement was noted in digit symbol-coding and trail making (both measures of working memory and speed of information processing) for the older adults who had received piano instruction. Based on these findings Bugos and colleagues suggested that individualized piano instruction may be an effective intervention for age-associated cognitive decline. Related research by Dieke Mansens and colleagues[82] reported that older adults singing or playing a musical instrument at least once every two weeks to be associated with better attention, episodic memory, and executive functioning, again leading the researchers to suggest that music making may serve as a protective mechanism against age-associated cognitive decline. But what happens when there is dementia? We take up that issue in the next sections.

Benefits of Music on Mild Cognitive Impairment and Dementia of the Alzheimer's Type

Musical activities are helpful in maintaining physical and mental wellness and, as noted earlier, may also enhance or act in a way that helps to maintain cognitive abilities. Recent studies examining musical activities as an intervention for mild cognitive impairment and dementia of the Alzheimer's type (AD) also suggest promising outcomes. For example, research by Kim Innes and collaborators asked older adults who reported subjective memory loss to listen to a program of relaxing classical music at least once a week for twelve weeks.[83] Results at the end of the twelve-week music listening intervention indicated significant improvement in self-report of memory function, as well as paper and pencil tests of attention, processing speed and executive function (i.e., digit symbol-coding and the trail making test). Further, these positive enhancements of subjective memory and cognitive function were sustained at a three-month posttest follow-up. Based on these findings, the researchers suggested that listening to relaxing classical music may beneficially affect functional and structural neurological elements associated with cognitive processing speed, attention, memory, emotional regulation and reward.

Music therapy has also been shown to have positive effects for individuals with dementia and their caregivers. For example, Teppo Särkämö and colleagues reported that individuals involved in a weekly group session of singing or musical listening for ten weeks showed improved mood, orientation, and short-term memory in comparison to participants who received the usual care that did not include these musical activities.[84] Beyond these effects in individuals with dementia, benefits were also found for caregivers who had been trained to continue with the musical intervention. At a second follow-up six months later, caregivers who continued the singing intervention on a weekly basis regarded the intervention as beneficial and reported reduced psychological burden of caring. Related research involving patients with AD[85] examining the effects of sung versus spoken lyrics on memory reported better recognition accuracy for sung lyrics immediately after stimuli presentation and at a one-week follow-up assessment. This work suggests that the melodic enhancement of words may broaden memory encoding processes as well as heighten arousal, thereby focusing attention and improving memory. Furthermore, a meta-review by Laura Fusar-Poli and colleagues suggests a global cognitive enhancement of music therapy for people living with dementia.[86] It should be noted, however, that across the various studies reviewed, intervention protocols varied, as did the reliability and validity of cognitive effects found, indicating the need for additional research to provide further understanding of how music may be used as a cognitive intervention.[87]

Music Intervention's Broader Effect on Anxiety and Depression Associated with Dementia

Memory loss is not the only problem presented by dementia. Often anxiety and depression are co-occurring conditions. Research by Stephane Guetin and colleagues[88] provides insight into how music therapy may benefit individuals with AD. In their research, nursing home patients with AD were randomized to either a treatment condition of music listening or to a control group, a condition without music listening. The music listening program lasted twenty minutes and was individually programmed so that it contained a selection of pieces preferred by the patient and was sequenced to induce relaxation. The music was streamed via headphones into patients' rooms and was administered once a week for sixteen weeks. At baseline, and every fourth week for twenty-four weeks, anxiety and depression were measured using self-assessment clinical instruments (i.e., the Hamilton Scale and Geriatric Depression Scale, respectively). Results indicated that in comparison to the control group, the music listening group attained a significant reduction in anxiety at week sixteen, and this effect persisted at the twenty-four-week assessment. Further, depression scores significantly declined in the music listening group from baseline to week sixteen and was found to be significantly lower from baseline at the twenty-four-week assessment. Other allied research has similarly suggested music listening as a practical therapy to help alleviate anxiety and depression in persons with AD.[89]

Research has also explored how music may help in eliciting autobiographical memories and thereby enhance well-being of adults with dementia. For example, research by Mohamad El Haj and colleagues involving young and older adults, and patients with dementia of the

Alzheimer's type (AD), indicated that listening to one's favorite music prior to memory assessment enhanced participants' recollections of autobiographical memories. These memories were more quickly retrieved, contained more detailed and more emotional information, and produced a greater positive impact on mood.[90] However, although young and older adults outperformed AD patients in how quickly memories were retrieved and how detailed the memories were, music listening facilitated the recollection of more detailed memories within the AD patient group, and that in comparison to older adults, enhancement of mood was largest among AD patients. This research suggests that these music-evoked autobiographical memories (MEAMs) may play an important role in supporting and enhancing the emotional well-being of individuals with dementia.

Similar MEAMs research by Lola Cuddy and colleagues investigated how listening to music may potentially reveal the positivity effect in individuals with mild to moderate dementia of the Alzheimer's type.[91] The positivity effect refers to a later life preference for and a recall of information that is positive in emotional content and is suggested to be a hallmark of healthy aging. The research design required participants to listen to familiar instrumental musical pieces and accessed how the music helped to influence mood and evoke memories of the past. Results indicated that in comparison to younger adults, the evoked memories of normal older adults and older adults with AD were rated as more positive, suggesting a positivity effect even for individuals with dementia. The findings led the researchers to suggest that despite the ravages of AD, a positive sense of self and a relative healthy-aging orientation has been preserved. Further, this research again reveals the therapeutic utility of music listening in aiding individuals with AD to reminisce and to find moments of enjoyment, despite ongoing cognitive impairments and disruptions to life. Moreover, it shows that long-term musical memories are relatively preserved in Alzheimer's disease. Therefore, in a very practical way, music listening evokes personal long-term memories and thus provides a source of cognitive stimulation that helps the individuals in expressing feelings and aspects of self, as well as providing an activity where they may maintain social and communication functions.[92]

Interpretively then, as proposed by Katlyn Peck and colleagues,[93] the effects of music exposure may innervate dopaminergic activity and arousal mechanisms that enhance neurocognitive networks involving attention, learning and memory, and longer term and autobiographical memories, and thus offer a nonpharmacological approach focused on maintenance of cognitive function and psychological well-being of persons with AD. Further, as suggested by Orii McDermott and colleagues,[94] music therapy and especially singing offer a nonpharmacological way to enhance mood and reduce behavioral disturbance in people with AD. In addition, as Alfredo Raglio and others report,[95] there are other positive behavioral effects of music therapy in persons with dementia, including reductions in agitation, anxiety, and depression. This whole-person approach is an important concern in music therapy and coincides with the philosophical orientation that recognizes dynamic connection between the inner personal experience and outer behavioral functioning. We will further explore the potential of music therapy in the next section as we take up interventions for other types of neurological impairment.

Music Therapy for Parkinson's Disease, Stroke, and Other Neurological Disorders

Walking and maintaining postural balance are both rather complex behaviors directed by neurocognitive systems that we often take for granted. With very fine coordination, these systems integrate incoming sensory information with outgoing motor commands, allowing us to perform a wide array of physical movements (e.g., standing up, walking across the room, dancing a waltz). As described by Dr. Aidin Ashoori and colleagues,[96] rhythmic auditory stimulation has been an effective intervention to treat the motor abnormalities that occur in Parkinson's disease or that follow a stroke or other neurological incidents that affect the complex neurological systems involved in movement and balance. The critical understanding of how music therapy helps restore motor function focuses on the underlying systems that are affected, such as loss or degeneration of neurons in the midbrain area of the substantia-nigra and basil ganglia, and how the rhythmic beat of music may direct inner timing patterns that control gait. As we noted earlier, musical tempo may entrain the brain, thereby producing a natural synchronicity between the external rhythms of the music and internal timing patterns that direct movements. A movement-focused entrainment also occurs when walking with a friend, where each person's step velocity and gait length come into synchrony, thereby allowing both persons to walk together at a relatively brisk pace or a more casual stroll. This connection between the musical beat and our inner rhythms, as well as other social cues, such as keeping pace with a friend in our walking example, also reflect the basic drive components of and the motivating influences of music on exercise routines and for more advanced athletic training programs. Indeed, music has a powerful influence over us, as many of us find it difficult not to tap our foot when we hear the excitement of a marching band or to want to move to the rhythms of a popular dance song.

A study exploring how external rhythm may influence walking tempo by musicologist Federik Styns and colleagues assigned young adults to conditions where they listened to slow and fast musical excerpts or just to excerpts of a slow- and fast-beating metronome.[97] The findings indicated that people synchronize their walking pace to slower and faster tempi. However, the synchronization and pace of walking were faster when music was present, leading the authors to suggest that the music affords a perceptual resonance in which the person's body feels the music and interpretively acts (e.g., walks or dances) in accord with the qualities of the music and its tempo. Allied research by physical therapist Joanne Wittwer and associates involving healthy older adults indicates similar synchronization effects, with faster walking observed when accompanied by music than when just the stimulus cuing of a metronome is provided.[98] Further, music may help individuals with Parkinson's disease. For example, music rhythm is suggested to produce automatic activation of the motor system (e.g., pre-motor and supplemental areas, basil ganglia, and cerebellum), which is affected in varying degrees by Parkinson's disease.[99] Further, music-based rehabilitation activities, where there is movement in coordination with music, are suggested to improve movement-related functioning as well as general quality of life in individuals with Parkinson's disease.[100] Indeed, research by kinesiologist Natalie de Bruin and colleagues, who involved individuals with Parkinson's disease in a thirteen-week walking-to-music intervention, reported that thirty minutes of walking, three times a week, while listening to an iPod containing an individualized playlist of songs, improved walking-gait velocity, stride time, cadence, and Parkinson's disease symptom severity at the completion of the intervention.[101]

Yet it should be recognized that the synchronization of walking with music is still a rather complex perceptual–motor process and, thus, when auditory pattern perception–motor timing coordination is affected, musical entrainment may be disrupted. For example, an investigation by music and health researcher Michael Thaut and associates involving individuals who suffer from Huntington's disease, a disease that results in brain cell death and disruption of mood regulation and other mental processes, indicated that participants could modulate their walking through a self-cuing or metronome-cuing of pace. However, there was lower pace modulation in the condition of walking with music, and this deficit increased with the severity of the disease, suggesting the perceptual–motor connectivity may be disrupted very early in Huntington's disease.[102]

Music therapy has also been suggested to be beneficial for individuals recovering from stroke and other neurological injury. For example, music listening has been reported to aid recovery of cognitive function in stroke patients,[103] indicating that through music's innervation of underlying neural mechanisms, resultant improvements in auditory and verbal memory, enhanced visual attention in individuals with visual neglect, and reduced anxiety during recovery may occur. Further, for individuals who have motor system disruption following their stroke that affects walking, music intervention to entrain sensory–motor coupling was suggested to improve walking speed and stride length in comparison to controls.[104] For individuals who suffer motor impairment of upper extremities as a result of their stroke, very brief music therapy that involved playing a keyboard or drum also suggested enhancement of motor function during their rehabilitation, as noted by improvements in gross and fine-motor skills.[105]

Other research has also suggested music therapy as a potential benefit in other areas where neurological function has been disrupted. For example, following brain or spinal cord injury, a twelve-week intervention in which patients were asked to write three songs that reflected on the past, present, and future self was suggested to enhance life satisfaction in the song-writing group in comparison to controls who received the standard care that did not include the music therapy intervention.[106] Further, treatment approaches that embrace the belief that everyone can benefit from music therapy have also demonstrated positive outcomes. For example, music therapy administered to prolonged coma brain-injured patients who had not recovered verbal initiative was noted to reduce psychomotor initiative and psychomotor agitation following an eight-week therapist-led music-improvisation intervention.[107] Music therapy, in the form of singing well-known songs, is also suggested as a way to stimulate cognitive functioning and emotional expression in older adults who suffer from frontotemporal dementia, a diverse type of dementia that affects the frontal and temporal areas of the brain.[108] Overall, various music therapy approaches used with these populations provide the benefits of music-related neurological stimulation, as well as opportunity for expression of emotions and personal meaning that enhances social involvement as well as meeting patients' psychosocial needs.

Singing a New Song

Perhaps the musical expression of Ken Medema, as we opened this chapter, is the most poignant reminder of music's gift and its therapeutic potential. His song, performed at a US Congressional Hearing of the

Special Committee on Aging, acknowledges the devastating effects of a stroke and the promise of music therapy to make the person whole again. It also reveals our human desire and quest to find self-fulfillment and harmony in our living. Ken Medema continues to sing his song of hope, living a life of advocacy that offers inspiration and aid to others. Blind since birth, Ken's lifelong involvement with music, first as a student, then as a music therapist, and later a professional musician and recording artist, provides us with insight into the power of music to make us whole, to enhance our quality of living, and to heal. Appearing often at spiritual retreats throughout the United States and still performing in his seventies, Ken advances through his music the importance of working for social justice, the courage of being, and the healing power of love.[109]

Apart from the restorative or rehabilitative benefits of music, music therapy may also serve as a palliative intervention. A palliative intervention focuses on reducing the challenges, struggles, or pains of the current moment. We recognize that each person has an indispensable need to communicate and to be understood. We also realize that there is much that family members and friends may do in providing an essential form of social comfort and in meeting this fundamental human need.[110] A first step in providing this indispensable aid is to be "present" to the other – that is, to continue to visit with, encounter, and interact with the person, treating them with respect and dignity. As we do this, we will gain a greater awareness of the changes we see our loved one or friend experience, and assist them and ourselves in the process of self-actualization – of discovering new understandings of the other as well as ourselves, and in finding a deeper sense of personal meaning and purpose in our living.[111]

In Chapter 5, we explore the role that resilience, recovery, and growth play when we face serious health challenges that affect our sense of who we are and our purpose in living.

5   Trio: Resilience, Recovery, and Growth

> Music broke down and rebuilt something or other in his head and heart.
>
> – Carl Sandburg, *Bath*

In 2017, Frank Vignola sustained potentially life-ending injuries as a result of an ATV accident. Spending nine months in a coma with his right shoulder broken in two places, a broken right arm, four broken ribs, and collapsed lungs, this renowned jazz guitarist was faced with the prospect of the end of his career. His recovery was one of reconnecting to his music and instrument. His journey was one of finding meaning again and a sense of identity as a musician. Undaunted, he indicated in a *JazzTimes* interview that he had to now focus on what he wanted to do musically. In this process, he worked on pieces by Charlie Parker. His journey back to playing was achieved by reaching small goals first, to play music he liked, and to learn the music thoroughly. In the interview, he remarked that the best therapy was to "practice as much as I can."[1]

Finding Meaning, Transformation, and Hope

Music is integral to finding meaning in one's life. It is the contextualized embodiment of the "human agency."[2] Indeed, music has had a long history and a connection to healing from the perspective of the musician but also from that of the layperson. For example, philosophers such as Aristotle and Plato believed that music affects the character of the listener. In Plato's *Republic*,[3] character was influenced by Harmonia (or modes), and music was the process by which humans realized their true form. In the medieval period, Boethius, for example, proposed that music was an all-pervading force (musica mundana) and a unifying principle in humans (musica humana) that brought the body and soul into harmony.[4] In fact, music was considered so important that it made up one of the four major areas of education in the medieval era (the Quadrivium: Arithmetic, Geometry, Astronomy, and Music).

Music is transformative. Music has the capacity to reach the depth of one's being and to provide purpose to one's life. Music can also open one to new experiences and to find a new way of living. This transformation can include a spiritual connection. Holistic approaches to healing have included the component of spirituality as a way to understand health and healing. Liturgical singing, ceremonial chants, and spirituals have been thought to be an integral part of a holistic process toward healing. Music unites us with the spiritual and helps us meet the challenges in our lives. The healing energy of music embodies meaning and a way to listen to our inner self. It handles the inner dissonance and leads us to live authentic lives.[5] For example, music therapists William Davis, Kate Gfeller, and Michael Thaut list the qualities of music that can inform research and music therapy, treatment, and intervention. The auditory experience of music provides a sensory stimulation that influences and moderates the attentional system, motor system responding, and other cognitive systems that may compel and influence a wide array of behaviors. Moreover, music may enhance and regulate affective experiences that are linked to motivational aspects of learning and adaptation. Further, considered from broader sociological and psychological orientations, Davis and colleagues indicate that music serves to facilitate group involvements, social exchanges, and interpersonal attachments. In combination, all of these channels of influence suggest many paths by which therapeutic processes may be coordinated. Thus, various forms of music therapy (e.g., active, passive, reflective, guided, with neurological focus) may effectively facilitate the individual's expression of feelings, needs, and desires. Music therapy can guide the maintenance of a regimen, lead to recovery, and facilitate rehabilitation. Indeed, there are many different approaches to music therapy and thus many ways to personalize the therapy for the individual. Therefore, music can be used to create a therapeutic environment that is nonthreatening and can address a variety of illnesses and disorders through its broad utility and adjustable implementation. This client-centered approach, which is an essential aspect of humanistic gerontology, takes into account and adaptively seeks to meet the different biophysical, communicative, psychological, and social needs of the person, holding at all times the central focus of enhancing well-being and quality of life.[6]

Throughout our discussion we have noted the positive influence of music to lift one's spirit and to enhance health and well-being. Indeed, music has a powerful influence on older people, and listening to music has been suggested as a "self-administered" form of emotional therapy.[7] For example, survey research suggests that when older people listen to music, they most often report that it makes them happy. Thus, music is strongly linked to mood regulation and general well-being.[8] In fact, the top-five emotions reported by subjects while listening to music were feeling happy, feeling enjoyment, feeling nostalgic, feeling relaxed, and feeling calm.[9] Therefore, various types of musical activities are noted to help regulate and maintain psychological well-being. For example, an investigation by psychologist Sarah Oetken and colleagues in a nondepressed sample of adults suggests that listening to music activates neurological systems that induces positive mood and enhances self-evaluation. At the neurological level, music listening activates amygdala and hippocampal areas, as well as other temporal brain areas.[10] Music therapy may also serve as an intervention to induce positive mood and maintain a healthy self-image when one encounters an illness that challenges coping resources.

Therapeutic Interventions

One of the most known techniques in the field of music therapy is the Bonny Method of Guided Imagery and Music. The Bonny method of guided imagery and music is an example of the humanistic perspective in music therapy developed by music therapist Helen Bonny.[11] Interestingly, it was initially designed as an alternative to other forms of psychotherapy.[12] The Bonny method is a music-centered, transformational approach to help people confront and find their way of being vis-à-vis their conditions. It utilizes specific programmed classical music "to stimulate and support a dynamic unfolding of inner experiences in service of physical, psychological, and spiritual wholeness."[13] The idea is that music has a healing energy that embodies meaning and provides a way to listen to our inner self. In effect, music allows us to adapt and to find new ways of dealing with the challenges in our lives. The guided imagery of the Bonny method creates a therapeutic relationship between the client and therapist with the goal of allowing the client to explore new ways of being, to understand the images and symbols generated while listening to music, and to recognize how the images and symbols lead to meaning, an inner sense of self, and hopefully to well-being and wholeness.

Thus, a major theme when looking at the role of music as it relates to healing is that music brings wholeness to the person. In many ways, music's function is to bring about an "alignment between the individual and the healthful, creative properties of music."[14] This perspective has its history in humanistic philosophy and psychology.

Humanistic approaches recognize that each person has the capability to reach one's unique potential. Deeply rooted in Eastern, Middle-Eastern, and classical Greek thinking, the humanistic perspective imbues meaning and value in people, and dovetails nicely with the role music plays in affecting health. The history of humanistic psychology is also traced to Buddhism, Taoism, Confucianism, and Zoroastrian writings and is prominent in the transcendentalists such as Emerson and Henry David Thoreau.[15]

As Brian Abrams outlines, humanistic music therapy has four tenets: The first is that it is client centered. Humanistic music therapy is an outgrowth of the approaches developed by Carl Rogers and others who recognize that each person has the capability to reach his or her unique potential. The person is in a process of becoming who they were meant to be. Through music, the goal is to become a self-actualized person. A second tenet is that music is a way of being. Music shapes character, and it is transformative. With regard to disabilities, music allows the client to transcend disability by challenging the client toward growth. A third tenet addresses the therapeutic goals, which are to allow the client to attain self-actualization and to achieve his or her unique potential. The client vis-à-vis music is a "contextually situated person" who stands in a relationship with self and community.[16] The goal is to achieve self-sufficiency and independence. The fourth tenet involves the therapy process. Any type of therapy is appropriate as long as it serves humanistic perspectives. These therapies allow the client to work toward self-actualization. A humanistic music therapy approach allows the client to "find his or her own musical way without fixed rules, structures, or theories."[17] This type of therapy aligns the individual to the creative and transformative properties of music. Such a perspective has profound implications for people with disabilities and acute and chronic medical conditions.

Expanding on this humanistic, person-centered approach, Natalie Rogers (daughter of Carl Rogers) applies it to other domains such as writing, art, movement, and music. The willingness to learn, to change, and to be open to new experiences is the focus of her expressive arts therapy. The relationship between client and therapist is all important. It is a relationship built on trust and an openness to change. The therapist trusts the client's ability to know and to express their own feelings. The role of the therapist is to help the client explore these feelings. Expressive arts therapy integrates art and movement with person-centered therapy. Rather than using art as the vehicle to diagnose and to treat, under a person-centered approach art is used as self-expression and a language between therapist and client. Here the client expresses feelings through art forms such as sculpture, painting, dance, and music. The client then begins to understand their feelings and sources of their discontent and begins toward a path to healing and openness to new experiences.[18] This chapter continues to explore the connection between music and healing and presents examples of resilience, recovery, and growth.

The Challenge of Diabetes

It is estimated that 34 million Americans are diagnosed with diabetes. Of those, 90 to 95 percent are diagnosed with type II diabetes. Risk factors include age, weight, and family history. Minorities are at higher risk. Complications that can arise are kidney disease, neuropathy, and risk of heart disease and stroke. Type II diabetes can be managed by diet, exercise, and medication. The goals of managing type II diabetes are to keep A1C, blood glucose, blood pressure, cholesterol, and weight at acceptable levels. Often diabetes management requires changes in eating and drinking habits, activity, and adhering to a medical regimen if medication is required.[19] Response and success of diabetes management can often vary. For some it is difficult to change the lifestyle that has contributed to the disease and that adherence to medical regimens can fail. Diabetes management not only requires the person to make changes but also that one has a supportive network to help the person. At times, we can look at those who have diabetes and possibly gain inspiration to keep going. Two such people are B.B. King and Clark Terry.

B.B. King: The King of the Blues

B.B. King (1925–2015) is one of the undisputed greats of the blues, and after diagnosis of type II diabetes he also became a prominent spokesperson for diabetes management. When B.B. King became aware of his diabetes, he worked to manage his type II diabetes.[20] He talked about engaging in a healthy lifestyle and, in his role as spokesperson, appeared in several commercials for glucose meters. Not only is B.B. King's story with diabetes one of resilience, but it is also intertwined with a story of growth and becoming, a continuing process of self-actualization that led him to mentor and to inspire others.

For example, over the years B.B. King took under his mentorship many young musicians, one of whom was Joe Bonamassa, who is a well-respected blues musician in his own right. Bonamassa's first touring gig with King was at the age of 12, when he opened for him in 1989. In a tribute upon King's passing presented in *The Guardian*, Joe Bonamassa stated:

Never again will there be another as good, gracious or as kind as Mr. King. It was this humility and this giving back to other artists that has stayed with me and it's something that I try and do with other artists in my career. His legacy in my life was that he gave me a stage and allowed me to play to his audience and some of his audience became my audience. I can never repay the debt of gratitude that I have for this man who befriended me and gave me that opportunity.[21]

Clark Terry: "Mumbles"

Clark Terry (1920–2015) was the first African American musician to be hired at the National Broadcasting Company (NBC). He spent 12 years on the *Tonight Show*. Earlier in his career, he played with Count Basie and Duke Ellington and was a strong influence on Quincy Jones, Miles Davis, Dianne Reeves, and many others. His endearing sense of humor and the energy he exhibited toward his music is evident in his trademark song and nickname, "Mumbles." Started as an improvisational piece on the *Tonight Show*, "Mumbles" was later recorded in the studio and included on a record by Clark and Oscar Peterson as they found that they had extra recording time in the studio to fill.[22]

Along with several other medical conditions, Clark lived with diabetes for sixty years and eventually underwent amputation of both legs. He was never a quitter and serves as an inspiration to all. His indomitable spirit pervaded all aspects of his music and relationships with others. Not only was he an accomplished musician but also a caring teacher. He loved his students, and many expressed their love and appreciation in return. He created youth bands comprised of students from all over the world, and sponsored more than sixty jazz camps each year. Many of his students went on to become accomplished and famous musicians. Through all his medical problems, he remembered to thank "Big Prez" (his nickname for God) for all he had been given. Having received many honors and awards, one that he appreciated the most was to be given a star on the Walk of Fame on Blueberry Hill in his hometown of St. Louis, Missouri.[23] Clark Terry passed away at ninety-four years of age.

Music and Diabetes Management

Following from these inspiring stories, we consider the role music can play in diabetes management. The question is can music be a successful part of one's diabetes management regimen? Specifically, how might music aid the person in managing this disease? To address these questions, we first look to studies that investigate the link between music and stress, and then the effect of music on diabetes.

We can start by understanding the link between obesity, metabolic pathways, and inflammation as factors in diabetes. Obesity can impact insulin sensitivity[24] and thus place the person at risk for other medical conditions such as atherosclerosis, airway inflammation, and fatty liver disease.[25] Inflammation is also linked to obesity and is associated with diabetes. In effect, obesity leads to signaling inflammatory pathways that in turn contribute to insulin resistance.[26]

Environmental and situational stress has also been implicated in type II diabetes. An early review of the link between stress and type II diabetes suggests that stress may trigger autonomic nervous system response (flight-or-fight), which impacts glucose metabolism and then affects adrenergic sensitivity in the pancreas.[27] For many of us, certain situations trigger stress and anxiety. For some it is flying, taking a test, going to work, or one of many other situations that we find potentially stressful. We think most find the prospect of going to the dentist as a particular example of a highly stressful situation even for a routine cleaning. It is no doubt, then, that many studies have investigated the role music has on reducing stress. Elevated cortisol levels are linked to stress. For example, listening to music particularly for relaxation reduces cortisol concentration.[28] It has also been found that listening to music with others reduces stress, suggesting that social cohesion and social support are important factors in stress reduction through shared listening.[29]

Music played in medical facilities can also be beneficial. For example, a review of studies by Timothy Lyendo shows that use of music in hospitals facilitates healing, improves memory and learning, increases immune function, and improves quality of sleep. It decreases preoperative pain and anxiety levels and lowers heart rate. It also improves postoperative experiences, reduces anger, and enhances positive feelings in patients with brain injuries.[30] Other research suggests that the music does not need to be identified as soothing or meditative. The key is that whether lively or more sedate, the music chosen and liked by the person leads to better stress reduction.[31] This may present a quandary for the dental patient whose dentist uses music as a distractor and comfort during the dental procedure, but the music played over the loudspeaker is not liked by the patient!

Numerous studies demonstrate a link between music and stress reduction. However, studies that attempt to find a direct link to diabetes have been mixed. For example, a study conducted on 100 patients in India with type II diabetes (ages 30 to 85 years) found a greater significant decrease in level of fasting blood sugar for the experimental group (33-point drop) that was on a protocol of diet, medicine, yoga/exercise, and 30 to 40 minutes per day of music of the individual's own choice compared to the control group (20-point drop) who received the same protocol with the exception of music.[32] Other studies have found no direct effect of music on blood glucose levels. For example, Susan Mandel, Beth Davis, and Michelle Secic observed pre-assessment to post-assessment lowering of systolic blood pressure, state anxiety, and stress in patients who received music therapy, but no changes were observed in A1C between the music therapy and nonmusic therapy groups.[33]

Another risk factor associated with diabetes is the threat of neuropathy and risk of amputation of the lower extremities, such as the feet. A study by Li Ji and colleagues assessed the role of music therapy along with exercise to improve blood flow to the feet. Chinese patients with diabetes engaged in an exercise program along with music therapy compared to control patients who engaged in exercise only. It was found that listening to music during an exercise routine not only improved adherence to the exercise routine but also displayed increased blood flow to the feet.[34]

This study importantly highlights the risk of peripheral vascular disease that can lead to amputation and that improved blood flow is facilitated by a combination of exercise and music therapy. However, curiously, the researchers reported fasting blood glucose levels of both experimental and control groups to be statistically the same at the beginning of the study, but they failed to report whether any changes occurred between the two groups at the conclusion of the study. We propose that music therapy may reduce one's stress levels and motivate one to exercise. Evidence is also suggestive that music therapy along with exercise improves blood flow particularly for individuals at risk for peripheral vascular disease of the lower limbs. Less clear is the link between music therapy and reduction in glucose levels. Certainly, more research is warranted toward understanding the relationship between music and symptoms specific to diabetes.

Music Therapy and Depression

Depression is a relatively common chronic illness, associated with physical and psychological disturbances that cause emotional and social impairment. Depression often occurs in association with other illnesses and is thus recognized as a comorbid condition likely to accompany neurological impairments such as various types of dementia, Parkinson's disease and stroke, psychiatric illnesses such as anxiety and schizoaffective disorders, as well as illnesses such as heart disease, diabetes, and rheumatoid arthritis. Thus, the occurrence of depression throughout the adult years is rather widespread, with as many as 14 percent of community dwelling older adults estimated to meet clinical criterion for mild, moderate, or severe depression.[35] Further, for older adults who live in poverty or face economic insecurity, as many as 1 in 5 may exhibit symptoms of depression.[36] Moreover, higher rates of depression in later life are associated with disability, neurological disorders, and other physical illnesses,[37] and older women are at a greater risk for depression than men.[38] Again, recognizing the occurrence of depression with other physical and mental illness, it is noted that a moderately high percentage (46 percent) of nursing home patients are reported to have some form of depression.[39]

As an intervention, music therapy has been suggested to be effective in reducing symptoms of depression. For example, in an intervention study with older adults residing in a care home, individuals who listened to music showed a lowering and improvement in both anxiety and depression symptoms.[40] Other research by Orti de la Rubia and colleagues employing interactive music therapy over the course of 12 weeks, where participants interacted with a music therapist in listening and concentrating on the musical task of remembering the song, its lyrics, and names of individuals in the group, found enhanced positive mood (e.g., being happy) and diminished negative mood (e.g., being angry, fearful, or sad).[41] In a similar fashion, Moon Fai Chan and colleagues reported that in a community-based sample of older adults where participants met once a week to listen to 30 minutes of recorded music and were also encouraged to listen to the recorded music each night before bedtime reported significant reductions in depression and blood pressure scores.[42]

Further, it has also been suggested that any type of music therapy (e.g., active or passive, individual or group) in conjunction with standard forms of care (e.g., drug treatment, health education, rehabilitation, and other clinical practices) helps to reduce symptoms of depression in older adults.[43] In addition, a variety of music therapies can serve as an effective nonpharmacological intervention to treat other behavioral disturbances in older patients with dementia.[44] Research by Jasmin Werner and colleagues involving older adults in a nursing home, where 47 percent of the sample met criteria for at least mild depression at baseline, indicated that older adults who received interactive group music therapy showed a reduction in depressive symptoms compared to older adults assigned to a weekly group singing condition.[45] Other research suggests, however, that a receptive, calming form of music therapy, compared to interactive therapy, was more effective in reducing psychological and behavioral symptoms (e.g., agitation) of dementia.[46]

Depression may occur as a result of or in conjunction with physical and psychological illness. When we consider depression as co-occurring with other disorders, research has suggested music therapy to be an effective intervention to help alleviate and relieve symptoms of depression. For example, group music therapy is suggested to be a beneficial intervention for individuals with post-traumatic stress disorder (PTSD).[47] PTSD results from experiences such as being physically or psychologically assaulted, being seriously injured, or fearing or witnessing injury to self or others and being terrified or helpless in responding. The symptoms often associated with PTSD include anxiety and depression. In a randomized control study involving individuals who were bullied, civilian casualties of war, or survivors of rape, childhood sexual abuse, terrorism, or torture, Catherine Carr and colleagues report that a weekly one-hour exposure to an active form of musical therapy over ten weeks, where the therapist provided improvised musical support and participants were free to use variety of musical instruments (e.g., drum, xylophone, guitar, piano) in making music, helped to ease symptoms of depression and helped to facilitate therapeutic group discussion. Subjects reported that playing music was soothing and relaxing, that it aided them in finding enjoyment in the shared social experience, and helped them to realize that they were not the only person with PTSD. Moreover, subjects reported that playing music helped them to remember earlier pleasant life experiences, and allowed them to express emotions, and other feelings.[48]

Depression often accompanies chronic illnesses, such as diabetes mellitus.[49] On a personal note, one author's Mom, in the last decade of her life, was diagnosed with type I diabetes. This type of diabetes requires daily administration of insulin to control blood glucose levels, and other accompanying illnesses (neuropathy, diabetic retinopathy, cardiovascular disease, etc.) that further intensify the illness challenge. As a result, for many people with diabetes, a real struggle exists in trying to regulate glucose levels and manage everyday life routines against the background of a chronic illness. The author relates: "For my Mom, listening to marching band music was a method she used for emotional self-regulation. Perhaps it was the power of the drum cadences that influence neurological rhythms that control heart rate and respiration, and that rouse us to move, that attracted her to this music the most. Certainly, it was her preference to listen to marching band music when she was feeling down, to use the music to motivate her in daily routines, and to find new inspiration to meet the challenges of living with diabetes." For many of us, too, it is possible that we will also come to a place in our lives where we might struggle and have to work through the difficult emotions of disappointment, sadness, or despair. Perhaps too we will find emotional and physical invigoration in the stirring sounds of the drum, rapturous harmonies of the orchestra, or heroic melodic lines of individual instruments in the music we listen to or make.

Music and Chronic Pain

Listening to music can also aid self-regulation of pain. Music as a distraction from pain has the goal of providing a positive emotional state, enjoyment, and increased motivation.[50] For example, Ann Gold and Ajay Clare in interview research report that although chronic pain often interferes with enjoying and being involved with music, music listening can improve emotional state in a way that is consoling, energizing, relaxing, and uplifting. One respondent reported how music supports them: "It would be to feed my spirits. A very sad piece of violin music or something, it could go into the soul and then sort of carry you forward . . . so that at the end of the piece of music, the situation [the pain] might not have changed but the way you perceive it does . . . . It helps to support you. It doesn't change anything, but it supports you."[51] Further, a survey investigation by Hillary Moss, exploring music listening in a hospital outpatient group of 107 participants who endure chronic pain, reported that 91 percent of the sample reported that music was somewhat important to them, and 69 percent reported a benefit from music listening. An analysis of narratives by participants indicated that listening to music helped with relaxation and coping. Although a small sample, attending hospital caregivers also indicated that music listening was a benefit and viewed music therapy as having a role in the treatment of patients with chronic pain.[52] Music listening has also been suggested to be effective in relieving pain as well as anxiety and depression in cancer patients.[53]

Other research similarly suggests benefits of singing in treating chronic pain. For example, research by Joke Bradt and colleagues involved adults suffering from arthritic, musculoskeletal, neuropathic, back, and other forms of pain, in an eight-week group vocal music therapy. Subjects were instructed on proper breathing and were led in vocalization training by a music therapist. At the eight-week assessment, reductions from baseline measures in self-ratings of how pain interfered with daily activities and how pain was perceived to interfere with accomplishing certain tasks despite the pain, were observed. This investigation also revealed that the vocal music therapy offered participants a way to self-manage pain through the relaxation, mood improvement, and self-nurturing orientation it provided. Further, beneficial social effects were found through the shared experience, social support, and the finding of joy and happiness in being with others that came about in group vocal music therapy. In addition, the therapy was seen as self-transformative as participants gained a sense of a renewed and capable self, as well as an enhanced sense of empowerment and a new way of being in the world that the vocalizing of music provided. Other outcomes expressed by participants were that music therapy provided the motivation to take control of their pain and to realize they are with others who experience the same challenges as they do.[54]

Research also suggests that music listening may reduce the perception of pain as well as the need for analgesic drugs during surgery, during management in intensive care, and during postsurgical recovery.[55] For example, patients randomly assigned to a music listening condition during the 24-hour postoperative period following nasal surgery reported lower pain, lower systolic blood pressure and heart rate, and used fewer oral pain medicines than did patients assigned to the control condition where no music was played.[56] Similarly, a study that explored music therapy as a pain intervention following hip, knee, or shoulder surgery where patients self-selected a form of music therapy (e.g., listening, recreating, composing, or improvising) reported immediate improvement in pain, anxiety, and in some cases less nausea throughout the patient's postsurgical hospital stay in comparison to control subjects.[57] Another study examining recovery from knee replacement surgery used music to support exercise adherence.[58] In this study, patients were required to perform a pedaling exercise to increase range of motion in lower extremity. Results did not show a decrease in self-reported pain but did suggest a decrease in the amount of observed pain during music-supported exercise. This mixed effect is also noted in a very selective review by Ciaran Grafton-Clarke and colleagues that looked at seven studies examining music therapy as an effective intervention to reduce pain following open-heart surgery. In their review these researchers noted that although a few studies reported significant reduction in postoperative pain, anxiety, and use of pain medicines, there was no consistent pattern of reduction observed.[59] These findings suggest that the efficacy of music listening as part of an effective nonpharmacological intervention specific to pain following cardiac surgery is still an open question.

Nevertheless, other research has indicated music therapy to be effective in comforting patients postoperatively and as a valuable therapeutic tool to help relieve pain. Indeed, research by Elyas Soltani and colleagues involving patients who listened to thirty minutes of their preferred relaxing music or receive standard care (without music) after undergoing coronary bypass graph surgery showed that patients receiving music therapy report greater physical, environmental, and psychological comfort at follow-up.[60] Further, a broader meta-analytic review suggests that a variety of music therapies are effective in reducing pain and anxiety before, during, and after surgery.[61] In sum, music therapy of various sorts, whether alone or in conjunction with other interventions, is noted to reduce the perception of pain and, in doing so, possibly reduce the amount of pharmaceutical intervention needed.[62]

Jim Weatherhead's Story

Many who live with daily pain recognize the challenges they face to effectively manage their pain. As we discuss music therapy for pain management, we ask again the question, "What does it mean to have 'quality of life' and 'to live the good life'?" The story of Jim Weatherhead, who has managed ankylosing spondylitis (AS), a very disabling and painful type of spinal arthritis, is both informative and inspiring. Born in 1958, Jim has lived with chronic pain since the age of 17 and was first diagnosed with AS at age 26.[63] As described in "My Surreal and Deeply Emotional Day – Jim's Story,"[64] we find further insight to our question:

It was 1988. I met with a very passionate and knowledgeable rheumatologist who was able to rekindle my hope with promises of future advancements in medicine. He said they were years from release but showed tremendous promise at a cellular level. We talked at length about strategies to keep moving and working. I quit drinking, and committed to a balanced, healthy diet and lifestyle. This is not to say that the next 27 years didn't include terrible pain, frustrations, and challenges, but the road was understood. I accepted that I didn't have control of the disease, but that I could, with help from good doctors, be a good manager of the disease. I've lost 18″ of colon, I've been within hours of death due to infections, I've had surgical corrections of my feet, I've got aortic scarring from inflammation, I've had my eyes impacted, I'm fused from hip to neck including my rib cage, my neck is a mess – it sounds like busted glass rolling around in there and it barely moves enough to safely drive.

Then in 2001, Jim went on a new biologic drug (TNF inhibitor) that changed his life.

Today, some 28 years after I had wished for a gun ... I thought about ... those very scary first years on this journey to a now satisfied mind, and the odds of me finding myself sitting here today ... nearly pain free, fulfilled, and truly happy. I am truly blessed. AS is not something I would wish on anyone, but I understood today that my reward for all my decades of hard work fighting my demons and this disease is not that I have survived and prospered, but who I have become.

Jim's story offers us insight into the question of how to live the good life, indicating that the challenges of illness and chronic pain need not derail us, but rather can be used to promote a process of becoming, of self-actualizing, and of celebrating life. Expressing a long-held interest in music, Jim notes, "Music has always been my spirit muse, my light of truth. Life with AS is an unyielding lesson in what's really important in life ... Faith, Love, Truth, Service ... there is no way one can successfully live with this disease without understanding the deeply spiritual walk of humility and service to others."[65] As Jim continues his advocacy and work to prevail over AS, he notes that "like a struggling musician that suddenly believes he *can* play, the long hours of struggle, practice and commitment *do* pay off."[66] Jim's story is a true testament of resilience, recovery, and growth. Now in his early sixties, he continues to champion a love for life and the successful overcoming of illness and chronic pain.

Other Disorders and Effects of Music Therapy

Music therapy is also used as an intervention to promote health and to enhance personal wellness in other illness conditions. For example, listening to relaxing music has been identified as a component of treatment to reduce blood pressure and thus lower risk of stroke.[67] A variety of music therapy approaches (listening, composing, recreation, and improvisation) have been indicated to reduce depression and improve quality of life in patients undergoing hemodialysis.[68]

Mel Tillis, the famous country and western singer who stuttered when he spoke but sang beautifully with a smooth flow of speech, is an example of how music may be part of the therapeutic intervention for disfluencies in speech. As noted by Anna Zumbansen and Pascale Tremblay, any singing can be the basis for a music-based therapy for aphasia or other motor–speech disorders that affect the expression and fluency of speech.[69] Music listening and reflection have also been suggested as innovative ways to rehabilitate memory in patients with dementia of the Alzheimer's type.[70] Further, a randomized control study by Ken-ichi Tabei and colleagues that included older adults in an exercise program that was accompanied by synthesizer-heavy dance pop music reported that older adults who exercised with musical accompaniment had subtle neuroanatomical brain enhancements (e.g., greater right superior frontal gyrus volume and greater preserved volume of right anterior cingulated gyrus, as well as left superior temporal gyrus and insula), leading the researchers to suggest that exercise with music induces greater positive effects than just exercise alone.[71]

Military Veterans and Music Therapy

The horrible impact combat has on human beings can never be fully expressed. Service members and family are left to deal with the physical, mental, and emotional damage that are the outcomes of war. Music therapy programs specifically designed for veterans and their families provide hope. One of the most comprehensive undertakings to incorporate music as part of a healing, rehabilitation, and recovery process was by the US military. In 1945, the War Department issued Technical Bulletin 187, which set forth a program of music to service members convalescing in army hospitals.[72] It outlined active (performing, playing) and passive (listening) participation as part of the program. The rationale was that music was a way to give service members a sense of accomplishment, emotional well-being, and sense of satisfaction that would contribute greatly to their recovery. Activities included physical therapy, such as music with exercise and individual and ensemble playing of instruments; occupational therapy, such as assembling instruments and improvised playing, or playing that emphasizes wrist, arm, and finger movements; education, such as movies and talks, lectures, music appreciation, music courses, recitals, and listening to recorded programs; and, finally, recreation, such as listening or participating in choruses, band music, recorded concerts, and variety shows. Insightfully this bulletin established that for a program of music therapy to be successful, three things should be kept in mind. The first is that because service members are often younger adults, the music should reflect their preferences. Allied research has indicated that music preference has been documented to be beneficial to healing.[73] Second, no evaluation of the music selected should be made. There is no "good" or "bad" music if it is the service member's preferred choice. Third, oversight of the program is important. The medical officer in charge is to be kept abreast of any changes in protocol.[74]

The success of this initial program is evident today. The American Music Therapy Association, founded in 1971, represents more than 6,000 music therapists nationwide and 30 countries. Under their aegis many programs in the United States provide service to active-duty members and 27 states plus Puerto Rico and Washington, DC, and employ music therapists in US VA hospitals nationwide.[75] Additional organizations such as Operation We Are Here provide a clearinghouse of resources for the military and supporters.[76] Included in this list of resources are many websites involving music, such as Guitars for Vets[77] and Music for Veterans,[78] to name two. Operation Music Aid, another organization, provides donated instruments to wounded veterans at Brooke Army Medical Hospital in Ft. Sam Houston, Texas, and Walter Reed Army Medical Center in Washington, DC.[79] Music therapy programs employ many different instruments, with some exceptions – such as drums, as they may sound much like bombs. The most popular among veterans is the guitar. The guitar can be played quietly if necessary but also transference of dominance to a different hand is achievable. For example, if a nondominant hand or limb is lost, a pick can be fitted to the prosthesis.

If the dominant (fingering) hand or limb is lost, retraining to fret the guitar with the nondominant hand can occur. In addition, the guitar, rather than being fretted with the fingers, can also be played slide style, requiring only the use of a pick and a slide (bottleneck, ceramic, etc.) to be held to play notes and chords typically in open tuning.

Veteran and active-duty musicians are playing their part in helping fellow soldiers as they deal with trauma. Active-duty service members of the prestigious US Army Band "Pershing's Own" formed a music outreach program for wounded veterans at Fort Belvoir, Virginia, and Walter Reed National Medical Center in Washington, DC. Here, service members use their skill in music to help other veterans toward healing and recovery.[80] Another story of resilience is that of Hank Bolden. Mr. Bolden was one of many African American soldiers subjected to secret nuclear weapons testing in the 1950s. He was placed with other soldiers only 2.8 miles from ground zero, given no eye protection, with only the trench he and other soldiers were laying in for protection. Over the years, many soldiers suffered numerous health problems as the result of these tests. In 1995, the US government officially apologized, and these soldiers were finally given some compensation for their unwitting participation in these atomic tests. Hank Bolden received and used a scholarship to complete his schooling at the Hartt School of Music and plays saxophone.[81] His is another story of resilience, recovery, and growth.

Williams Syndrome and Precocious Musical Genius

We can find further testimonies of resilience, recovery, and growth in folks diagnosed with Williams syndrome. Williams syndrome is a neurodevelopmental genetic disorder caused by the spontaneous deletion of 26 to 28 genes on chromosome #7. As a result of this deletion, people with Williams syndrome are missing one copy of the ELN (elastin protein) gene in each cell. A loss of the ELN gene is associated with connective tissue abnormalities, such a joint problems and loose skin, and cardiovascular disease, particularly supravalvular aortic stenosis (SVAS), a heart defect present from birth that is characterized by a narrowing of the large blood vessel that carries blood from the heart to the rest of the body. Other physical problems are associated with Williams syndrome, such as cardiovascular, kidney, heart and blood vessel, low birth weight, slow weight gain, dental abnormalities, and increased sensitivity to sound. Those with Williams syndrome experience developmental delays, increased anxiety, learning differences, and cognitive challenges. However, they may show remarkable strengths in speech and long-term memory. Children with Williams syndrome can be very sociable, exhibit social closeness, show an increased propensity to approach strangers, a greater use of social language, and more sensitivity to other's emotions. They also may show a deficit in fine motor skills and spatial relations.[82] Importantly, children with Williams syndrome show a strong affinity toward music and respond with a greater range of emotions compared to children not diagnosed with Williams syndrome.[83] Thus, children with Williams syndrome are often recognized as musical geniuses.[84]

The affinity toward music in children with Williams syndrome is the catalyst by which therapy using music leads to intellectual and personal growth. Music is akin to language in that to be completely immersed in music is to "think" musically. Multimodal approaches (visual, auditory, somatosensory, and movement) to teach children with Williams syndrome to learn to play an instrument have been successful. Included in this process is for the child to imitate the therapist (e.g., drumming, tapping), to apply musically appropriate strategies that recognize perceptual–motor processes (e.g., visualize where to place fingers, exposure to live performances), and to stress the importance of learning to listen to music.[85]

Enrichment programs such as the Music and Minds program have also been successful, using enrichment experiences focusing on individual learning styles, prior experience, talent development, and educational needs of children with Williams syndrome. The Music and Minds program is based on the School Enrichment Model (SEM). This model identifies traits in gifted children, such as above-average ability, task commitment, and creativity. Under the Music and Minds program, these components are incorporated into an immersive enrichment experience specific to music. Students find the experience more educational and enjoyable when they can select their own topics that are creative and challenging. Enrichment opportunities such as dances, open-mic nights, and self-designed music performances result in these children becoming more open and willing to interact with others, to become more willing to engage in problem solving, and to increase their competence in other areas such as mathematics.[86] These findings have implications for education. This model can be employed to develop the talent of the child, to use a positive approach that addresses the strengths and not deficits or negative symptoms, and to dispel the students' own negative self-beliefs about their own inability to succeed. The research is clear that music helps folks with Williams syndrome cope with emotional and physical challenges.

A semi-structured interview by Ewie Erasmus and Liesl van der Merwe of three individuals with Williams syndrome can shed light on the mechanisms by which music provides a way to cope. They uncovered four themes important in the musical experience of these individuals. One theme was passion for performance. The interviewees exhibited great passion to perform. This allowed for personal growth, confidence, and improved self-image. Performance also gave them a connection with the crowd. The second theme was fostering friendships. Music provided a way to make new friends and interact with others. Music was an important factor toward gaining social acceptance by others. The third theme was coping with challenging situations. Music helped them to regulate negative moods and to cope with daily challenges. Finally, the fourth theme was musical dependency. The interviewees could not imagine life without music and that music was a significant component in their lives.[87] In summary, we now know that folks with Williams syndrome are focused and have a greater attention span for music, can retain melodies and pick up and play tunes by ear, and can transpose music to different keys. Often, they show these talents in greater proportion than their counterparts not diagnosed with Williams syndrome.

Less studied is the impact of Williams syndrome on older adults. A multisystem study of 20 adults (age range 30 to 51 years) found that medically associated problems from Williams syndrome continued.[88] Organ system compromises, cardiovascular disease, diabetes, decreased bone density, and increased anxiety were found in this cohort. The study also suggests that mild accelerated aging was implicated in this group. Although this was a small group of participants, the researchers indicated increases in medical and cognitive problems with age. Other researches have confirmed that accelerated aging is associated with increased anxiety.[89] Relatedly, earlier age-associated declines in long-term episodic memory occur in individuals with Williams syndrome compared to others with unspecified intellectual disabilities.[90] It should be pointed out that studies finding earlier age-onset deficits for individuals with Williams syndrome compared to other groups were largely cross-sectional studies. Cross-sectional studies can tell us about differences between groups. If we want to understand changes that occur within a group, we must conduct longitudinal studies of individuals over time. One longitudinal study of individuals with Williams syndrome found no clear age-related decline in function early in adulthood, but suggested that age-related decline may begin and then precipitate after ages 50–55 years.[91]

Although the importance of studying older populations with Williams syndrome has been recognized by researchers, even less is known about the role music has in the lives of these aging individuals. However, if we wish to find a positive testament of aging, musicality, and folks with Williams syndrome, we look to Gloria Lenhoff. Diagnosed with Williams syndrome, Gloria Lenhoff, age 63 at the time of this writing, is a lyric soprano and plays accordion. She has a repertoire of more than

2,000 songs and sings in 28 different languages in many different styles. She has performed worldwide, with various performers, as a soloist, and with several opera companies. The book *The Strangest Song: One Father's Quest to Help His Daughter Find Her Voice* tells of Howard Lenhoff, who recognized his daughter's musical talents and soon was on a quest not only to help his daughter but also to raise awareness of Williams syndrome. At first, ridiculed by the scientific profession, he was finally vindicated when his own research and the research of others became compelling and demonstrated the incredible musical talents of those with Williams syndrome.[92]

Music: The Path to Resilience, Recovery, and Growth

Overall, the research reviewed here suggests that music, in all the ways with which one may engage it, promotes a way of being that assists individuals to go beyond the difficulty and challenges of their illness and to aid them in charting a path to familiar and comfortable moments of living. Whether playing an instrument, singing, or listening, the act of music involves some of the highest forms of cognition. We see in the examples of Frank Vignola, B.B. King, Clark Terry, military veterans, folks diagnosed with Williams syndrome, and countless others that music, indeed, "builds up something in the mind and heart." Music provides resilience to adversity, contributes to the recovery process, and is a source of growth in the individual.

We take a holistic view of music, wellness, and aging in this book. Just as they are intertwined, they are also to be viewed as more than the sum of their parts. Music, wellness, and aging are taken as a gestalt. Although this chapter does not provide a comprehensive overview of all areas where music and music therapy are important to our wellness, these examples emphasize the role music plays in our well-being now and in older age. Music allows one to find meaning and purpose in life. It stirs the imagination, leads to new ways of thinking, listening, and being, opens communication between others, and provides comfort, reassurance, and ultimately, peace.[93]

6 Tutti: Music in Relationships and Communities

And let there be no purpose in friendship save the deepening of the spirit.

–Kahlil Gibran, *On Friendship*

Music is a social experience. Our shared musical experiences tap into an inherent need to be with others that is basic to our makeup as human beings. Shared musical experience in our view can take place between performer and audience, a mentor and student, among musicians, among listeners, in music and singing groups, and even between listener and performance media such as social media, CDs, and videos. These shared experiences are an important part of our relationships with others and continue throughout the life span.

The importance of shared musical experiences can be illustrated in many ways. One way is to think about social support networks. According to social psychologists, social support networks can provide us with tangible, emotional, and informational support. We will discuss each in turn. We also present the role of social norms, motivation, and conscious planning in our shared musical experiences, as well as mentoring, community musical organizations, and social justice. Also presented are stories about our own mentors. It is often in stories that we come to understand our relationships with others and gain insight into our human existence.[1]

Social Support

Social support networks can provide tangible, emotional, and informational support. Tangible social support, also called instrumental support, is the type of support where we as receivers of support obtain specific things from our support network. This instrumental support can be in the form of monetary aid or help in other ways, such as shopping for groceries or mowing the lawn. Another form of social support is emotional. Here, support comes from those in our network being there for us. This form of support, too, allows us to cope with events in our lives. Finally, we utilize our support networks for information. We can gain valuable information about resources, educational opportunities, and other support groups available to us.[2]

Social Norms, Motivation, and Conscious Planning

As presented, social support networks provide tangible, emotional, and informational support, but they also can motivate us to change and to be more intentional in our actions.[3] For example, Paschal Sheerhan and Sheina Orbell found that intention to achieve a health goal is a key factor in success toward one's goal.[4] This concept of intention is from a theory called the Theory of Planned Behavior, where behavior (motivation toward or achieving a goal) is based on several variables. One is *attitude* toward achieving the goal. One must indicate that the goal is a good thing to reach. Another is *subjective norm*. Subjective norm means that one is motivated to achieve the goal and that one agrees with others who believe that this is a worthy goal to achieve. A third variable is *behavioral norm*. Here one agrees to perform the behavior and has the resources to achieve the goal. For example, one has a car or other means of transportation to a doctor's appointment. However, research finds that these variables, except *behavioral norm*, only indirectly predict if someone will achieve their goal. The entire model hinges on the person stating their specific *intention* to achieve the goal.[5]

As important as one's stated intention to achieve a goal, other research has found that as part of the intentional process, having a well-defined plan adds significantly toward achieving a goal. For example, Paschal Sheerhan and Sheina Orbell[6] integrated Peter Gollwitzer's[7] Implementation Intention model of planning into the Theory of Planned Behavior. Gollwitzer's model proposes four components that lead to goal achievement. These components are willingness to achieve a goal, a cost–benefit analysis of reaching the goal, the stated intention of achieving the goal, and importantly, an articulation of a plan to achieve the goal. In a series of studies, Sheerhan and Orbell compared the Theory of Planned Behavior to Gollwitzer's model on whether women will attend a cervical cancer screening within a 6-month period. They found that intention to attend a screening highly predicted the actuality of the goal in 62 percent of the women in the study, but also having a plan increased achieving this goal in 92 percent of the women in the study! In our own research predicting health goals of older individuals, we found that having a well-articulated plan of action allowed older adults to be more success-ful in achieving health goals within 3 months.[8] Another important finding in our research is that many participants cited that the person most important in helping them form and keep to a plan is a spouse or significant other.[9] Other research, too, finds that survivability after significant heart surgery increased in those who had a confidant – a person whom they trusted implicitly and who would always be there for them.[10] It is clear that having a plan is important in achieving a goal.[11] In a similar way, when applied to music, our stated intention and planning strategies toward music-related goals such as rehearsals or practice sessions are also associated with achieving those goals.[12]

Although social support networks are often thought of as a positive thing to have, keep in mind that support networks can be detrimental as well. We can have support networks that engage in deviant behavior, provide us with misinformation or malicious information, and can create situations of emotional turmoil and codependence. In this chapter, we focus on the positive aspects of social support in the context of our musical relationships with others. We will further investigate the link between music and social support networks, and how both help us cope with stress in our lives. It is well understood that effective coping is crucial to emotional stability but also plays an important part in our relationships with others.[13]

Music, Social Support, and Coping with Stress

Positive social support networks can serve as a buffer for stress. Feelings of stress are common to everyday life, and we can often become overwhelmed and feel a loss of control regarding events in our lives. Chronic stress can result in profound physiological, cognitive–psychological, and behavioral outcomes. Physiological responses to stress are a suppressed immune system, elevated heart rate, elevated blood pressure, and autonomic nervous system responses (the classic fight-or-flight response). Changes in thinking and acting associated with stress include problems with memory and attention, increased irritability, anxiety, and depression. Behavioral changes due to stress include increased substance use and abuse, poor nutrition, disrupted sleep, decreased compliance with a medical regimen, delay in treatment seeking, or not seeking treatment at all.

Music and Response to Stress

As noted in Chapter 5, music may be helpful in reducing stress and anxiety.[14] To aid in understanding the complexities of the stress response, Lazarus and Folkman proposed a Cognitive Appraisal Model.[15] This model emphasizes the relationship between the person and the environment in response to stressful events. The first part of the model is primary appraisal. Here, the person determines if the event is positive, negative, or neutral. Is the event perceived as a threat, as harmful, or a challenge? Once the event is categorized along these dimensions, the person engages in a secondary appraisal. This secondary appraisal is a self-inventory-taking process, where the person asks, "Do I have the coping abilities and resources to resolve the event?" If the person cannot sufficiently cope with the event, then stress is experienced.

In addition to the appraisal process, we engage in two types of coping responses to stress – problem-focused coping and emotion-focused coping. Problem-focused coping involves taking specific actions to deal with stress as a problem to be solved. For example, a person may ask what they can do to reduce the stress associated with performing at their clarinet recital. Using the problem-focused approach, the person might warm up with a series of exercises that will prepare them to handle the challenges of the recital piece. They may adjust their performance goals if they feel they are not quite ready to play the piece or that it is a particularly difficult piece. A common problem-focused approach when encountering a difficult passage for a horn player hitting a key high note within a phrase is to remember to be relaxed as they begin the phrase and to make minor adjustments to posture, embouchure, wind pressure, and tonguing that will allow the note to be played.

Emotion-focused coping is adopted when the person feels the stress cannot be readily resolved or is something that is to be endured. The persons may use relaxation techniques that will allow them to remain physiologically relaxed (i.e., calm) and psychologically confident (i.e., thinking "I've got this") before and during their recital.

As part of problem-focused and emotion-focused coping, we also utilize other cognitive and behavioral strategies. For example, problem-focused coping can also include active coping, where we engage in actual effort to do something about the stress. We also might engage in planning, where we think about and consider strategies to reduce stress. We also might undertake suppression of competing activities, where we focus our concentration exclusively on the problem at hand. We might also demonstrate restraint and wait until the right time to address the situation or to seek out one's support network for specific, tangible ways to help.

Similarly, emotion-focused coping can involve seeking moral and empathic support from one's close social networks by discussing one's feelings with family or friends. Emotion-focused coping involves positive reinterpretation, where we look for the "silver lining" in the stressful situation. Other cognitive–behavioral processes include acceptance, venting, denial, and mental disengagement. For example, acceptance is to learn to live with the situation. Other emotion-focused coping is to turn to religion and seek the help of a higher power, or use prayer, or meditation. Venting is an emotional expression that involves letting one's feelings out. Denial is refusing to believe that the stressful event is happening. We can also practice mental disengagement by creating distractions or behaviorally disengage by reducing our efforts toward solving the problem or just give up. Finally, people may use or abuse substances to cope.[16]

Along with these problem- and emotion-focused examples of coping, we recognize that involvement with music is another positive way to cope with stress.[17] The impact that music has on stress reduction is well documented. Indeed, the simple act of listening to music can reduce one's stress response.[18] Therefore, involvement with music should also be considered a coping response. In the following sections, we will relate a few examples of how music and social support go hand in hand to reduce stress and to help us find pathways to recovery and growth. We will also investigate the role music has in the positive results of relationships involving mentorship, music therapy and family relationships, social–community relationships, social justice, and prosocial behavior.

The Intersection of Music, Wellness, and Aging

As we begin to consider how music intersects with broader aspects of our living, it is important to recognize the power of music in the lives of older adults, particularly in their relationships with others. We noted in earlier chapters the many physical, cognitive, and behavioral changes that occur as we age. But another aspect of our aging to emphasize is our own self-identity and relationship with others. As noted in the previous chapters, music can provide a positive influence and a potential buffer to any negative changes that occur as we age. Indeed, a review by Andrea Creech and colleagues found many positive outcomes associated with becoming involved in music as we age.[19] These positive outcomes can be a greater sense of social cohesion, empowerment, personal and spiritual development and a positive outlook on life and a sense of purpose. Even negative myths that present aging as a time of decline and infirmity are dispelled by studies that investigate older adults who are involved with music. Creech and colleagues further found that older adults have a capacity to develop new musical skills and to maintain them with age, dispelling a myth that as we age we lose the capacity or become limited in our ability to progress or to learn new things.[20] One social benefit of involvement with music and music groups is the sense that one is a valued contributor to the music group.

Intergenerational benefits occur as well. Playing music with younger members dispels stereotypes and facilitates peer learning and sharing of expertise. The cognitive benefits include rising to new challenges, acquiring new skills, and improving concentration and memory. Creech and colleagues also address barriers to playing in groups. These barriers are physical access to facilities, perceptions of elitism, financial constraints, time of day, lack of information about opportunities, caregiver responsibilities, willingness to socialize, confidence, and motivation. They offer some remedies. Groups need to be welcoming and inclusive, facilitators should establish mutual respect and provide appropriate challenges to the players, and facilities are to be accessible. Mentoring of new members or a "buddy system" can go a long way in creating a successful and enjoyable musical experience for all.[21] In Chapter 5, we highlighted B.B King and Clark Terry as important mentors to up-and-coming musicians in the context of health. We further explore the role of mentorship through more examples.

The Gift of Mentorship

Anyone who has played in a band or orchestra – whether in school, college, or in the community – can possibly identify a person or persons whom they consider to be a mentor. A mentor is someone who teaches something more important than just how to play an instrument. Through their guidance, they convey the fundamentals of being a professional and how to conduct oneself on the stage, playing field, or parade marching. Mentors can demand much from the student, but in order for the student to say that this person was a mentor is to recognize that that person nurtured that student and is considered a friend. A mentor such as this has given the student a gift that can never be taken away – the art of reading, interpreting, and playing music. A mentor not only opens the student to new musical experiences, but also broadens the student's world by showing how to act professionally along with providing a rich array of historical and socially relevant perspectives. Like new music that seems to push the boundaries of what is possible versus the constraint of the preexisting tonal or melodic or rhythmic structures, good mentorship too can help us find a balance in exploring our creativity and adhering to convention. In the same way, a mentor may lead us in a nondirective way to explore our potential as a person, find a balance between the restrictions of musical forms and conventions, and the freedom to explore and develop our own approach to playing, singing, and living. In a manner of speaking, mentors introduce us to a resilient mindset where we successfully face challenges and constructively work with others. This mindset lasts a lifetime. Fortunately, we can maintain it throughout life or rediscover it as we become involved with others in community bands or with old and new friends in other formal and informal playing situations.

One such mentor was William Schaefer. Mr. Schaefer was one of the author's high school band directors. Along with his duties of rehearsing concert and marching band, he also conducted afternoon rehearsals of different sections and in the summer would invite students to the school for individual instructions. The author relates: "I was fortunate to have him as a mentor. I recall that during our sectional rehearsals he would often stand behind us eating cheese and peanut butter crackers as he called out the rhythm and melodies. His teaching later became invaluable when I switched from trumpet to French horn. He taught me how to read rhythms that often were the province of the horn. These rhythms would involve playing back beats or playing in 6/8 time where the eighth notes often sounded like a cantering pony to me. As a result of these sessions, I learned a strong sense of rhythm and timing. Before he retired, he had begun to have medical problems. A few times during a parade the ambulance would be called as he was having a respiratory event. I also recall in one parade he pulled behind him an oxygen canister to help get through the parade route. After retirement he supplemented his income with occasional piano gigs at the Lion's Club or other civic events. His memory and the gift of music that he gave me would always live on."

Learning music is a social experience, and mentors provide a glimpse into a world beyond our family, school, and local community. One of the authors also describes his experience with mentors: "My first band teacher was Joe Bozzi, a trumpeter who often came to my parochial school in the same tuxedo he had worn while playing at the Playboy Club the night before. Beyond receiving a foundation in the rudimentary aspects of music, his notoriety of playing in a nightclub provided an opportunity for me to consider and to look beyond into the broader social community. From my elementary school encounter in the 1960s, and at this present writing, Joe's career has offered insights into possible career paths in music, as a music educator and performer, and how music can still be an activity in later adulthood, as he is still performing at area clubs and music festivals in the St. Louis area.[22]

"Another music teacher, Dr. Henry Orland, also provided students opportunities to think beyond their present point of reference. In fact, even though the subject of the courses I had with Dr. Orland were about music history, I credit him with also teaching about various aspects of psychology and social justice in his classes. His life story is exceptional: As a young man, Dr. Orland came to the US in 1939, leaving Strasbourg, Germany, with his mother and father as Nazi Germany sought territorial expansion and the Second World War was beginning. He would later return as a member of the US Army to help rebuild Europe under the Marshall Plan. After his military service and again back in the US, Dr. Orland completed his graduate studies in music at Northwestern University. He later worked as a college professor at St. Louis Community College, served as music reviewer for the *St. Louis Globe-Democrat*, and conducted several area community orchestras and musical ensembles in the St. Louis area. Dr. Orland was also a member of several professional associations and from 1975 to 1985 served as a member of Urgent Action Committee of Amnesty International, St. Louis. His lectures often reflected his interests and earlier world experiences. In his class you gained a deep appreciation of how people find their place in the world, and how we might best treat one another. One memorable concept he shared was to 'become a renaissance thinker.' That is, to seek to develop one's musicianship, and greatest human potential, by also learning about history, literature, philosophy, and the sciences. Dr. Orland died in 1999, but in retirement he continued his role as an educator, teaching German as a language. For his students he has left a wonderful legacy of working for social justice."[23]

Another mentor was Warren Bellis, symphonic band director at the university. One of the authors relates: "I was a college student auditioning for the trumpet section in the symphonic band one semester; there were about 12 trumpeters, so it was pretty stacked. Dr. Bellis asked me to come by his office after the auditions, and he indicated that they did not have a tuba player, and he asked if I would be interested. I think I might have been placed as 2nd trumpet at best, or maybe 4th trumpet. I indicated that it would be interesting to try a new instrument, and he relayed a belief and a way of operating that was illuminating and that resonated with me still. He said, 'Take the tuba and the music home, and come back in two weeks. If it doesn't work out, I'm a big guy (referring to himself), I can handle it.' I did, and went on to play tuba for the rest of the next two years in the symphonic band. Later I played the baritone horn for one year. He offered me a great way of framing the challenge, and expressed a sense of trust in me that was very much appreciated. In a subsequent semester when I was in another ensemble conducted by a different professor, he popped in to listen to our rehearsal. He again asked me to stop by his office as he left at the end of the session. I went to see him, and as I entered his office he said, 'I just wanted to let you know that you were doing some really nice things musically, and playing great during the rehearsal.' Receiving the positive feedback and sensing his continued support for the initial challenge and how I was developing in my tuba playing was great. I would call Dr. Bellis one of my many informal life mentors – his approach to teaching and guiding students, his suggestion on how he might frame a life challenge, and willingness to take a risk, have stayed with me to today!" Conveying his teaching approach once to a newspaper reporter, Dr. Bellis indicated, "One must arouse the interest and curiosity and the mental activity of the student. It is a mixture of experience, enthusiasm, knowledge, and hard work. As with everything, the thing to do is to try to achieve excellency, which is the result of hard work and the discovery that there are 24 hours in the day and seven days in the week."[24]

Mentorship in an Intergenerational Context

Often mentorships are intergenerational, typically where an older mentor nurtures a younger mentee. However, intergenerational experience can also be found in bands and choirs that invite larger numbers of older and younger participants. Earlier we noted that intergenerational music programs can not only dispel the negative stereotypes younger people have of older people, but also these programs and experiences can dispel negative stereotypes older people have of younger people. Intergenerational programs can span an age range that can go as young as five or six years to the nineties. Key for successful intergenerational experiences and mentorship is establishing mutual trust and respect between younger and older individuals. Here, one can think of active-listening approaches of the Rogerian perspective. For example, a climate of unconditional positive regard is a key component of successful mentorships. One can challenge the mentee but in the context that allows the person to explore new ideas, gain self-confidence in playing, and be allowed to fail without condemnation from the mentor. It is an old but true adage that the student should hope to eventually outshine the master. But it is also true that a jealous mentor is no mentor at all. In effect, the goal is to create trust that allows the mentee to become authentic as a musician. The concept of unconditional positive regard also can be successfully applied to intergenerational programs involving a number of younger and older persons. One major concern of both young and old is feeling they are accepted and belong. Apprehensions and anxiety regarding acceptance by young and old can be dispelled in a well-thought-out music experience.[25] Borrowing a term from vocal teacher Janice Chapman, "reciprocal empathy" can occur across generations in that young and old understand the shared fears, apprehensions, anxieties, hopes, and feelings of each other.[26]

Often overlooked in establishing and fostering quality relationships through music is the organization of the physical space. It is not surprising that we are the most comfortable in our own space, whether that is in the office work space or the one we create in our own home. We have a personal comfort zone, so that when we are outside of it, we experience anxiety and apprehension. These negative feelings we have when we are outside our comfort zone can in turn inhibit our interactions with others. Having a large, spacious area to play music contributes to comfort, particularly for older individuals. A musical experience can be less enjoyable for players when they have set themselves up in the most comfortable way only to have to readjust because other musicians arrive late and or require more space than planned.

Physical space also involves access. The facility should be easily accessible. Accessibility can involve location, time and effort involved in getting to the facility, and even the location of doors and access to restrooms. The ability to move about is also important. It is found that older adults have a more positive experience in intergenerational programs when they can move freely around the room and also to other areas of the facility. Comfortable seating and effective arrangement of chairs and tables are important. An obvious example, but that occurs more commonly than one would think, is that a chair with arms is detrimental to a musician's ability to play an instrument such as a saxophone, guitar, or a French horn. But also appropriate arrangement – example, face to face – allows musicians and singers to watch each other and to anticipate changes. Other factors that facilitate intergenerational musical experiences are to provide breaks that allow participants to bond informally. Finally, the timing and dates of rehearsals, meetings, and recitals are to be designed to be the most accessible to all members.[27]

As we hope to underscore throughout this discussion the importance of music in our relationships, a story offered by one of the authors is illustrative: "All my family members took music lessons, even Mom and Dad. Mom and Dad's interest in music was key in recognizing music as a form of social expression. We shared and celebrated our common love of music. Coaching and providing support to each other, we offered insight to technical challenges presented by various pieces of music, and the various instruments we played. As a family we attended school band and professional orchestral concerts and, listening closely, heard the composer's portrayal of life's earnest concerns, and the deepest human feelings that can be experienced. Even in the fledgling sounds of the fourth-grade band, one may recognize the deep emotions that the music reveals, hear the noble intent of the elementary school students to convey the composer's artistic intention, and the conductor's close interest and care for their musical expression. Music, whether listening to or in its making, *really* is a social experience!"

One of the authors also relates the story: "When my dad took me to the music store to buy my first 'real' guitar, I immediately gravitated toward a snow white guitar with three pickups and enough switches to handle a train yard. While I tried it out, I overheard my dad discussing the price with the store owner. I heard him ask 'how do you get the 'country' sound out it?' My dad really wanted to hear a steel guitar sound as he was very fond of country and western music. The owner explained that the guitar was not a pedal steel guitar. I took the guitar home along with a solid state amp that I later found to be woefully inadequate in volume and tone. But the bonding experience my dad and I had that day cannot be put into words. As long as I played a little bit of Johnny Cash's 'Folsom Prison Blues' every once in a while he was happy."

The Sister- and Brotherhood of Jazz

One of the cultural components of jazz music is the comradery that occurs among jazz musicians. However, also famous are the "cutting contests" of the big band era, where groups sparred against each other and the winner was determined by the audience and allowed to play the rest of the evening, or individually, where competitiveness would lead a musician to try to upstage another. A common, possibly apocryphal story is that during a rehearsal or jam session a band would "test" any new musician who thought he could stand with the band by having the band constantly change the key as they played through a song to see if the "newbee" could keep up. One story told to one of the authors by a friend who tried to make it in New York City is that he would go to a club where a piano player well into his eighties was playing. This friend was hoping to move into his place when this musician retired. As he watched the pianist perform, he noticed another older man listening and watching the piano player intently. He approached this gentleman and struck up a conversation with him. He later found out that this person too was waiting for the piano player to retire, or in the words of the man "to die," and that he was next in line for the gig. It was then that this friend decided that trying to break into the New York City jazz scene was not for him.[28] Few gigs and more musicians to fill the gigs could create a climate that might be viewed negatively but can also allow musicians to engage in a process of honing their craft to a high degree of musicianship. We focus more on the positive comradery that occurs among musicians.

One of the most iconic photographs in the archives of jazz music is Art Kane's "Jazz Portrait Harlem 1958." Shown in this photograph, taken at 17 East 126th Street, are some of the most famous jazz musicians of all time.[29] The comradery captured in the photo of these 57 jazz musicians is unmistakable. We see in the photograph Dizzy Gillespie with his arm around J. C. Heard and Roy Eldridge turning back toward Dizzy possibly sharing a joke. We see Marian McPartland and Mary Lou Williams in conversation with each other. A favorite part of the photograph is Count Basie sitting on the curb flanked to his right by 12 children from the neighborhood. The unlikelihood of assembling so many of the greats at 10 a.m. is historic, but importantly captured in this photograph is the love, mutual respect, admiration, and friendship that they had for one another.

To illustrate how this well-loved photograph can project beyond itself and foster positive relationships with others, one of the authors relates an experience he had in a conversation with a student. "I had this photograph hanging on my office wall at the university. I was in a conversation with one of my students and he happened to notice the photo. I told him a bit of the history behind the photo and where it was photographed. When he heard the address, he immediately said, "I thought I knew where that was taken – it is about two blocks from where I used to live." This picture represents more than a love of jazz and history. It is an extension in time and space that establishes a connection to others and nurtures a comradery and commonality beyond its historic context.

Music Therapy, Social Support, and Family

As we have noted in the previous examples, music is a form of coping and is an important component of social support.[30] Music enhances interpersonal experiences we have with others. It can unlock our deepest emotions and allow us to communicate with others in a deep and profound way. We have discussed previously that music therapy can be an effective tool to help the individual toward recovery from trauma. Music can also be incorporated into family therapy to provide insight into the dynamics of family interaction and communication and allow for a sharing of emotions, building of mutual trust, and modeling of positive relationships, roles, and parental functioning.[31] For families of very young children (two to thirty-six months) who die of chronic illness, music therapy in the form of background listening or movement to music may aid functioning of surviving siblings and parents, whereby the "music helps mourners express that which may be inaccessible to the spoken or even the written word."[32] Similarly, music therapy in the form of singing, listening, or performing on an instrument has been reported to successfully aid women survivors of domestic violence by enhancing personal awareness and self-esteem, and reducing feelings of guilt and anxiety.[33]

Research involving dementia patients and their caregivers indicated that during periods of music therapy involving singing, dancing and playing percussion instruments, there is a positive shift in caregiver engagement and initiation of physical touch with Alzheimer's patients.[34] Thus, music therapy may effectively facilitate meaningful interaction between dementia patients and caregivers.[35] In a similar manner, music therapy, in the form of singing, listening, or performing along with the music therapist, is effective for couples when one partner is hospitalized.[36] This couples' oriented music therapy can help create a safe place for each person that facilitates communication, and produces soothing and calming effects. In addition, the therapy allowed a chance for the couple to reminiscence about the relationship and express feelings about being in the hospital. For medical professionals, music listening with reflective discussion has also been suggested to be beneficial. Indeed, music therapy used in medical education was suggested to aid medical students in becoming more reflective practitioners via the opportunity to discuss feelings that cannot be talked about during medical training.[37]

Playing or listening to music connects us to others and reveals to us our shared hopes, failures, and importantly, our humanity. Music plays a consoling role for the individual[38] as well as for the community.[39] Music connects to our deepest personal experience and reveals to us what Carl Jung referred to as the collective unconscious.[40] Indeed, music provides a language that conveys our deepest psychology, brings to life cultural myths and archetypal figures,[41] and gives us a way to communicate that is comforting when we encounter illness.[42] Further, for midlife and older adults, music is important in the development of identity, social connection, maintenance of well-being, and a way of expressing and experiencing spirituality.[43] At times, however, and depending on the style of music, there may still be negative stereotypes of getting older in the lyrics of songs.[44] However, as discussed here and in earlier chapters, music, as a therapeutic tool, plays an important role in positive aging.[45]

Social–Community: Town and Community Bands

We have emphasized throughout this chapter that music is a social event. The positive outcomes of the social aspect of music are peer support, sense of belonging, a giving back to the community, a sense of pride, and positive reinforcement. Broader themes that emerge are a sense of purpose, autonomy and control, and social affirmation (positive social relationships, competence, and recognition).[46] There is no doubt that interactions with others through music provide a buffer to social isolation and loneliness. Earlier in this chapter we provided examples of the positive outcomes of interpersonal and intergenerational aspects of music through mentorship, playing and singing in ensembles, and the relationship between younger and older musicians. We continue in this section by investigating the role that the community can play in the wellness of the person through interaction with music. We will explore specific examples such as New Horizons and the important role and function of town bands and other music groups in contributing to the wellness of the individual and wellness of the community.

The town or community band has enjoyed a long history. Primarily comprised of volunteers, the town band is typically a not-for-profit organization that is self-funded through playing events and/or contributions by the community. The town band is missioned as an inclusive organization that often has no auditions and accepts musicians at any skill level and any age. In a town band one can often find amateurs, professionals, retired folks, and past and present band directors. Many town bands include several generations of a family, where siblings, parents, and grandparents play together.

One of the authors belongs to the Shippensburg Town Band – an all-volunteer organization. This group was established in 1922 and performs on average 50 events per year. The band also is comprised of suborganizations: the Blakepelle Shippensburg (German Band) and the Shippensburg Swing Band. The author describes how he became involved with the community town band: "I was probably in my 2nd or 3rd year at the university and was at the time sitting on a university-wide committee. I was talking to a professor from the biology department and through the course of the conversation we began to talk about music. She mentioned that Shippensburg had a town band and that because I played a variety of instruments, I should join because they needed more French horn players. I told her that although I had played the horn in high school, I had not touched one in over 35 years and besides, I could not afford one anyway. Her husband for a time had been an interim band director for the university band and later started his own band instrument repair shop. The following week she came in carrying a horn case with the horn inside. She had asked her husband to come up with a suitable horn for me to borrow, saying 'now you have no excuse not to join.' I eventually was able to purchase my own horn and have been in the town band for almost 20 years. In fact, I play in all three groups: Town Band (French horn), German Band (Eb alto horn), and Swing Band (guitar)."

The New Horizons Organization

Another community musical organization is New Horizons. New Horizons is an international organization that welcomes musicians fifty years of age and older, at all skill levels. Its goal is to be age inclusive so that older musicians can engage in creative musical endeavors. Older musicians can continue their musical development by participating in a variety of workshops, classes, and ensemble playing.

The first New Horizons program was started at Eastman School of Music in Rochester, New York, and founded by Dr. Roy Ernst, Professor of Music. His philosophy is that "anyone can learn to play music at a level that will bring a sense of accomplishment and the ability to perform in a group."[47] The organization's goals are to be supportive of musicians with no competition or intimidation. Dr. Ernst's educational philosophy is "your best is good enough." It is important to note that organizations such as New Horizons promote the idea that music is connected to wellness. Dr. Ernst believes that music and playing in ensemble groups challenges mental activities, fosters social growth, and fulfills the need to be a member of a group. The link between music and health is clear in his statement that "a musical instrument is an exercise machine for the brain."[48]

Currently, there are more than 180 New Horizons chapters nationwide.[49] New Horizons chapters offer a variety of programs and other educational opportunities in the area. New Horizons reaches out specifically to seniors in the area to reestablish, learn, or hone their music skills in a nonthreatening and supportive environment. Senior adults, often coached by former band directors, members of the band, or other instructors, can refresh and pick up new skills or learn to play a new instrument, often in a concert band setting along with other adult learners.

The New Horizons in Chambersburg, Pennsylvania

In 2010, Paula Hepfer (then executive director of The Cumberland Valley School of Music, CVSM) contacted Carl Sponenberg to be band director of New Horizons in Chambersburg, where he was teaching instrumental lessons at CVSM at the time. Mr. Sponenberg went to Eastman from 1969 to 1972 and graduated with a Master of Music degree. The program initially started with 11 members on September 23, 2010. The next year, membership rose to 14. Mr. Sponenberg served as band director there for several years.[50] He is also the current director of the Shippensburg Town Band.

An Interview with Members of New Horizons

We sat down for an interview with Heather Gateau McEndree, the current executive director of the Cumberland Valley School of Music and the contact person for New Horizons in Chambersburg, Pennsylvania, to discuss the importance of this program for the participants and for the community.

Tell Us about New Horizons in Chambersburg

We started the program offering band rehearsals and group lessons. We obtained grant funding and then expanded from there. Presently, we have 25 members in the program.

What Programs Are Now Offered?

We now have band, string orchestra, and we are piloting a choir and a chamber ensemble.

Why Chambersburg?

As you know from living in this area, there are many fine and talented musicians. Chambersburg seemed to be the place that was centrally located to serve the needs of musicians in the area.

What Do You Personally Get from the Experience?

The satisfaction that we offer support for older musicians who want to learn to play an instrument or want to get back into playing music with others. I also experience the sheer joy of watching them play and perform. One of our oldest members is 95 years old and likes to say that his saxophone is "85 years old."

What Do You See for the Future of New Horizons?

It is thriving and I expect it to continue. We offer a low-cost program that allows older adults to continue making music. It continues their life-long learning of an instrument or allows them to start playing either anew or if they have laid down the instrument in their youth and desire to take it back up again.[51]

Endorsements abound as to the importance and impact the New Horizons Band experience has on an individual. Here, a few of the New Horizons members in Chambersburg provide their personal testimony:

Testimony 1: "I am in two of the New Horizons ensembles, The String Orchestra and the Band and did the Chamber Ensemble this summer. I joined them as someone relatively new to the area, as both a way to meet more people in the area and a way to be more involved in the community. I also love the opportunity to explore my musical abilities more deeply. I play upright bass or violin or piano in the string ensemble. Violin is the instrument with which I have the least experience, but it is a 'safe' place to make mistakes and take risks. I have maybe 12–18 months of lessons on this instrument. I have just started playing bass clarinet in the band. I have only played this a few weeks, but have played clarinet for a number of years, about 10–12. I really enjoy the people. They are new groups, so they are very welcoming to newcomers. The groups are also full of people who are exploring their abilities, so mistakes and missed notes are the norm. You are challenged to work at whatever level you come in at, whether that is an experienced musician or a new beginner, there is a place for everyone. I've made some great friends who have carried out beyond the hour we meet each week and I've even brought a couple along to the Ship Town Band."

Testimony 2: "I learned about New Horizons from Carl (the 1st director). I offered to help with the clarinets and then decided to play in the trumpet section. I play trumpet with NH. I inherited my grandfather's cornet some years ago but didn't have a reason to play it or a group to play with. NH provided that. I have since purchased a trumpet but still have the cornet (made in 1906). It still has a wonderful sound. As you know I also play clarinet with the Shippensburg Band. I played in school and didn't play for over 35 years before retiring in 2001 and joining the Ship Band. NH gives me a place to play a second instrument. The music is at my level for trumpet (grades 2–3). We have had many opportunities to play for various groups (usually the band is not paid). I have made new friends in the music community through NH."

Testimony 3: "I joined the New Horizons band to relearn my B-flat clarinet. It was so much fun as I was really surprised at how quickly the fingering came back to me. It was good for my lungs, too, because I've improved my breathing a lot by playing my horn. I play the B-flat clarinet. I began in 5th grade which the school district I lived in started a band program. I played from then until I graduated from high school. After that I occasionally played, but never for any length until I joined the New Horizons band about 10 years ago. I have personally gained a lot of benefits especially better lung capacity as I mentioned. Also the friendships have greatly enriched my life because we are an active group and lead interesting lives. I also play with a New Horizons Band in Hagerstown, and we mostly play at nursing homes. We did play at the VA Center in Martinsburg, and that was quite rewarding because many of the patients were severely handicapped, and I hope we brought some cheer to their lives. I feel that music keeps my brain active and more alert as I age."[52]

Music, Community, and Social Justice

In Chapter 1, we investigated the intersection of music, social justice, and the wellness of a society. Music that advocates for social justice contributes to a well society. It calls out injustice and compels us to fight for social change. It also implies that we are each responsible to advocate for social justice. According to Paul Westermeyer in his book *Let Justice Sing: Hymnody and Justice*, we understand that at the deepest level of our being we are called to be fair and just, to be caring and compassionate.[53] In this section we expand our discussion by considering the role of music within the community as a vehicle for social justice.

Social justice is often a key feature of religious hymns and folk songs. Music serves as a conduit to work for social justice and is found in the songs and lives of people such as Woody Guthrie and Pete Seeger.[54] In addition to calling out social oppression, poverty, and racism, composers, singers, and musicians have a sacred task of sharing the voice of hope.[55] With regard to this desire to share hope, we find many songs celebrate life helping young and middle-aged people to see later life as a time of possibilities and not as pathology. One social justice issue that listening to or playing music dispels, then, is the negative stereotype of old age that suggests inability, incompetence, and decline. As one moves into the later part of life, social justice through music can promote an awareness of the subtle physical, cognitive, and social changes that occur, as well as the positive experiences that may be realized. In a similar manner, seeking exposure to new forms of music may also broaden our understanding of others. For example, the older adult who endeavors to explore rap music, learn about world music, or to experience the tonal structure of Polynesian music also may discover many common connections to their own life and shared human experiences.

Music is a basic way of communicating within a social structure.[56] It conveys a vast array of social and cultural information. It is a vehicle to express personal preferences, values, and traits, and facilitates social bonding.[57] Indeed, music is a conveyance of culture, history, ideology, religion, emotion, education, social class, and social norms. According to Minette Mans, "It is an instrument of both diversity and unity."[58] The tripartite model of music presented by ethnomusicologist Alan Mirriam posits a bidirectional relationship between behavior, music, and cultural concepts, suggesting that listening to or performing a particular style or type of music also influences the behavior of the listener and performer (e.g., gestures and movements), as well as the cognitive concepts that we associate with the music, culture, and behavior (e.g., personal virtues, cultural values, communal ideals). Thus, music opens a pathway for the person to become aware, to explore, and to attain insight into and an understanding of different cultural groups.[59] While music making and listening afford opportunities to learn about ourselves as well as different peoples, music making and listening should also be recognized as a way of practicing social justice.[60] That is, music as social justice pursues the principals of equality, fairness, and justice for each person; embraces universal human rights, where there is an equal valuing and respect expressed for each person; and fosters an acceptance and equal valuing of diverse ethnic and multicultural perspectives, ideals, values, and ways of living.[61]

This perspective of music as social justice echoes the concern of community psychologist Julian Rappaport,[62] who introduced and promoted the concept of "empowerment," the principle that individuals and communities should express their representative autonomy and self-determination. Thus, just as Rappaport expresses in "Community psychology is (thank God) more than science," music is more than an art. Music is also a medium to advance human rights and a form of social dialogue that may advance concerns for human rights, and personal and communal well-being.[63]

One response to social justice ideals and universal human rights was the founding of the first racially integrated symphony orchestra, the Symphony of the New World, in 1966.[64] Founded by Benjamin Steinberg, the musical director and conductor of the orchestra, the Symphony of the New World sought to move beyond the ignorance and cruelties of racism toward a society based on the principles of equality and respect for all persons. In its mission statement, the goals of the symphony were to create as many job opportunities for conductors and classical musicians from nonwhite groups who were underrepresented in the music profession. Further, the symphony would give concerts in low-income communities. Finally, the symphony was to serve as a "cultural beacon" to other countries, particularly Asia, Africa, and Latin America.[65] One author had the honor of briefly meeting one of the early members of the orchestra, Julius A. Miller (born July 7, 1936; died November 11, 2017) just a few years ago. Julius played the viola, and starting at age eleven pursued a classical music career that saw him earn diplomas from the New York High School of Music and Art (currently,

Fiorello H. LaGuardia High School), Ithaca College, the Manhattan School of Music, and Rutgers University. In the mid-1960s Julius began a thirty-year career in music performance and teaching. During a historic time that began to address policies that held in place racial segregation and its pernicious discrimination, Julius toured with Nat King Cole and for twelve years performed with the Symphony of the New World, serving in the esteemed position of Symphony Orchestra Librarian. He continued his career as an assistant professor at Stockton State College (currently, Stockton University) and as an orchestra member at resorts and Bally's for performers such as Frank Sinatra, Sammy Davis, Jr., and Tony Bennett. In a musical career that celebrated both diversity and unity, Julius performed at many venues, including Sing Sing Correctional Facility, the Palace Cathedral for Reverend Ike's (Frederick J. Eikerenkoetter II) religious service, and the Apollo Theater for James Brown. Old age is a time when ensemble playing and teaching may fulfill the psychological needs of belonging, contributing, and leaving a legacy. Late in his career Julius taught in New York City Public Schools, performed at the Church of St. Mark and All Saints in Golloway, New Jersey, and for smaller events. Although the Symphony of the New World was disbanded in 1978, the good works of Benjamin Steinberg and Julius Miller still serve as a guide to how we might individually respond to and advocate for social justice through music.[66]

Music, Empathy, and Prosocial Behavior

When we consider the wellness of the individual and society, we recognize that playing an instrument or singing together, even the simple "Happy Birthday" song, fosters social bonding and thus serves as an important evolutionary mechanism supporting the community. Through music, we become connected to each other. We experience a social closeness. Often this closeness cannot be articulated but instead is sensed at an unconscious level. A further example of this phenomenon is when musicians play together and they are so "in sync" with one another that they form a gestalt where each individual becomes merged into a unit, a group that goes beyond the sum of each person's contribution.

Positing that our evolutionary history guides our behavior, research by Daniel Weinstein and colleagues examined whether social bonding, as defined by feelings of inclusion, connectivity, positive affect, and release of pain-blocking endorphins, would be influenced by singing in a choir. Results from this pretest–posttest study indicated that although there was no variation in release of endorphins across small or large choir conditions, choir members' self-report of social closeness was greater when singing in a small choir (i.e., groups ranging from 20 to 80 members) than in a large mega-choir (i.e., a group of 232 members).[67] Allied research exploring the evolutionary function of music examined the effects of musical activities such as singing, dancing, drumming, and listening on the release of pain-blocking endorphins across a series of studies. The main finding from this research suggested that singing, dancing and drumming all triggered release of endorphins, while listening and low energy musical activities did not.[68] Moreover, it is evident that music making and music-inspired dancing are essential community bonding mechanisms.

Other research suggests that involvement in a racially integrated choir and singing a program of racially diverse choral music may introduce shifts in attitudes concerning the social cohesion produced by African American and European American hymns.[69] Further, qualitative analyses indicate that approximately one-third of the choir reported that the opportunity to participate in a racially inte-grated choir represented a community-building event, bringing together diverse cultures that made the singing experience more meaningful.[70] Further research found that music making and music listening promotes prosocial behaviors. For example, research by Idil Kokal and colleagues, asking if synchronous drumming helped people feel united, showed that the ability to synchronize with the leader's drumming resulted in activation of reward-processing centers in the brain, leading to greater prosocial commitment to others,[71] again suggesting that music has a powerful influence on brain processes that are tied into evolutionary functions such as prosocial behavior.[72]

Other research by Shannon Clark and Giac Giacomantonio involving young and older adults explored the relationship between music prefer-ence and empathy as predictor of prosocial behavior.[73] In this study, older adults preferred reflexive and complex music (e.g., classical, blues, folk, and jazz genres), and younger adults intense and rebellious music (e.g., alternative, rock, and heavy metal genres). For each age group, it was their music preference that was most predictive of empathic concern. Perhaps it was the lyrical content of these selections and not the genre itself that may broaden perspective taking of various social and moral issues. In a similar fashion, a series of investigations by Tobias Greitemeyer using college students reports that listening to songs with prosocial messages enhanced these students' accessibility of prosocial thoughts, interper-sonal empathy, and helping behavior.[74] Further, related research by Greitemeyer has suggested that exposure to music with prosocial lyrics reduces aggression.[75]

Research investigating the effect of long-term musical group interaction (e.g., playing games of music imitation, improvising rhythm) on
empathy in children report that children exposed to musical group interaction showed an increase in empathy scores from baseline and had
higher scores compared to children who instead engaged in a story-
telling activity.[76] Other research using adults similarly suggests that
music may modulate emotional arousal as well as emotional
contagion.[77] Thus, the connection between music and empathy has
important implications for how people view other cultures. For example,
listening to the music of an unfamiliar culture (e.g., Indian, West African)
may create a shift in cultural attitudes.[78] Listening to culturally diverse
music may evoke empathy and affiliation in listeners. Individuals high in
dispositional empathy were found to be more likely to entrain to the music
and to display an unconscious preference for the ethnic group's music to
which they were exposed. Thus, music making and listening is more than
an aesthetic practice. The harmonies and expressions of beauty found in
music arouse brain centers involved with emotional and empathic
concerns.[79] Music serves as a conduit to explore ethical thought, and
moral and spiritual values.[80]

And, What of Love Songs?

And, what *of* love songs? This chapter has described social relationships
from the perspective of mentoring and family relations, ensemble playing, and social justice. But certainly music is also a part of our deepest
and most intimate relationships, too. Indeed, we know that music may
evoke a whole range of amorous feelings and set the mood for romantic
encounters. Moreover, with great elan and celebration, we often share
with our spouse and intimate others the statement, "They're playing our
song!" Therefore, before we leave this chapter on relationships, we
would like to briefly ask how music helps create the mood for
romance. Certainly, music has been shown to affect emotions[81] and,
across cultures, feelings of intimacy are suggested to be elicited by
various styles of music.[82] Accordingly then, love songs and expressions
of hope are found within all cultural settings, and research has suggested
the positive or negative mood of music to set the mood and influence
sexual intimacy, but there is no clear linkage of music directly to sexual
arousal.[83] However, research exploring music as a moderator of interpersonal attractiveness suggests jazz music influences women's interpersonal attraction toward and judgments of men's attractiveness, and
rock music videos involving women as focal characters were found to
augment men's sexual arousal.[84] Other related research has suggested

that music that contains or expresses misogyny, sexual aggression, or violence against women influences males' acceptance of violence against women.[85] Certainly, personal and cultural preferences are likely to be moderating influences of how music may be perceived, and how it may be linked with sexual attractiveness and become part of sexual intimacy. Songs such as "I'm in the Mood for Love"[86] or "Por una Cabeza,"[87] the tango song that accompanies the beginning dance scene of the film *Scent of a Woman*,[88] are both examples of how music is an expression of, and intertwined with, our romantic feelings and deepest intimacies. Given that romance and the deepest feelings of belonging are such central expressions of ourselves, this is an important area for continued research. And, as the authors strongly suggest, there is great need for more love songs! For songs that sing of caring and compassion, of hope and new insight, and of understanding and respect between persons and communities.

The Bond of Music

The relationships we establish with others through music are unique and special, ones that are not necessarily experienced in other social interactions. Music is important for our well-being, happiness, contentment, and peace. A study that interviewed older adults (some in their nineties) found that for these participants, music helped them to stay focused, occupied, and gave them a more youthful outlook on life. They believed that music helps to slow the aging process and provides a way to achieve spiritual, intellectual, emotional, and cognitive wholeness.[89] Our relationships with others through music are indeed transformational and transcendent. They can shorten the distance between us in age, class, and background. Young and old can experience a bond that disregards age. People from one culture can connect with those from another. We become better people through music, recognizing our shared hopes, experiences, fears, and failures. Music forms friendships – a "deepening of the spirit." Through music we find inclusiveness and tolerance. Ultimately, we learn something about each other and, most importantly, about ourselves. In Chapter 7 we continue to discuss the ways music deepens our self-actualizing experiences in the work we do and in retirement.

7   Rhythm and Blues: Work and Retirement

> In the labor of engines and trades, and the labor of fields, I find the developments, and the eternal meanings.
>
> – Walt Whitman, "A Song for Occupations"

The jobs we undertake and the work we do provide us an opportunity to explore and realize our highest potential in life. Indeed, as Walt Whitman's "A Song for Occupations" notes,[1] it is often through our work, as we provide for our families and make contributions to our communities, that we find a deeper purpose and meaning in our living. But many jobs can be full of toil and challenge, leading us to seek out moments of respite and relief. In the flow of the work-a-day world, however, music becomes a key resource and provider of moments of release and celebration. For example, the long tradition of singing while you work alludes to how music may lift our spirits and help us discover pleasure and a sense of accomplishment in our jobs.[2] Music may also help us do our best on the job as well. For example, research exploring how music may affect our work suggests that the rhythm of music increases heart rate and respiration, and helps focus our attention and improve our job efficiency.[3] Beyond music's ability to enhance the coordination and efficacy of our work, it also may promote wellness and provide relief from the draining pressures of our jobs.[4] Thus, as Todd Rundgren's antiwork song "Bang on the Drum All Day"[5] seems to suggest, if work were only *more* like music – a celebration of our living and everything we love – then our everyday labors would not be such toil. Accordingly then, what we do for a living and how we think about our jobs is a complex issue. Our occupations serve at least two ends – the practical objective of making a living as well as the deeper psychological objective of expressing and finding meaning and fulfillment in our work. This understanding of how work has dual functions is important to embrace as we think about careers and retirement. As noted in previous chapters, music offers a raison d'être, a reason for living. Thus, in this chapter we will discuss how we may find a reason for living in our careers and retirement, and offer how music may be intertwined in this process.

Dreaming about Work

Our interest in having a particular kind of career begins in childhood, but employment opportunities and the types of jobs we undertake are a central concern throughout adulthood. Career choices, according to the economist Eli Ginzberg, tend to grow from dreaming about future possibilities in childhood and shift to a more realistic understanding of what we have to offer and where we will fit in during adolescence.[6] So in childhood, career choice tends to be fantasy oriented, where we are dreaming about what the future may be like and imagining what is possible. Maybe our earliest dream is for the "celebrity life" of being a rock star, or the next great opera singer, or another type of high-status career. Through the backing of parents and other family members, children are supported in their pursuit of this dream. There are music lessons and recitals, and all the necessary preparations to make the dream into a reality. Yet, as the song "Dead End Kid" by rock musicians Howie B and Robbie Robertson portrays,[7] for some children and adolescents these early dreams and hopes are not supported, and the message they hear is one that is demeaning and discouraging.

Like other rhythms in development, with continued growth the dream-like orientation gives way to a more tentative stage in adolescence and young adulthood. Adolescence is a time in development when we become aware of ourselves in relation to others in new ways. Further, it is a time, as Erik Erikson postulated, that we are involved in the process of forming an occupation-oriented identity.[8] This formation of identity reflects psychosocial dynamics involving ego synthesis and gender orientation, coupled with processes of social comparison and self-evaluation that allow us to appraise our dreams and hopes in life in relation to our deeper sense of who we are, and the specific talents, capacities, and values that we may possess. With a continued and burgeoning sense of "who we are," our initial self-assessments give way to a reappraisal of what we might become, what is realistic. An example of this reappraisal is when we observe the early adolescent dream of being a "rock star" fade, and the young aspiring virtuoso recognizes, "Gee, I'm not sure I am going to rise to the level of 'the greatest of all time' – but I know I can become a pretty good musician!" Thus, reflecting a developmental rhythm, our appraisals and reappraisals of what might be possible involve an exploration and trying out of available careers, and result in a sharpening of our focus onto career areas that correspond to our abilities and then selecting a specific job field or career path to enter.

One idea to consider about Ginzberg's youth-oriented model is that it may have application in later times of development as well. In fact, some of us in our forties, fifties, and sixties may still at times return to the processes of evaluating our career interests in relation to our talents, capacities, and values, and thinking about what is possible. For example, when businesses downsize and jobs end, we may again dream about a new job or how to establish a start-up business and once again evaluate our interests in relation to our skills and values, as we hope to find new work that is realistic and fulfilling for us. In later life, too, in our seventies and beyond, we may still "dream" about a new career and the possibilities that would flow from a novel involvement. Further, in later life we might also think about this model in relation to pursuing avocational interests, taking on various pastimes or new endeavors that are more like having fun than the toil of "work" – for example, following their dream of singing in a barbershop quartet or church choir, playing in the community orchestra, or joining a "garage" band.

A Long Way to the Top

An allied career model that complements Ginzberg's and extends into midlife comes from psychologist Donald Super.[9] Again reflecting developmental rhythms, Super's Career Self-Concept Theory suggests alterations and restructuring of one's vocational self-concept from adolescence to young adulthood, through midlife, and all the way to the time of retirement. Probably most of us have a sense of how our career orientation has changed as we have moved from our teenage years into young adulthood, and now as we look back on our early path of development, we may recognize a connection with the heuristics of Super's models. For example, during adolescence we develop beliefs about what type of work meshes with our burgeoning self-concept. These first thoughts about our career originate through our early work experiences and are accompanied by the chorus of "What are you going to do when you grow up?" that we hear from family and friends. A bit later, again echoing the developmental rhythms of later adolescence and early adulthood, there is a narrowing of choices and the initiation of behaviors that begin our selection and preparation to enter a particular field of work. For music students, this time in development might include the narrowing of career focus to becoming a music educator or considering fields such as accounting, business administration, law, medicine, or other career areas suggested by parents and counselors.

Subsequent career advancement portrays an edging forward that coincides with completion of education and training, and entrance into the "real world" of work. From this point on and throughout young adulthood, our career choices are based on the practicalities of entering into a career and starting our job. This is often a time in development where the tempo of living may be very excited and fast. It is also a time when career decisions are perhaps most influenced by external factors, such as what others (family, employer, peers) expect from us, or our quest for fame, or to be "in" with a particular social group. This is also the stage in which the person begins to establish themselves in particular job roles and responsibilities. For individuals who encounter difficulty in their first career choice, there may be a rethinking of their selection; a return to the earlier decision-making process; and reselection of a new job or career. For example, the difficulty of making a living while trying to establish a career as a professional musician is well noted, and being able to "make it" requires strong motivation, successful coping, and often the enduring assistance and support of family and friends.[10] It is at this point, when a particular type of career may seem like it is going nowhere, that the person may be compelled to adopt their backup plan. For example, the aspiring musical concert performer may opt for a career as a music educator or some other more viable and better paying type of work.[11]

Another shift in the developmental rhythm occurs at midlife, as careers become more established. In our thirties and forties, life's tempo may have slowed down somewhat from the allegro of young adulthood to a pace that is more moderato as we gain the sense that "we made it," found success in maintaining our job, begun to advance up the career ladder, and settled down or started a family. Yet, during this time we may still seek to advance our careers and reach for better paying, higher status positions, or work that allows greater self-actualization. This is also a time that often requires perseverance and continued on-the-job learning to adjust to new innovations and changes in job requirements. Thus, much like the song titled "It's a Long Way to the Top (If You Wanna Rock 'n' Roll)" by the rock band AC/DC suggests,[12] there is an awareness of the need to keep pace, to persevere, and to carry on in one's work. It should be noted, however, as we reflect and take inventories of ourselves and seek greater personal growth, that midlife is a time of reorientation as well. As Carl Jung suggests, midlife is a time of shifting our focus from the external world onto our inner life, and the new adventure of seeking a deeper understanding of ourselves, and the cultural and spiritual backgrounds of our psychological "self."[13] Midlife, as Jung suggests, is also a time of changing expression of masculine and feminine psychic components. Thus, in midlife we may adopt new roles and realize new potentialities as we rebalance intrapsychic needs and our tendencies to be easy going or aggressive, deferential or domineering, nurturing or neglectful, compassionate or indifferent.[14] This may also be a time when we pivot onto a different career path as we move on to a job that better reflects our personal interests and values, and thus is more fulfilling. In the middle of life, too, we might come to a full stop in our career and have to look for new work due to economic downturns that force businesses and corporations to downsize or close or due to change in our abilities to perform our jobs. Thus, as noted by James Fowler, midlife can be a time when, having experienced and coming to know the "sacrament of defeat," we undergo transformation and reorientation in how we construct the purpose and meaning of our lives, and how we relate to the world in which we live.[15]

In the years immediately before retirement, another change in the developmental rhythm is suggested to occur. Here the tempo may slow even more, from moderato to adagio. This phase of career development involves a more explicit planning for retirement and the separating from work. Finally, at "retirement," as this stage is aptly named, the person stops working full time.

Both Ginzberg's and Super's conceptual models are very useful to explore with teenagers and young adults, but they also can offer insights into midlife and older adults, too. Nevertheless, it is important to note that these models seem rather one dimensional in the sense that they suggest "careers" to be those full-time jobs that pay money and from which we may make a living or raise a family. Certainly, there are many nonpaying jobs and careers – for example, being the stay-at-home parent, or a volunteer, or amateur musician. Additionally, it should be recognized that there is tremendous variability in how a person selects, enters, and continues in their career, and thus not everyone may follow or move through these career phases exactly as they are laid out. Moreover, having the same career throughout adulthood is not as likely in the twenty-first century as it may have been in earlier times. Indeed, one problem with Super's theory is that, due to a variety of contextual and sociohistorical factors (e.g., equal access and opportunity to a career field, technological advancements, outsourcing of formerly in-house jobs) as well as personal concerns (e.g., development of interest in other job areas, job burnout, health problems), not everyone may be able to enter or stay in the same career throughout the adult years. Thus, just as we consider the validity of Ginzberg's and Super's models, at different times in adulthood we may need to again reassess how our current job "fits" our interests and undertake the process of selecting, finding, and reorienting to new employment or to the status of an ex-worker or retiree. Fulfilling one's highest potential may mean taking on a job or pursuing a career that allows one to use all of their toolbox of skills, be their true self, and allow for their best to shine.

A "Part" Just for Me!

Our inexorable quest to express ourselves and tell our life story through music[16] directs us to ask how we might best satisfy psychological needs and motivations in the work we do. The psychologist John Holland's Personality Type Theory seeks to do this.[17] This "pigeonholing" theory proposes that to be happiest in our work, it is important to match one's personality to a particular type of job. The central idea is that when the "person–job" fit is good, the individual is more likely to enjoy the work, work more productively, and stay in the job longer. Conversely, a mismatch between the person and the job is likely to lead to less satisfactory outcomes and to singing the "work blues." The personality-occupational categories Holland offers include "realistic," where the person expresses a personality orientation that fits with jobs where we work with our hands or become involved as concrete problem solvers. Another is "investigative," which refers to an orientation where the person is more task oriented (the "get 'er done" orientation) or enjoys thinking in critical ways, pursuing leads, and seeking solutions like a detective or scientist. A category that matches with a person's enjoyment in working with people is labeled "social." Categories that might overlap a bit with these include the "conventional" orientation, which refers to a style of personality and job demands where the workplace is highly structured and the person is happy to follow directions from others. Another is "enterprising," which refers to a personality orientation and job fit that requires good verbal and leadership skills. The last category Holland offers is called "artistic" and refers to a personality orientation and job fit where there are many opportunities for self-expression and the freedom to work in a relatively unstructured manner. Naturally, most musicians as well as music lovers fit in this artistic category. Realizing the multiplicity of ways we might express ourselves, however, leads to the understanding that there may be many career areas that a person may find suitable. If you consider what you really like doing, perhaps longing for the job that you have always dreamed of or thinking about making a "comeback" as an amateur or professional musician, certainly this personality-occupational-fit concept is useful to explore. Even in later life, one may gain a new perspective on what is still possible and where one might find a "good fit" with pursuits such as part-time employment or consulting work, volunteering, or involvement in community artistic projects, musical groups, and involvement with various artisan guilds and hobby associations.

But, how good of a fit? So often we might feel like a square or star-shaped peg trying to fit into a round hole – both ways seem awkward. Finding the right job is a creative process that optimally may provide opportunities for self-actualization and transformation. Research by psychologist Paul Costa and colleagues, applying Holland's theory and asking about aging effects, suggested that younger adults (under the age of fifty-five) are slightly more realistic, artistic, and enterprising in their orientation than older adults (age fifty-five or older).[18] Further, Costa and colleagues report women are more likely than men to express social, artistic, and conventional orientations, yet vocational interests are highly stable for men and women throughout adulthood. In interpreting these age and gender variations in occupational orientations, Costa and colleagues suggested they are likely to reflect the influence of acculturation processes for men and women. In a related manner, a very important criticism of Holland's theory is that different ethnic and sociocultural groups have not been involved in research.[19] The very specific concern here is that some gender, racial, and cultural groups have historically been denied or had very limited access to particular careers. Thus, Holland's theory appears to have overlooked both subtle and not-so-subtle biases and the social context of vocational choice. Another criticism is that there is no accounting for changes in personality and related occupational orientation with advancing age, changes that may stir the person to pursue other career areas. Nevertheless, matching the person's values, needs, and interests with particular organizational roles and activities is likely to lead to an enhancement of greater satisfaction in work and with involvements later in retirement.[20] Thus, taken as a whole and noting well their rather caricatured outline and attendant criticism, the career models described here provide us some insight into the processes of career development and how taking into account various transformations, adjustments, and fit with roles and activities can lead to satisfying outcomes for the person.

The Deeper Orientation of Our Work: Social Relationships and Societal Concerns

As we alluded at the beginning of this chapter, in many ways work is like music in that it expresses and reflects our deeper psychology and communal orientation. Indeed, our job is often an aspect of our identity, intermixed with and reflecting deeply held personal values and social expectations (e.g., being a loving provider by holding down a job) as well as the higher social status that is associated with certain types of jobs (e.g., physician, nurse, musician, engineer). Thus, what we do as our "work" supports our self-concept and identity as a person.

Yet again considering the rhythms of development, there are certainly cost–benefit trade-offs to note, especially when we examine career and nonwork life goals in relation to identity and purpose and meaning in life. These trade-offs vary from person to person, but usually the more difficult, stressful, unrewarding the work, the poorer the quality of work-life. Moreover, the higher the perceived costs (e.g., too stressful, low pay, poor working conditions) the greater likelihood that we would rather be doing something else instead. Thus, work interests and opportunities may change as we move through the life course. But beyond just having a "job" to do, we recognize that work involves relationships and social connections, and that throughout our living we experience many gains and losses in these aspects as well. Perhaps the most significant losses we experience as we journey into midlife and old age are the losses of grandparents, parents, brothers and sisters, partners, and spouses. In our work, too, it might be a loss of a trusted co-worker who moves on to another job or retires, or a great boss or inspiring mentor who retires. Thus, these social aspects of our lives, and how they intersect with our day-to-day job and impassion us to rise to new heights in our work and influence our living, are important to acknowledge, cherish, and celebrate.

Job Performance Concerns

An old joke circulating around rehearsal rooms and music amphitheaters asks, "How do you get to Carnegie Hall?" This seems to be a reasonable question – if you are looking for driving directions. However, the punch line plays on our naiveté: "Practice, practice, practice!" When we think about being successful in our "performing," however, it's not just rehearsing that is important, but our physical capacities, psychological temperament, and adaptive skills as well.

As noted in an early foundational work by Edward Stieglitz, an imminent professor of geriatric medicine of the last century, the capacity for physical work is generally observed to decline throughout our thirties and forties, with a steeper decline beginning at around age fifty.[21] It is noted that most professional orchestra and classical musicians retire in their sixties and seventies, although some exceptionally gifted individuals, like pianists Vladimir Horowitz, Arthur Rubenstein, and Rudolf Serkin, continued into their eighties and beyond.[22] With regard to the capacity for mental work, however, there is generally a continued enhancement from around our mid-twenties into our fifties and sixties, and many individuals continue to be quite productive in their intellectual and creative expression well into their eighties and nineties.

Thus, as noted in earlier chapters, declines in physical, sensory–perceptual, and cognitive capacities occur with advancing age; these may most impact professions demanding high levels of physical endurance and mental alertness, such as airline pilots, as well as those that require great strength and physical stamina, like construction workers. As we mentioned in earlier chapters, too, the gradual loss of physical and mental capacities might be a good reason to sing the "Getting Old Blues."[23] However, most of the jobs that people hold are not so demanding that they are unable to compensate for decline in physical and sensory–perceptual/cognitive functions. In fact, often the older worker performs at levels well above younger workers, with peak productivity among workers occurring in the forties and fifties, with gradual declines thereafter.[24] It should be noted further that older workers are less likely to be injured on the job, but when they are injured, there is a longer period of convalescence. Thus, older workers are less likely to be absent from work, but those with health problems have higher absenteeism.

When we consider many creative fields, we recognize the very high and masterful quality of work that may be done later in life. For example, the classical music composers Johannes Brahms, Phillip Glass, Leos Janacek, Leo Ornstein, and John Williams are all recognized for composing some of their greatest works later in life. Similarly, if we look across the many different musical genres (e.g., jazz, rock, country, pop), we recognize the continued involvement and creative contributions of musicians like Johnny Cash, Miles Davis, Aretha Franklin, Dizzy Gillespie, Mick Jagger, Dolly Parton, Pete Townshend, Neil Young, and many, many others in the latter half of the life cycle.

Even the singing group "New Kids on the Block," beyond their similarly named debut album in 1986,[25] have continued on the musical scene, albeit members have matured and gotten older, and are performing concerts at this writing. However, in other areas that require high levels of muscular strength and stamina, we may see older adults at a disadvantage. For example, decline in physical abilities is the primary reason for retirement of professional athletes in their thirties. Thus again it is important to note that in many occupations, as Stieglitz has alluded, intellectual capacity for work continues into later life and work performance remains relatively stable with age. However, when we consider age and job training, and the speed of acquisition of new skills, we recognize that older workers do take longer to train, but the difference is modest.[26]

Moreover, in employment or job-seeking situations where retraining is required, older workers may require special accommodation.[27]

A Labor of Love or Inordinate Drudgery?

When we consider the social and relational aspects of our job, we start to become more aware of the importance and benefits of work. Certainly there is a richness found in the relationships we form with the people with whom we work, as well as an understanding of how we have benefited or have been challenged, and have grown as a result of particular work relationships. Moreover, the involvements we have with younger and older co-workers help us to gain new insight, to become inspired, and to realize a deeper awareness about others and ourselves. As the gerontologist Leo Missinne notes, "We need to meet all kinds of people so that we can find ourselves. Young people need older people just as older people need young people in order to become more themselves and more human. That humanizing process will teach us that there is a child behind the mask of each older face, just as there is already an older person behind the mask of each young face."[28] Indeed, it is in our social encounters with others from diverse backgrounds and of different ages that we may embrace social influences that allow us to reconfigure our inner person, to embark in new areas of creativity, and to discover our greatest potential. Moreover, as noted by the humanistic psychologist Carl Rogers, the process of self-actualization occurs through our actions – our actions to be creative, to be involved with others, to seek and to understand the influence of intrinsic and extrinsic forces that sculpt our personhood in this process of becoming who we were meant to be.[29]

Yet throughout life, each of us will have to find a balance between these intrinsic and extrinsic forces. Thus, beyond the conceptual models presented earlier, we again note a variety of developmental changes in careers across the life course.[30] These changes occur due to failing to master successfully the developmental tasks of the first career, finding a career that is a better job fit and more satisfying, and changing life goals due to divorce, widowhood, or sudden unemployment. Research on midlife adults suggests that most often people change careers due to external circumstances (34 percent) or experienced external pressures (26 percent); fewer people change careers just because they want to (17 percent).[31] Nevertheless, career change is most often motivated by desire to find a job that fits better with one's personal values and that is more meaningful to the person.[32]

In general, intrinsic and extrinsic factors are important in determining whether we find a deeper fulfillment through our work, or regard it as another unpleasant four letter word. Moreover, social and work-related factors influence the person's perceptions of quality of work life and nonwork life, as well as whether the job can be considered a "labor of love" or an "inordinate drudgery." Certainly, as we work we may develop a sense of job satisfaction. Research on job satisfaction generally suggests that the person will stay in a job longer if they like it, that better paying jobs usually provide more satisfaction than do low-wage jobs, and that satisfaction is higher when the job is a reasonably good dispositional fit with the person.[33] Further, with advancing age, work becomes less of a focus in one's life and thus it may take less to keep one satisfied. As a result, differences in experience, contexts, and the person's stage of development are all suggested to be related to the person's report of job satisfaction.[34] When we again consider the times of young adulthood, middle, and later life, we note that younger workers are often happy to have a job, but are more likely to quit if they do not enjoy the work.[35] Further, older workers may find greater satisfaction in work and are more likely to contend with difficult work situations because other work is not easy to find. In general, over the adult years, job satisfaction is noted to increase due to more income, higher status jobs, greater job security, and stronger commitment with advancing age.

Other Career Challenges

Many career challenges result from changes in technological and social factors. For example, technological advancements continue to transform work sites and work–skill requirements, and economic downturns often put people out of work and necessitate finding a job in a new or different field. Further, our jobs may not always be the job we expected, and thus we are awakened to this concern and encounter the reality shock of what we had expected and hoped our job to be like, and the realization of what exists in the "real world." Thus, one's early career choices may become reoriented due to unrealistic expectations or due to the person's apprehension to remain in a particular job. For example, one of the author's early music teachers, Salvator A. Piazza, was a French horn player and a highly regarded school band director in the St. Louis metropolitan area. As a gifted young musician, in 1940 Sal auditioned for the famous conductor Leopold Stokowski's All-American Youth Orchestra. This was a great opportunity to "show his stuff." But Sal did not make the cut to join the touring orchestra, many of whose horn players later went on to become principal members of symphonies in Chicago, Philadelphia, and St. Louis. Sal remarked that he was so nervous at one of his early auditions that his legs were shaking – but because he was wearing very baggy trousers, no one seemed to notice. Yet despite these early setbacks, Sal later joined and played with the New Orleans Philharmonic Orchestra. Later, discussing the challenges and stresses of being a member of a professional orchestra, Sal related how he reappraised his professional calling and opted to become a teacher. He subsequently had a successful career as a music educator in the public schools that spanned four decades.[36] Thus, a related concern has to do with the person's ability to cope with job pressures and various career challenges that the person encounters. Indeed, not everyone will join a professional ensemble, become an orchestra leader, or reach the status of vocal soloist or instrumental virtuoso. Thus, we should keep in mind that there are many more amateur than professional musicians and that the "real" way to be "successful" is in continuing to find ways to adapt to and overcome life's challenges, and continue to learn.

One of the big problems for older workers is age discrimination.[37] Age discrimination refers to denying an individual a job, a promotion, more pay, or other desired work benefit solely because of his or her chronological age. Age discrimination still occurs and continues to be a problem in the workplace. For example it is suggested that ageism is expressed in the age restrictions that indicate employment opportunities are just for those composers who are below the age of forty.[38] When we seek to understand age discrimination, we delve into the influences of social cognitive processes and related age stereotypes. Age stereotypes refer to attribution biases that often negatively stereotype older workers as untrainable, uncreative, or out of date.[39] For musicians, rather subtle age stereotypes are reflected in lampooning expressions such as "the only people that still listen to that style of music – are my grandparents" or "this is an evening show– can your band stay up that late?" or "our audience wants to groove with a hip and 'youthful' act – not the geriatric set." These stereotypes arise from age prejudice and ultimately lead to discrimination directed at the older worker.[40] We should keep in mind that skill, health, and motivation are better predictors of job performance than merely age.[41] Further, governmental protections, such as those in the United States against age discrimination, are outlined in the Older American Act of 1965, which defines an "older" worker as one at or past the age of fifty-five, and the Employment Act of 1967, which prohibits the denial or termination of employment to individuals over forty because of their age. In addition, the Employment Act of 1967 was amended in 1986 to prohibit job termination on the basis of age, at any age. Yet, there is still much to be done to make the workplace a fair place for everyone.

Concerns for Equity in Employment

There have been many changes in jobs and careers since 1900. One notable change is the number of women who are now in the workforce.[42] This increase in women working outside the home means there are more working mothers and many more dual-career marriages. Certainly these changes have occurred in response to practical needs but also in relation to societal changes that allow everyone to have greater opportunities in life. When we consider practical needs, we recognize the extent to which the income and other benefits obtained through work gratify such nonwork-related needs and wants as food, housing, clothing, and recreation. Further, when we contemplate the person's desire for self-actualization, we recognize the extent to which work is gratifying and enjoyable for its own sake, in that it leads to greater opportunities for personal growth and in finding deeper purpose and meaning in life.

There has been an historic increase in the number of women in the traditional workforce. But research also indicates a gender variation in the type of work undertaken and at what point in the life course the work is performed. For example, men are more likely to work outside the home throughout the life course, whereas women take time off to raise children.[43] Just considering work outside the home, however, is an incomplete representation of the division of work between men and women – the spouse who stays at home to take care of children and the home is as much actively involved in work as the spouse who works outside the home. In fact, changes in roles and work economy suggest that men and women are becoming more alike in types of work.[44] Across all age groups, however, there are greater numbers of men in the traditional workforce than women, and women are on average paid less than men for performing the same type of job. What hopefully we understand is that women are a very important part of the labor force and also play a fundamental role in family life, raising children, or in charge of the home. Further, there is often variation in terms of the need to find a balance between career and child-rearing.[45] Some women do only career, some women only child-rearing, and other women do both. Again considering the balancing of child-rearing and work, we note that working mothers are more likely to experience conflict and stress when partners do not support their careers, when there are long work hours, or when career aspirations are higher than the job currently held.[46] In addition, it should be noted that women who work may be no less satisfied with life than those women who opt to raise a family, nor are they less competent employees than men.[47] Yet, women who work and raise a family are more likely to encounter biases with regard to employer's perceived attributions of their work and assessed potential for advancement, and may find greater difficulty in meeting obligations in both work and family areas.[48]

Thus, as noted in Benjamin Steinberg's work to establish the first racially integrated orchestra, the Symphony of the New World, and other efforts to integrate and include women in professional ensembles, there is still much to be done to address the social justice concerns in the workplace to make every type of career accessible to all, regardless of a person's age, gender orientation, ethnicity, race, color, religion, or disability.[49] Further, it is now widely recognized that gender can no longer be thought of as a binary construct. As we presented in Chapter 1, a well society is one that expresses concern and fights for fairness of all people. Discrimination in the workplace has been well documented against LGBTQ+ individuals. It is reported that at least 20 percent of LGBTQ+ individuals have experienced discrimination based on gender identity when applying for a job.[50] The recent US Supreme Court decision (cited in Chapter 1) provides equal protection under the law against discrimination of LGBTQ+ workers and is an important step toward becoming a well society.

Economic Concerns and the Transition to Retirement

A person's wage earnings throughout the years of viable employment affect Social Security retirement benefits as well as pension plans and personal retirement savings. When we consider the economic status of older adults, we note that with advancing age comes lower income and greater rates of poverty.[51] There is also an exacerbation of poverty due to ethnicity and gender.[52] In fact, in old age there are more persons of color below the poverty line than whites, and more older women than older men. Some of the US government programs that have aided older people and are hoped to continue to do so in some form or another include the Social Security Trust Fund, Medicare, and Medicaid.[53] The Social Security Trust Fund is a fund that all US workers pay into that provides a very basic income after they retire. Medicare refers to a government health insurance program for people sixty-five years of age and older that helps pay for basic health-care services. Medicaid refers to a government health insurance program that pays for health care for eligible low-income adults, pregnant women, elderly adults, disabled or blind, and families with dependent children.

Some of the popular concerns about Social Security benefits and Medicare/Medicaid health insurance plans are that a country's ability to meet economic demands and provide assistance to older adults is a function of the increase in nonworkers as measured by the dependency ratio. The dependency ratio is the number of individuals ages sixty-five and older and below the age of sixteen, in proportion to the number of individuals considered to be of working age (those individuals between sixteen and sixty-four years of age). It is expected that an increasing number of older adults, especially adults over the age of eighty-five, will place greater demand on programs that provide specialized health services, housing, and nutritional programs for older individuals. Currently and in the future, changes in the dependency ratio will challenge the ability of governmental programs to meet the needs of individuals of all ages vis-à-vis retirement accounts, health programs, and other social insurance programs. Important questions in the Social Security and health-care reform debates are: "How will we cut up the pie of resources to be fair to all generations?" "How will we be fair in treating and providing for older adults?" "What more could we do – what more should we do?"

Certainly, there is a special role for musicians and music lovers in these and other moral debates. Indeed, we may serve to "beat the drum" for and write the songs of social justice – songs that sing out for an equitable distribution of resources for everyone. We might also lend our ear to and provide support for musical programs that seek to promote human rights and strive to be inclusive in providing educational opportunities to build bridges that will connect diverse groups of people. For example, to promote social justice concerns, we could attend concerts and provide support for the activities of groups such as the Human Rights Orchestra. Founded by Artistic Director Alessio Allegrini, the Human Rights Orchestra is made up of professional musicians from across Europe who, through their fund-raising concerts, offer support to aid humanitarian and social justice projects around the world. Their mission is to inspire everyone to recognize our shared humanity and the basic human rights of all persons, and to take action to meet the needs of people at society's margins.[54] One could also support and attend concerts by such groups as the Black Pearl Chamber Orchestra, located in Philadelphia, Pennsylvania. The artistic and educational mission of the Black Pearl Chamber Orchestra is to promote diversity, inclusion, and equity. Founded by Artistic Director Jeri Lynne Johnson, the first African American woman to win the Taki Concordia Conducting Fellowship, an international conducting prize, this orchestra seeks to involve all ages and all communities in a variety of musical experiences that connect countries, cultures, and communities.[55] We can also offer support for projects such as OrchKids, a music program for underserved youth in Baltimore, Maryland. Started by Marin Alsop, the first woman to become music director of the Baltimore Symphony Orchestra, this program is designed to create social change through greater educational and career access for Baltimore City children.[56] Thus, through our music making and support for orchestras and educational programming, we too can become active participants in the social justice concerns that affect us all.

Retirement

In a history of music course in college, after listening to the Italian composer Gioschinni Rossini's heraldic "William Tell Overture" and contemplating the beauty and excitement of his music, one student asked, "What ever happened to Rossini?" The professor simply responded, "He retired." The student, confounded, asked, "How could such a gifted composer simply retire? How is that possible?" Rossini had written 39 operas in his relatively brief career, and in 1824, at age 32, was regarded as one of the most brilliant composers of the time. Yet he would not write another piece of music after the premiere of his *William Tell* opera in 1829.[57] In biographical accounts of his life, one reason offered for Rossini's early retirement at the age of 37 was due to the speed with which he composed, producing a burnout or "exhaustion" of his genius.[58] Other influencing factors may have been the loss of his mother in 1827 and the despair he felt or the tepid reception of his *William Tell* opera by the critics. But Rossini's poor health at the time, and untreated venereal disease, are also key factors that likely led to an early end to Rossini's career as a composer. Rossini lived another 40 years, never to publish another piece of music. He died in 1868. Certainly, the factors associated with retirement are often complex – most of us probably think that retirement will be a time when we can do the things we enjoy the most. In a way, we want to believe that retirement will be a time to "smell the roses" and enjoy the time we have left to live. But perhaps that is more of the "dream" of retirement – the actual "reality" of retirement may be much different and include economic restrictions, failing health, and feelings of being excluded and obsolete. Some years later, the music student mentioned earlier came to understand that jobs and careers do not always take a particular set course, nor are they easy and always fulfilling in the ways one had hoped they would be. And, though many of us dream that later life will be a time when we can live out our "golden years," various health issues, along with the worry about access to afford-able health care and prescription medicines, often take commanding and central positions in our everyday living.

Nevertheless, retirement is a time of life most people look forward to, but for different reasons.[59] Some people retire because they've reached the age where they can receive retirement benefits, while other people retire because they have the financial ability to do so.[60] Other folks may retire because of poor health, and some retire to pursue different opportunities. Further, due in part to long-standing economic inequalities and the resultant financial insecurity that is encountered, one study of retirement confidence reports that 30 percent of American workers are apprehensive about their ability to retire and the economic disadvantages they would endure.[61] Moreover, as a point of reference and comparison, when we broaden our view to look globally, we find that in the developing countries of West and Central Africa fewer than 10 percent of older adults have access to retirement or pension programs.[62] Thus, for many older adults, retirement may be postponed or never really be realized in the same way it is by older adults who enjoy greater financial security.[63]

The Rhythms of Retirement

Conceptually, as the social gerontologist Robert Atchley has suggested, the many years of retired living may be construed as a developmental process, consisting of various phases or rhythms of retirement.[64] There are many models of retirement, however, and a variety of considerations for when we might end formal employment.[65] But if we look closely at Atchley's model, we may gain a useful understanding of what might occur and the issues that we might confront in retirement. These are not inevitable phases or responses to retirement by any means, and undoubtedly reflect the Western-industrialized context, yet like Ginzberg and Super's career models, they provide a heuristic conceptualization that is useful in organizing ideas about retirement.

Retirement is a key event in the life course. As we get older, we can see it on the developmental horizon. So an early stage is termed "preretirement." That is where many of us may be now – hoping that at the end of our work careers we will have the freedom to do some of the fun things we always dreamt about doing. This preretirement phase contains *remote* and *near* aspects. The remote aspect is the time in our thirties, forties, or fifties when we think about retirement in a relatively positive way. In contrast, the near phase of preretirement is a time when the person orients themselves toward a specific date for retiring. This is when individuals may develop a "short-timers" attitude and gear themselves up for ending work, relationships with colleagues, and exiting the social situations that they were involved with during their career. Individuals may also develop a fantasy about what retirement will be like and how they will enjoy their retirement. If one's expectations differ from reality, then the transition into retired life will likely be a bit bumpy. Often worries about retirement revolve around income and health, and, usually, there is little concern about missing the job. Thus, sometimes the retiree's attitude may reflect the strains of the famous country-western song "Take This Job and Shove It," written by David Allen Coe and sung by Johnny Paycheck.[66]

The last day of work and the retirement ceremony officially mark the beginning of retirement, the time when job routines and responsibilities will officially end. As retirement begins, Atchley proposes possible phases or rhythms occur, each which corresponds to a time and feature of retirement.

The honeymoon phase refers to a euphoric period involving the first days of retired life where there is more free time to do the things you have always wanted to do. This moment of retirement is usually an exciting and happy time, where there are many well wishes extended to the person, noting the culminating point of one's career and duty to one's job. There is often an expression of personal gratification that is celebrated as the person is glad to have "given the best they had" and "graduated" to the next stage of life. A very busy schedule, filled up with different activities and extended travel, is a common itinerary in the honeymoon phase. However, not everyone goes through a honeymoon phase; it requires money and a positive attitude, and eventually gives way to the construction of an immediate daily routine now that work is over.

The immediate retirement routine is a phase of realigning one's daily routines with activities that provide satisfaction. It might mean having more time to rest and relax. The rest and relaxation aspect refers to a period of low activity that is in marked contrast to the more active honeymoon phase. After a long period of work, many people seek a respite and want some time to "take it easy," but after this "time-out" many people return to the same physical activity level they had before. Further, due to a decrease in one's level of stimulating intellectual or creative challenge or loss of enjoyable physical routines and social involvements, as the honeymoon or rest and relaxation phases begin to wane, some people may become disenchanted with the retired life, thus reflecting the sentiment of the song written by Jerry Lieber and Mike Stoller, and recorded by Leslie Uggams, "Is That All There Is?"[67] Some people may wish to continue and keep on doing the work routines and long for the social involvements they had just a few weeks or months earlier.

The phase of disenchantment refers to the experiences some people, who do not find it easy to adjust to retirement, encounter. This is a time when the person may find that retirement is not all that it was made out to be. Disenchantment usually arises from the awareness that retirement, while it is a time of reduced work, often is also a time of reduced income.

Other sentiments such as feeling a loss of being involved with co-workers, or of being valued for the work they have done, or that one would rather "wear out rather than rust out," or that the happy times with family or friends may not be as attainable as previously envisioned may also crop up.

Again, for some older adults, as the honeymoon phase slows down, the rest of retirement may not be characterized the same way, and this often leads to a period of letdown or depression.[68] Yet this experience of disenchantment is not inevitable. One early cross-sectional study suggested that only 10 percent of retirees reported being disenchanted at any given time.[69] Longitudinal analyses too suggest that disenchantment is even more rare.[70] Those who become less positive toward retirement do so usually as a result of disability or failing health, as well as a lack of economic and interpersonal resources.[71] Again, it should be noted that, for most people, retirement brings a reduction in annual income. Yet, individuals who held higher-level and better paying jobs generally tend to regard retirement more favorably because of better retirement savings or generous pensions.[72] The adaptive and forward movement in retirement is to find a new routine. Whether the person is always happy at the beginning of retirement or becomes disenchanted in some way, the next phase is important in providing a sustainable structure to retirement.

The reorientation phase is a time of finding new activities to take the place of the work routine. This is a time where despite the turbulence of the moment, one recognizes and feels the currents of life pulling us forward. These new routines and involvements may include developing new hobbies and interests, or working part-time, or volunteering. This reorientation may also thrust the older adult more deeply into inter-dependent family roles, continuing to serve as family leader, provider of housing and economic support, and teacher and life advisor for adult children and grandchildren.[73] In previous chapters, we noted how joining the band or choir, or having more time to explore music through listening, or by having more time to create or compose became sustaining activities for some older adults. Thus in retirement, key music involvements such as playing in the community band or singing in the community choir may take prominence and become a centering activity that brings about opportunity for positive social interactions, personal reflection, and self-actualization. The challenge of the retirement routine is to balance abilities and limitations, thus becoming or remaining as self-sufficient as possible. Moreover, although the retirement routine may follow from the honeymoon or rest and relaxation phases, others may reach it through the painful reassessment of personal goals during the disenchantment phase, and others may never reach it. Developmental trajectories have beginning and ending points, and that is true in retirement as well.

The last aspect of retirement is called the termination phase. This is the end of retirement and occurs when there is change in health or functional status so that instead of being regarded as a "footloose and fancy-free retiree," the person is more likely to be considered a "patient" or "nursing home resident." Conceptually then, this phase reflects the movement of the person from the independence and autonomy of retired life to the dependency and restriction of illness and disability.

Certainly, during retirement many adults experience changes in health that require adjustments. There are also stereotypes of retirement that suggest healthfulness declines when people retire; or, that retirement reduces the quantity and quality of friendships; or, that people become less active when they retire. Like other stereotypes, these are unfair and inaccurate depictions of older adults in general. A well-noted example of the possibility of music becoming a central feature of the life of the older retired adult is the Young@Heart Chorus, whose members since 1982 have performed to audiences around the world, dispelling stereotypes of "how retirement should look" and reimagining what is possible in later life.[74] Further, when we consider adaptation, we note that social relationships buffer the stress of retiring, and intimate relationships and social involvements such as the community chorus or band, or opportunities to attend concerts, are important sources of connection for the retiree. Thus in general, although vulnerable individuals do encounter health challenges, retirement is often a time of good health and positive well-being for many.[75]

Making a Comeback

As we have discussed developmental rhythms in careers, and mentioned "making a comeback," it is interesting to consider a couple of fascinating cases. One involves two blues musicians, Sterling Magee (born in 1938) and Adam Gussow (born in 1958), who formed the Harlem, New York, street-performance duo of "Satan and Adam."[76] Sterling is a blues guitarist who in the 1960s played with Marvin Gaye and James Brown, and recorded on Ray Charles' Tangerine label. However, expressing a sense of disenfranchisement with the commercial music industry, he took on the appellation "Satan" and became a street performer in Harlem in the 1970s. Adam was a Princeton University graduate who played harmonica; he discovered Sterling during a sidewalk concert in the 1980s and asked if he could "sit in." From that moment on, a professional relationship between the two developed – as teacher and apprentice – that would later lead to studio recordings of their music, and take them from the sidewalk performances in Harlem onto stages across the United States and Europe. In many ways their story is as much about their close relationship, founded through shared musical interests, as it is about career development. But the latter is important to consider here as it suggests what is possible and helps us recognize the many bumps, bends, and junctions in the "career road." Thus, Sterling and Adam's career as a blues duo evolved and included periods in which they did not perform together – and a time when both encountered health problems. Further, for the duo there were times beyond their early career when Adam took on a new job role as professor of American and African American literature at the University of Mississippi and Sterling moved into a nursing home in Florida, continuing all the way to a time of reunion and musical comeback with new bookings and a 2019 release of an award-winning documentary film, *Satan and Adam*,[77] which summarizes their long and ongoing relationship. Their inspiring story celebrates the joy of music. It also directs us to realize the potential of intergenerational and interracial exchange, the ways we might help one another to acquire greater mastery and overcome physical and social obstacles, and ways in which we may find a deeper meaning and purpose in our living. It also poignantly reminds us of the many small steps and occasional large leaps we take in the long journey of our careers: the initial point of beginning, the many steps and moments of ascendance or decline, the broadening horizons of mastery as we become "established" in our work, and the personal growth that our social connections afford. Indeed, their story depicts the very helpful relationships formed between co-workers, teachers and apprentices, and others who offer moral and emotional support, provide practical assistance, and aid each other in the process of becoming.

Another exceptional "comeback" to consider is that of Hailu Mergia.[78] As a young man in the 1970s, Hailu was a member of the Africa jazz group Walias Band and a star in the music scene of Addis Abba, Ethiopia. Hoping to escape the oppressions of the Derg government and the Ethiopian famine of the 1980s, and seeking an opportunity to propel their career even higher, the band left Ethiopia and emigrated to the United States in 1981, eventually taking up residency at the Ibex Club in Washington, DC, and traveling in a van to play road gigs. But "making it" was difficult, and by 1983 the band had disbanded, with some members returning to Ethiopia. Hailu remained in the United States, however, later enrolling in classes at Northern Virginia Community College and studying music at Howard University. Through the assistance of an associate he met at Howard University, Hailu recorded a solo album in

1985, titled *Hailu Mergia and His Classical Instrument*. But by 1991, making a living by playing music was not a practical option. So Hailu took on other work, including driving an airport cab and carrying passengers to and from Dulles International Airport outside of Washington, DC. Yet his involvement with music did not stop: He used the time between fares to practice on a portable keyboard. With a growing popular interest in African jazz music, Hailu, in his early seventies, was "discovered" again with a rerelease of his early recordings in 2014. Hailu now celebrates his newly found success and no longer drives a cab. Rather, concerts are being planned that will take Hailu and his jazz ensemble to cities throughout North America and Europe. Hailu's inspiring story points out moments of beginning and departing, adjustment and transformation, challenge and success. It is a story about overcoming obstacles again and again with the help of others, and suggests to us once more how a career in music may lead us to new insights and understandings.

Marking Life's Milestones and Leaving a Legacy

We began this chapter recognizing the link between work and music, the dream of what is possible, the perseverance it takes to "make it" in our careers, and the strong drive and personal quest that lead us to fulfill our greatest potential. We end by recognizing that our jobs and retirement represent key milestone events in our development throughout the adult years. They reflect where we have been and how we have become. Similar to the times of graduation, engagement, marriage, and loss of loved ones, we recognize the importance of all our career and retirement events in telling a story about who we are and what we are about. We often mark special points along the way with the celebration of music, hoping to realize an insight and gain deeper understanding into the changes and losses that occur. Perhaps it is reflection in old age on these life milestones that we come to look beyond ourselves, hoping to leave a legacy. The music we make, and all the songs we have sung, represent one aspect of that legacy. In our ongoing development we often try to see past the horizon and find a glimpse of what may come next. Thus, in this looking ahead, as the theologian Henry Nouwen suggested, "The vision of aging can lead us beyond the limitations of our human self ... a vision that invites us to a total, fearless surrender in which the distinction between life and death slowly loses its pain."[79] How we mark our path and transcend through life to death will be discussed in Chapter 8.

8   Requiem: Spirituality and End-of-Life

The world may be known without leaving the house.

– Lao Tzu

In the attempt to articulate an experience we, in some way, destroy or at least alter the experience. Any attempt to recreate the experience is now constrained by the way it has been defined. No doubt at times we can recreate the initial experience, but if we force ourselves to experience it again – particularly once it has been defined in a prescribed way – we may fail. Experience in this way is understood in similitude to other things. For example, when describing an experience, people often say, "It was like – " or "I felt that – ." The experience cannot be described directly but only in metaphor or simile. However, we believe that *experience can only be experienced.*[1] That is, we are removed from and live outside our experience when we try to define and categorize it. The experience of the spiritual too puts us in a quandary. Spiritual experience often cannot be defined or categorized in a definitive way. As Carl Jung notes, spiritual experiences come upon the person "from inside as well as outside," suggesting a phenomenon that is both an aspect of our mind as well as social and supernatural events.[2] Thus, spiritual experience defies our meager attempt to explain it.

What Is Spirituality?

Recognizing this conundrum, we understand that spirituality can be experienced in a variety of different ways. For the purpose of this chapter, we define spirituality to be "a person's expression of ultimate meaning and concerns of life, of their faith beliefs or affiliation with a religious institution, their sense of the sacred and connection with nature, and their attitudes about their relation to others."[3] Spirituality is important in many peoples' lives and provides a basic context of living. Spirituality can aid us as we encounter illness, experience changes in functional abilities, witness declines in the capacity to participate in society, and as we face death. This common focus on pathology, symptom, and disease is part of a biomedical model of health. Although it is important to understand the causes of illness and disease, an alternate approach is to take a more humanistic perspective that focuses on human potential, individual growth, and self-actualization. Spirituality is given a central place then in this humanistic perspective. Indeed, "all life purposes and needs stem from that spiritual center."[4]

Although spirituality has practical social and psychological aspects, it is also the transcendent awareness of something beyond us. Our understanding and experience of the spiritual is often incomplete because it is articulated in a contextualized universe of our religious orientation, personal philosophy, connection with nature, or the experience of the here and now. We may never get at the true essence of what it means to be spiritual but only reach an approximation. However, spirituality can transcend these constraints and, although explained and interpreted through these varied lenses, we can in rare moments experience the divine. In the following sections, we discuss where spirituality, music, and aging meet. Music and spirituality have had a close connection not only in the sacred but also in personal experiences that could be described as transcendent. We also look at the connection between aging and music and aging and spirituality. Finally, we understand the important intersection where all three meet. In this intersection, we explore feelings of the presence of others, thoughts on death and dying, and our approach to living that gives us comfort, hope, and a sense of finality.

Spirituality, Music, and Aging

As we begin to explore the intersection of music, aging, and spirituality, we wish to first connect spirituality with a few theories regarding how people may approach aging in the context of society. These theories are common to the area of social psychology and aging. Our approach is novel in that we offer a new view of these theories by inferring a spiritual component that is woven through and embedded in them not heretofore articulated. Thus, as we consider the "success-oriented" social theories of aging, we will point out how aspects of spirituality are represented. These theories are often portrayed to be at odds with each other but can, from our perspective, be seen as more complementary and even conceptualized as embodiments of the yin and yang dynamic of life noted in earlier chapters. Two early success-oriented theories from the 1960s were Activity Theory and Disengagement Theory.[5] These theories attempted to explain how older adults could experience a fulfillment and satisfaction as they neared the end of their careers and throughout the years of retired life. Activity Theory posits that older adults who are able to remain active in their everyday life routines would be more likely to live out old age as the "golden years." Early research supporting this perspective indicated greater social activity in old age to be associated with greater satisfaction with life. In contrast, however, a competing perspective was born from the observations that many older adults seem to be watching the world go by from their front porches and apartment windows. This competing perspective, Disengagement Theory, posits that in later life there is a process of mutual withdrawal between the older person and society, and that a decrease in interpersonal activity is both satisfying for the person and helpful to society. Further, like Activity Theory, early research supported Disengagement Theory. When older adults are able to slow the pace of life a bit and reflect more on personal experiences, even reduce job responsibilities, they are also more likely to report greater satisfaction with life.[6] Although these theories offered competing perspectives when they were first introduced, they might better be considered as complements of one another.[7] That is, an older person may find satisfaction in greater activity in things they enjoy or that hold current interests, while at the same time disengage from social settings or routines that have become too cumbersome or no longer hold importance. Moreover, as we noted in earlier chapters, when we consider later-life maturation and the processes of gerotranscendence offered by the gerontologist Lars Tornstam,[8] we should recognize that a deeper existential awareness and insight exist, as well as satisfaction and fulfillment in living, through both "action" and "inaction." Certainly there are times in life when we are more active (e.g., when we are young and in good health) and times when age-related changes in physical abilities or health require a readjustment of social routines and a reduction in activity levels. Yet this type of "inactivity," due to declines in physical abilities or health, might still allow the person to live a very full and active life. An example of this type of inactivity is when a person is unable to attend religious services due to poor health. To continue to be involved in their spiritual practices and expressions, the person may then substitute physical attendance with home-based activities. Watching worship services on the television or other spiritual practices (e.g., listening to sacred music, praying or meditating, reading sacred texts, receiving a visit from clergy in the home) and social activities (e.g., telephoning or exchanging e-mail with friends in lieu of meeting in person) may take the place of attending a religious service. Thus, we should be aware that "activity" might mean different things to people who are healthy, and to those who are experiencing changes in physical or mental capacities that restrict everyday functioning and socialization.

Similarly, we should be aware that what we observe in terms of physical activity might not reveal the deeper and very active inner life of the older person.

Two additional theories that are reflective of and akin to a person's spirituality are Exchange Theory and Continuity Theory. Exchange Theory posits that we interact with other people to the extent that the rewards we receive, both material and nonmaterial, are in balance with or exceed the costs we incur.[9] This theory suggests there is an underlying interpersonal economy that we are concerned with, and when the social exchange is unbalanced, usually when the cost is too great, we readjust by perhaps disengaging to some degree or end our social interaction all together. However, so long as there is a sense that we are breaking even or even benefiting in the relationship, we will likely continue the social involvement. One example of a costly social exchange is when a friend or family member demands too much of our time or other resources. You may have had an experience like this when you had to tell a friend, "I would like to join you at lunch and catch up, but I don't have the time (or emotional resources) right now."

Exchange Theory also offers us a model that we might consider in the context of our faith beliefs and family relationships. We might consider the way we find our faith beliefs, or a particular faith orientation, comforting and supportive. For example, at a public forum to discuss inter-generational connections and viewpoints held at the local university attended by one of the authors, it was fascinating to follow the conversation between two older adults who responded to the question of how they regarded religion at their point in development. One discussant offered that she was raised in the Catholic tradition, had her children baptized and confirmed in the church, sent them to Catholic schools, and followed the traditional practices of the church throughout their upbringing. Yet, at this moment later in life, she reported, it was difficult to embrace her earlier faith orientation. In fact, now in later life, she felt like she had more questions than answers about her faith. Suggesting an imbalance in the costs and benefits of her faith orientation, she ended her remarks by describing herself as a "fallen-away" Catholic. At which point an older gentleman sitting across the table remarked that he did not "find" religion until age fifty-three, and he too had many questions about his faith. Yet, he continued, there seemed to be some benefit and comfort in his beliefs. How we may weigh the cost and benefits of our spiritual practices and beliefs is an intriguing question – one that might lead us into a deeper realization of our spirituality as we get older.

The exchange model also might tell a bit more about the underlying psycho-economics of family relationships. Like many families, we often meet regularly for holiday celebrations. And, we enjoy these get-togethers – most of the time. Yet the cost–benefit exchange of these celebrations may change as family members develop and mature. For example, both younger and older family members may feel at times that they have other more interesting or important things to do, such as being with classmates or best friends, working, or pursuing other personal interests. Certainly, there seems to be a shift in the perceived social exchange within the ritualized family celebration for adolescents and young adults, who may express boredom and dissatisfaction when they are with older adults. This may create a problem for the organizers of family celebrations, in that they may prefer everyone to attend for the whole time, but some younger persons leave early because they find the cost of staying for the entire celebration greater than the benefit. In this example, finding a way to optimize the intergenerational social exchange is an important concern. Sometimes turning off the cell phones and personal computing devices allows the kind of face-to-face conversations that make the social experience more enjoyable so that everyone stays to the end of the celebration. At other times it might be important to remind family members why they have gathered – why it is important to be together – and to reflect upon the shared values and beliefs they hold together that constitute and reflect the deepest expression of their faith.

Another theory very much akin to the spiritual and deeper psychological orientation of the person is Continuity Theory.[10] Continuity Theory proposes that the person's self-concept is developed through early social and interpersonal experiences, and that over time people develop a strong sense of who they are and attempt to maintain this sense of self by placing themselves in environments that support their self-concept. It is through our earliest spiritual yearnings and religious instructions that we come to know and describe ourselves. Even in later life these aspects of our spirituality are still recognized as important facets of self, as noted in the remark of the older women who had fallen away from her faith. In a similar way, the person who was a member of the band or choir, or played sports, in high school often continues to have interests and involvements in these areas during midlife and in old age. Similarly, the high school basketball player still enjoys shooting hoops with grandchildren and attending local games in the community. The person who played an instrument in high school band may continue to find enjoyment in a community band. In all of these examples we find that there is continuity and maintenance of a defining aspect of the self, where one's spirituality is a central feature. So much so, that the philosopher Paul Griffiths has proposed that our faith orientation is so central to our self-concept that it represents *comprehensiveness* and continues to provide a system of meaning that is foundational and relevant to all aspects of life.[11] Thus, Griffiths suggests spirituality is so essential to our meaning, making that it is relatively inescapable and suggestive of a continuity of self that cannot be abandoned. In this way then, we recognize our faith orientation as an essential aspect of how we know and view the world. Thus, we find spirituality as a defining structural thread within the social models of activity, disengagement, exchange, and continuity.

Music and Transition to the Sacred Moment

Most of us know now that we do not just go from being a young person to being an older person. There is no immediate shift from middle age to old age. It is gradual. All along the way, we might always feel "youthful." Our recognition of the wonder of the world, our personal growth, and the ups and downs of life we have experienced seem to reflect a sacredness of our human experience, so that when we consider the paths we have followed, we might feel "that's the way it was meant to be." Much like the modern composers Gustav Holst and Oliver Messiaen, we might seek spiritual solace, discover a sense of wonder and awe, and find comfort in nature and in our connection with the universe that surrounds us.[12]

For example, as noted by Holst in the 1920 premiere, a mystical and spiritual connection between heaven and earth inspired his symphony *The Planets*. "These pieces were suggested by the astrological significance of the planets; there is no programme music, neither have they any connection with the deities of classical mythology bearing the same names. If any guide to the music is required, the subtitle to each piece will be found sufficient, especially if it be used in the broad sense. For instance, Jupiter brings jollity in the ordinary sense, and also the more ceremonial type of rejoicing associated with religions or national festivities. Saturn brings not only physical decay, but also a vision of fulfillment. Mercury is the symbol of mind."[13]

Similarly, the music of Messiaen, which is famous for its use of birdsong as a thematic compositional element, is suggested to convey the symbolisms of theology.[14] Further, as Messiaen alludes, composing music reveals and reflects mystical aspects of spirituality: "I compose for the pleasure of internal hearing at the precise moment of composition. There is the notated rhythm, imagined, internally considered, as one might reflect on a few lines from a book of theology or philosophy. There is even the rhythm conceived by a single individual in a unique moment, solely for the intellectual pleasure of numbers, an absolutely personal rhythm, like a prayer – and as incommunicable."[15] As the compositions of Holst and Messiaen demonstrate, the experience of music provides entry into the sacred and is a reflection and a realization of the sacredness of life.

Yet throughout our development and at the end-of-life, we make transitions. We become transformed. One of the authors recalls a transition and sacred moment when a loved one died: "It was a cold but sunny January morning when we attended the funeral of a dear family friend. As we entered the church through its great doors, we were soon upon the casket, near the church's entrance. The church was silent. We passed by the casket, down the center aisle bathed in the glow of brilliant colors radiating from the stained-glass windows. The congregation sat quietly until the ringing of the altar bell and the beginning of the Mass. The congregation then stood as the priest entered and walked to the back of the church. He sprinkled holy water on the casket and escorted it down the center aisle to the front of the church. As the Mass began, the priest explained that as we come from dust, we will return to dust, and today is a welcoming home of the deceased. Then, without any accompaniment, the cantor began to sing, proclaiming a musical offering of prayer – a psalm for the deceased, the 23rd Psalm. The funeral mass and its music, stirring our memories and deepest emotions, is a sacred moment – another transitional and transforming moment in our life journey."

Power in the Presence

The passing of a loved one and the resultant funeral represents a sacred moment and a transition that provides a sense of finality and closure. Although these experiences are designed to allow us to "let go," people do claim to still feel the presence of the recently deceased. The felt presence of friends and loved ones who have recently died is a very powerful, moving, and sometimes frightening experience. The presence can be as vivid as a claim to have actually seen the person or to a vague sense that somehow you have connected with the person's spirit. For example, the singer Celine Dion reported sensing the presence of her husband, who died from cancer in 2016.[16] Often, our contact with deceased loved ones occurs in dreams. It is reported that in dreams, those who have died may deliver messages or give the mourner a chance to say goodbye.[17]

It is commonly reported that people have witnessed and believed that deceased family members come to their aid especially in times of crisis or when they are in distress. These more positive sensations seem to out-weigh any distressing, disturbing, or negative reports involving the presence of someone deceased.[18] This feeling of presence might just be sensed or it could be more specific, such as smelling something or having feelings of being touched.[19] It is unexplained, yet many of us have had these experiences. Within many faith traditions, these experiences reflect our sense that we are interconnected to each other, and that this connection is not broken upon death. We distinguish feelings of presence as being different from hallucinations or delusions of seeing those who have died. A hallucination is perceiving something that does not exist; a delusion is based on false thinking. The feeling of presence is linked more to a real connection to the person in a way that goes beyond sensory deception or faulty thought. Musicians, too, find a special connection to those with whom they have played and who have inspired them. When bandmates pass away, we try to honor them by carrying on in their absence. Tribute concerts, dedications, establishing a foundation, or commissioning a musical piece in the person's name are examples of how we can honor someone. But we can carry that person's memory in more subtle ways, such as thinking of the person while playing a concert. At times, a thought or memory of the deceased person breaks through in the middle of a performance. Special events, venues, and dates may also remind us of the person. We believe these experiences go beyond nostalgia but instead reflect our real need to keep something special with us about that person. Because they are no longer with us, we feel it is our duty to carry on and to play as an honor to them. And, yes, we often have the feeling that they are still with us.

In an earlier chapter we described Frank Vignola's potentially life-threatening accident and his long road to recovery. He related in the same article in *JazzTimes* of his experience of the presence of Les Paul (who died in 2009). This sense of presence occurred at the Iridium in New York City when he began playing again. Frank Vignola played with his good friend Les Paul at the Iridium for eighteen years, off and on. On the night of his return to the Iridium, Vignola relates that he felt Les Paul's presence, which gave him the encouragement to restart his career.[20]

One of the authors relates the story of his father, who passed away in 2014 after a hard-fought battle with ALS and Parkinson's disease: "On the night he died, I was playing with my trio at a local restaurant. I had visited him in hospice, 100 miles away the day before. I knew then that his time was near. I was sitting quietly at the bar, having a drink as I waited for my two bandmates to show up. I had the strong feeling that he would pass away that evening, and although I knew I could not be there, I was going to dedicate my playing that night to him. He died while I was playing that evening. I knew this even before I arrived home and was given the news by my wife. It is that inexplicable feeling when you know someone you love has died, and you feel their presence. While I was playing that evening, I did feel his presence at the time. I felt that on his way, he stopped by to look in on me before he took his final journey.

Although my Dad passed away in 2014, I have felt his presence many times, particularly when I am feeling troubled or need his advice on what direction my life should take. For example, I was feeling a bit down in the summer of 2015, wondering if I should continue playing music. I was not sure I was doing anything worthwhile with it. I asked Dad for a sign to let me know if I should continue or give it up. That summer I was playing at an outdoor concert with a twenty-piece big band. At the concert were two young ladies who had some form of developmental–intellectual disability. They were dancing and clearly having a great time. At the end of one of the songs they came up to the stage and we exchanged high fives. It was then I knew that Dad had asked God to send these two angels as a sign to let me know that my playing was providing happiness to others. After that I never worried about how much I was making or if I was getting enough gigs – I realized that any chance I had to play, I would play joyfully."

End-of-Life

One way to think of end-of-life is as a transition from one state to another. Some people have described this transition as a liminal space between life and death. Liminal space is the in-between of living and dying.[21] It can also represent a place of uncertainty, ambiguity, and conflict.[22] Fear of death and dying is common. However, like the yin–yang conceptualization, liminal space involves other distinctions, such as those between science and religion, health and illness, transitions from young to old, as well as life and death. Our experience of these transitions, we believe, can lead to possibility, transcendence, understanding, and spiritual peace.[23]

We also gain insight into the transition from life to death by understanding the end-of-life visions and dreams that are commonly experienced. Not only do we understand life in relation to our spirituality, but our spiritual beliefs provide us a way of understanding the end-of-life and conceptualizing what may occur after death. End-of-life visions and dreams (ELDVs) allow us to find meaning and a sense of comfort, peace, and acceptance. A qualitative analysis of the dreams and visions of sixty-three hospice patients uncovered six themes involving ELDVs. People report that their dreams contain a comforting presence of friends, relatives, and pets. Preparing to go is another theme. Here the ELDVs can involve traveling, whether by car or flying, or other means of transportation. People report that they may feel that loved ones are present and watching over them. A sense that loved ones are waiting for them is another theme that is represented in ELDVs. However, distressing and anxiety- raising experiences are reported too, such as past traumatic and negative experiences, or abuse. Finally, the person may report that the

ELDVs contain unfinished business.[24] What we know from the research is that these dreams and visions at end-of-life are normal. They are a part of the healing process and transition for both loved ones and the person at the end-of-life. ELDVs are intrinsic to the transition from life to death; they occur close to death, the content is varied, and content may be influenced by a person's culture.[25]

It seems self-evident that music can be an important component of a peaceful transition from life to death in hospice and palliative care. However, the effectiveness of music therapy at end-of-life seems unclear. Although substantive evidence exists that music therapy is effective in improving physical and psychological function, studies on music therapy and palliative care come from noncontrolled and unpublished studies. Joke Bradt and Cheryl Dileo, looking at five carefully controlled studies on palliative care and music therapy, could not offer a conclusion of the effectiveness or ineffectiveness of music therapy on end-of-life. Clearly more research is needed.[26] One possible intractable problem arises when conducting research on folks in hospice and at end-of-life. Ethical considerations are important when considering therapy at end-of-life or withholding therapy as part of a research agenda without considering the moral and ethical ramifications and the wishes of the patient and family; this is possibly why most of the research in this area does not withhold treatment (i.e., a control group).

Comfort, Hope, Finality

Although we have previously discussed the feelings of the presence of loved ones and friends who have passed and that end-of-life is not an end but a transition, we also wish to discuss how spirituality can connect with music while we are living. In the teaching of the Buddha, the path of eight right practices (the noble eightfold path) are right view, right intent, right mindfulness, right speech, right conduct, right diligence, right concentration, and right livelihood. We understand that these practices are designed to enrich one's life in the context of Buddhism. Conceptually, however, it should be noted that these basic guides for living are also represented in some form within all world religions as well as in psychological therapies. Thus, we also ask, how can we musically incorporate these practices on a path toward wellness?

Music is an experience based on perception. We can hear, feel, and express music in many ways. Music can become so much a part of us that it is indeed part of our consciousness, our existence. *Right view* is to understand and correct erroneous perceptions. Right view is an "insight we have into the reality of life."[27] When we perceive music through listening or playing, we should keep in mind the concept of right view. We become conscious of the music within us. With right view we can ascertain if the music we listen to or play is right for us. Music that is not true to oneself leads to discord and unhappiness. We can then apply the concept of right view to understand when music is right and when it is wrong. Punk jazz may not be our thing. Through deep self-reflection we can understand the source of our dislike. Perhaps we prefer more melodious arrangements or a more traditional approach. It does not mean that it is wrong; it just does not fit with how we see ourselves.

As we get older, the concept of right view can involve our understanding that there are various ways to perceive something and that these views are neither correct nor incorrect. This idea does not support that everything is then relative – quite the contrary. We can work through our misconception of ourselves and others. We practice right view through mindfulness, reflection, learning, and experience. We begin to see things as they are.[28] We understand that we have both healthy and unhealthy elements of who we are, but we begin to see the goodness in others and in ourselves and begin to nurture that goodness. Ultimately, we become free, allowing us to love and to experience peace.

When we engage in *right intention*, we know what we want and strive to achieve it through persistence and single-mindedness.[29] Recall in our discussion of the theory of planned behavior that a key component is a stated intention to achieve a goal. Also, having an action plan is important. Thus, successful goal attainment involves intent, planning, and persistence. Perhaps we are thinking about going to music school or joining a town band. However, often in trying to achieve a goal, our planning can go awry because we often waste time on anxiety, worry, and fear. Thoughts of what if I get rejected? Am I too old? Or will I be ridiculed? can paralyze us. This is irrational thinking. Thinking in a rational way allows us to identify whether our thoughts are useful or harmful. The impact of our harmful thoughts is presented in the work of psychologist Albert Ellis, who proposed that emotional disruption and unhappiness are the result of engaging in irrational thinking. We engage in irrational thinking as musicians when we make statements like "I should be a better musician than I am," "People ought to play better than they do," "We must play a piece exactly the way it is written." The goal of his Rational Emotive Behavior Therapy is to retrain one to identify irrational thinking and to come to a more rational assessment of one's source of problems.[30] Thus, through rational thinking we can address the three statements in this paragraph by practicing in a diligent, focused way; mentoring and helping others to become better musicians; and working slowly on a piece until it can be played to everyone's satisfaction, or at least to a "happy compromise."

Another outcome of right intention is to live in the here and now. Again, this idea is also expressed by the work of Carl Rogers, a proponent of client-centered therapy. In this approach, Rogers proposes that worries of the past and the future are detrimental and that to become an authentic individual is to live in the here and now.[31] To be authentic in one's music is to experience it in the moment. Whether listening or playing, nothing else should matter, not where you left your car keys or whether you folded the laundry. Accordingly, right intention allows one to be in the present and can result in peace and harmony in thought and action.[32] The experience of music in the moment through right intention can be a source of health.

Through the use of *right mindfulness* we direct our attention to the here and now. The practice of mindfulness allows us to come back to the present when our mind wanders. When we practice right mindfulness, our attention is on the present moment. We become inattentive when we focus on something that takes us away from the present moment. The practice of mindfulness leads us to a broader understanding that we are connected to each other. It should be noted that the concept of mindfulness is found in other religions. For example, mindfulness is embodied in prayerful meditation or centering prayers in Christianity, in a branch of Islam called Sufism, in Judaism, and in Hinduism.[33]

The use of mindfulness in listening, singing, or playing can result in more positive emotions and outlook.[34] When we practice mindfulness as it relates to music, we become aware of the present moment, we no longer think about the past or future, and we become attentive to the source and form of our thoughts and not the content. Mindfulness comes from a Buddhist philosophy, but it also is used in modern psychological therapy and allows one to explore the source of one's distress or suffering. One example of the use of music and mindfulness to help patients with breast cancer undergoing adjuvant chemotherapy is the work of Teresia Lesiuk. In this work, she proposes a mindfulness-based music therapy approach applying four attitudes of mindfulness. They are *nonjudging*, to refrain from evaluating the feeling or object; *beginner's mind*, to see things in a new way (i.e., to attain a sense of wonder in all things); *suspend judgment*, to not be critical initially when experiencing something; and *acceptance and letting go*. Incorporating these four attitudes in a music-based therapy program, Lisiuk found that women in the program reported reduced anxiety, a more positive outlook, reduced symptoms of distress and fatigue, and importantly, allowed them to be more assertive with regard to doing those things that they felt were important in their lives.[35]

The practice of mindfulness represents a mindset that has practical application for the musician and for the listener. For the musician, the practice of mindfulness can help reduce anxiety or stage fright associated with performing. It can also increase satisfaction and quality of the performance. This mindset allows the musician to be more spontaneous, to take more chances, say in soloing, and to reach a higher level of musicianship. With regard to the audience, the practice of mindfulness while watching or listening leads to a closer attentional focus on the music and thus more involvement and enhanced enjoyment.[36] Thus, for both musician and audience, the practice of mindfulness creates a bond between each that allows for the channeling of a positive experience, growth, and a sense of oneness.

Music is communication. *Right speech* is communicating with love to resolve conflict and discord and not to speak cruelly, which encourages further suffering in us and in others.[37] With regard to music, right speech is to musically speak the truth. This seems evident; if we claim that the music we listen to is the music we like and represents who we are, otherwise why listen to it? The same goes for playing music. Musicians should play music that is true to who they are. If they are inauthentic through their music, they are sowing the seeds of discord. Authenticity through music thus creates peace and happiness in oneself and others.

The musical world provides many examples of authentic musicians. A few that come to mind for us are Bob Dylan, John Coltrane, and Miles Davis. When Dylan moved from a pure folk music to include electric instruments, there was a great uproar from his fans. However, this was a move that flowed naturally from his creative process. John Coltrane's magnificent work "A Love Supreme" reflects this idea of speaking truth through music. Of course, Miles Davis was one never to back down from what he believed was musically his path. From incorporating more electric elements in his groups to the groundbreaking use of modes in "Kind of Blue," he blazed his own path to speak truth through music. The concept of authenticity is implied in music educator Donald Hodges' "Why Study Music?" We make music to express and to grow in our identity as musicians. As we have presented, music is transcendent and, as Hodges expresses, is life changing and "provides powerful insights into our private, inner world."[38]

A reverence for life and the practice of nonviolence is the center of *right conduct*. Flowing from right conduct are generosity and compassion. Taking responsibility in our relationships with an awareness of how our actions may affect others is engaging in right conduct.[39] Through right conduct we practice social justice. We abhor killing, we call out instances of abuse and neglect, we denounce corruption and stealing, and we work toward generosity, compassion, and protection of the vulnerable. Throughout our lives we are called to right conduct. Education, sources of worship, and relationships with family and others should focus on instilling right conduct in us. In a society that practices right conduct, right conduct springs within us. In a society that rewards wrong conduct, wrong conduct prevails.

How and where do we direct our energy? When do we feel our most energetic? When do we feel focused and feel that sense that we are going in the right direction? At times, we may be focusing our energy on the wrong things. Perhaps it is on working to the point of becoming a workaholic or perhaps on having fun to the exclusion of our obligations to others. In these cases our energy is dissipated, and we can be left with a sense of ennui or even loss and dissatisfaction with life. Striving in the wrong direction can waste our effort. *Right diligence* is following a middle way. It involves balancing our energy to avoid extremes. How do we know we are practicing right diligence?

For the musician, playing music may be exclusively for money and fame. The musician may be consumed by greed and the desire to get ahead of others, taking others' good fortune as a slight toward attainment of these goals. Resentment and hatred may be the result. If we do not experience three components – joy, ease, and interest – we are not practicing right diligence.[40] Joy and interest can be intuitively understood. If we do not feel joy or become uninterested in what we do, perhaps we are directing our energy in the wrong way or toward the wrong end. Ease is more difficult to understand.

A way to understand the concept of ease is with the following anecdote. One of the authors was listening to a concert by a famous big band with his wife and a friend. The band consisted of highly accomplished musicians, and over the evening each was given an opportunity to take a solo. Every soloist displayed an astonishing command of their instrument. The solos were full of energy and seemed to flow with ease from each musician. Astounded, I asked my friend, "How does someone become this good?" Of course, his reply was "Practice." I said, no, somehow this gets "poured into your head," because I indicated that I practice a lot and will never reach that level of musicianship. Somewhere the answer is in between, and this is the experience of ease. There is a certain amount of aptitude that will lead one to music, but it must be nurtured through practice. The key is right practice: finding the right teachers and the right colleagues to play with – those who nurture joy and interest. One does have to work hard at one's craft. Practicing is the key. But wrong practice is wrong diligence. If you find that practicing results in feelings of frustration and tiredness, then reexamine your practice. There is a concept in psychology called "flow."[41] Basically the notion is that when we are in a flow experience, we are in the here and now; concerns of past and future fall away and we experience the immediate. When we experience flow, all thoughts of mechanics such as scales and chords are ignored, and we no longer concentrate on those things but instead our musicianship comes through with joy and ease. Musicians and listeners describing this flow experience express it as "being in the groove," "grooving," or "jamming." Those who experience this state will tell you there is "nothing like it!"

Active concentration involves paying attention to what is going on in the present moment; selective concentration is focusing our attention on a particular object, thought, or problem to the exclusion of all other stimuli.[42] When we concentrate, we want to attain evenness in our concentration. We do not become overfocused nor do we want our mind to wander. Mindfulness and *right concentration*, then, are connected concepts. When you fully concentrate in the right way, you are living in the moment. One frustration that many musicians express is losing focus during practice, rehearsal, or in a performance. With the practice of mindfulness we can identify why we lose focus and bring about ways to regain concentration.

As noted in Chapter 7, a large part of our identity is often derived from and based on our livelihood. Our work can be a way of experiencing satisfaction and a sense of who we are. It is important, for physical and psychological health, to engage in *right livelihood*. That is, we do not engage in work that results in harm to others or ourselves.[43] Violations of right livelihood can be inherent in the work itself or can come from our own wrong reasons for engaging in a certain type of work. For example, if we work for companies that blatantly harm the environment, or others, then this is wrong livelihood. However, seemingly harmless work can be harmful if we engage in it for the wrong reasons. Again, a music example works here. Music is intended to be a source of joy for ourselves and others, but if we engage in the practice as a livelihood with the goal of getting ahead at the expense of others (e.g., cheating others on contracts or using others for our own ends – also examples of wrong diligence), then we not only create the conditions of suffering in others but ultimately create suffering in ourselves. Wrong livelihood destroys the spirit. Right livelihood uplifts the spirit.

Spiritual Needs, Aging, and Music

As noted at the beginning of the chapter, when we seek to articulate an experience, we lose the capacity to relive that experience again in the same way. Although we can recall past experiences, we recall them through the lens of the present. Again, recalling the past also confronts us with the duality of time; we are in the past and, at the same time, in the present and future. Our recollections of past experiences may be bittersweet or filled with gratitude, pleasant or unpleasant, defeating or inspiring. Recollections of past experience can be distorted, misremembered, and possibly fabricated. We also think toward the future. We may contemplate what the future holds for us and make plans to achieve the future we envision. We may also feel discouraged and fearful as we look toward a future that we perceive to be bleak and nonprosperous. Often, we look for spiritual guidance to reconcile these perspectives. Many spiritual and religious teachings thus seek to bring the past, present, and future into balance. Our lives are a mystery in many ways. For example, we contemplate the existential questions of why we are here, what is our purpose, where are we going in life, what happens when we die? We ask these questions because we live within and are guided by a limited world view where our understanding is incomplete. These questions lead us to consider the divine and are intertwined with the spiritual needs for meaning and purpose, the need for love and belonging, and the need for forgiveness.[44]

The need to find purpose and meaning in our life is linked to our self-identity and sense of dignity. Erikson, in his psychosocial stages of development, described the last stage of life as one of integrity or despair, where one may look back on life with a sense of accomplishment or with regret and despair over opportunities lost. Further, as we continue in our development and near death, as Tornstam suggests, what were construed as positive or negative aspects of self or of our life experiences may no longer hold the same importance or concern. Indeed, the freedom of gerotranscendence leads into the light of a "new" day. Thus, throughout our life the need for love and belonging may take many forms. Love that is self-interested and transactional (e.g., if you help me, then I will love you) is harmful to social relationships and the self-concept. Conditional love (e.g., I love you because) can impose a burden to deserve or earn the other's love and the fear of losing the attributes that one is loved for. However, love that is unconditional that is given despite of one's faults, habits, or history (i.e., the Agape love of God) satisfies this spiritual need. Unconditional love promotes self-worth, joy, security, belonging, hope, and courage.[45] We need to be forgiven. We need to reconcile our lives and experiences with ourselves and with others. This includes resolving a guilty conscience or sense of shame, overcoming life's regrets, and seeking and receiving forgiveness for broken promises. We note that the power of forgiveness, both for the person who receives it and the person who gives it, is uplifting. Mother Theresa notes: "Forgiving is an act of love, forgetting is an act of humility." Without forgiveness there may be psychological consequences in the form of feelings of worthlessness, hostility, psychological stress, defensiveness, and paranoia.[46] Living spiritually brings the past, present, and future into balance. We learn to acknowledge our past and if possible correct mistakes or ask for forgiveness. We learn to live in the here and now to find joy in our everyday experiences, and we look toward the future with hope.

Life Review and End-of-Life

Through a life review of our personal history, we find meaning in our lives. The famous medical gerontologist Robert Butler first noted that older adults often are involved in reminiscing about their life. Recognizing the importance of reminiscence in later life, life review was developed as a method to facilitate a deeper understanding of self and to find integrity about the life one has lived. Life review is often used by therapists working with older adults but may also be informally facilitated by just being available and listening to the older person. In general, life review is suggested to have a wholesome effect on the older person and society. Indeed, life review helps the older person tell the story of their life and provides a method whereby others can know about and appreciate the many contributions made by the person. The therapeutic effect is in revealing how all the events, experiences, and circumstances fit into the person's worldview and thus become integrated into a philosophy of life. Life review brings the future into focus, as the person thinks about what they will do with the time left in life and the material and emotional legacies that will be left to others. Life review also helps to reintegrate unresolved conflicts and fears, expiate guilt feelings, reconcile broken family relationships, and prepare the person for a peaceful death.[47]

Contact with the spiritual, through religion, faith, the sense of the sacred, and especially music, provides us a way to understand sources of suffering in ourselves and in others. It is through love, compassion, and giving that we achieve individual and social wellness. There is hope. Through our outreach, awareness, shared concerns, and connectedness to one another, despite humankind's theological and political differences, we may find a way to build peace between people and to achieve peace within ourselves.

9 Coda: Defining, Directing, and Celebrating Life

I celebrate myself, and sing myself,
And what I assume you shall assume,
For every atom belonging to me as good belongs to you.
–Walt Whitman, "Song of Myself"[1]

When one looks back on life, it is not the things we have done that we necessarily regret, but the things we have failed to do. In many ways, a life review entails a counterfactual process of thinking about what might have been – those events and outcomes that could have happened if we had made a different choice than the one made. Research shows that the most frequently stated regrets are omissions – such as not taking a chance, not spending more time with loved ones, or not making a financial transaction. It may seem that omissions that lead to regret increase with age. One reason they can be more regretful is that these inactions may still be unresolved, and that leads the way to an endless number of counterfactual possibilities that could have occurred if the person only acted. Commissions, or those things we did, and regret, are more easily reconciled or the person may have learned something from them.[2] Although we may come to regret things in our life and may ruminate over them and view older age as a time of despair and decline, we try to face the challenges confronting us and work toward changing or at least compensating for setbacks and frustrations in our lives.

We can embrace what we call a wellness mindset in later life in that we seek to adapt to life changes, and when necessary reinvent ourselves while remaining authentic and without illusion about our own aging. This is also true for amateur and professional musicians. Aging musicians, as with all of us, face an array of cognitive, behavioral, and emotional changes that can affect playing ability. Here it is important for one to understand those changes and to either overcome or compensate for those changes. We will have ups and downs in engagement and energy. It is important to note that energy levels and our willingness to stay involved with music will vary at times. The important point is to stay engaged. This possibly requires adjustments to be made to one's playing

159

or singing, to one's performance schedule to accommodate changes with age, or to engage in new technologies to reach an audience.[3]

As we have related, maintaining social support networks is important. For musicians, maintaining connections with fans and fellow musicians and creating a new fan base is important and strengthens support networks. As discussed in Chapter 6, becoming involved in music groups, community groups, and going to concerts allows one to stay socially engaged. Also important is life review. A review of our lives, what we have done and what we have failed to do, provides meaning and serves as a basis to make necessary changes in our lives and to stay invigorated, inspired, and connected to others.

Defining, Directing, and Celebrating Life

The importance of authenticity and living that is true to self cannot be overstated. True self, whether we believe that it comes from God loving us into existence[4] or by other means, is indeed the essence of who we are. In a world where we face many challenges, finding one's true self can be difficult. Indeed, the challenge of finding one's true self may involve a movement away from defining ourselves using earlier comparison metrics of success or accomplishment, or looking back and dwelling on the past. We seem to be confronted with a paradox. That is, we exist in a liminal space, a constant transitioning from living to dying. We are also confronted with the past. There exists a conflict within us between thinking and living with the past but at the same time looking toward the future. One response is to reject and to let go of the past – possibly those things that have held us back, our regrets, our ruminations about what might have been, our self-defeating thoughts and behaviors. All of these threaten our authenticity as a person.

As we consider the phenomena of music, we recognize it can lead us onto and be a path to authenticity. Through music we may discover how to face changes as we age as it provides comfort to us in times of difficulty and increases our joy in times of happiness. As a thought experiment, try to contemplate a world where music does not exist. Now listen to the sounds around you. If you live in an area with a lot of traffic, such as a city, or in more rural area – listen. Sort out the many sounds around you. Hear the honking of horns or the banging of the garbage truck as it compacts the trash. Listen to the birds in your yard as the wind blows through the trees. Now put the sounds together and listen to them as you would a musical composition. Hear the repetition of sounds and sounds that are "played" once or twice. For lovers of music, we see that a world without music cannot exist. It is created in the symphony of sounds around us. Therefore, listen, and celebrate the song of life – from cradle to the grave. When we confront misery and difficulty as we will, music can provide comfort and healing.

Getting older also presents challenges. It too is a paradox. Not only do we still think about past, present, and future, but we also consider our state of health as we contemplate getting older. Other challenges such as financial stability and quality-of-life issues will occupy our time and present challenges to us. Later life can be a time of involvement and simultaneously a time of uncertainty and change. What is important is how we respond to those challenges. When we embrace a wellness mind-set, instead of framing changes in health, abilities, finances, and social experiences as defeating and limiting, we can treat these as challenges to overcome. Aging then is ultimately a process of finding new insight, recognizing our inner strengths, and of becoming. We often hear older adults say, "I am 87 years young – and looking forward to what the future will bring!" or "I am a retiree with memory and health problems, but I still love my spouse and we are thankful for each other. Each day we hope to find a way to celebrate – and now more than ever before, we enjoy our living!"

Avoiding the "Entrapments" of Aging

Indeed, people have fears and challenges as they face the prospect of getting older. One of the greatest fears that a person has of getting older is not fear of death but the fear of loss of independence and becoming a burden upon others.[5] Disability exists, decline exists. As we begin to experience some of the natural and disease processes of aging, we might notice that people start treating us in different ways. As we consider aging, we also want to discuss what we call the entrapments of aging. These entrapments have their origin in the norms and mores of society, one's education, or family experiences and can influence one's views of getting older. But once aware of these entrapments and how they contribute to our negative views of aging, we can work on moving beyond them toward a more healthy and realistic view of getting older.

One entrapment is to view aging as something negative. When we engage in self-defeating or negative behavior or thinking, we can become unwell. To believe that aging is a steady state of decline can be detrimental to our overall well-being. But we also do not want to fall into the entrapment that successful aging is a norm. We all age in different ways, and when we try to compare our state to an eighty-four-year-old pole vaulter or the ninety-year-old still running half-marathons, we are not helping ourselves when we have just been diagnosed with a serious medical condition or struggle with cognitive and behavioral changes.

Another entrapment is that we do not reduce human experience to solely neurobiological and brain processes. In fact, our thinking could arise from the conscious–unconscious mind, and this could be the cause of a preponderance of neurobiological activity. The conundrum is does thought create neurological activity or is it neurological activity that creates thought? Indeed, fMRI analyses of someone listening to an orchestral work shows that all parts of the brain become activated when listening to music but not at the same time. Interestingly, different parts of the brain are activated at different points in time in the music as well.[6] Although this issue has been apparently resolved in some circles (e.g., the mind is the brain), we feel that it is still an ongoing enterprise. For example, we still cannot find the connection between concepts such as experience and consciousness in brain process, in what some would call the "hard questions" of consciousness.[7] More elusive is the connection between musical experience and consciousness.

Another entrapment, we believe, is the medicalization of aging. Here it is important to understand the distinction between normal process and disease process. For example, in Chapter 3, we made the distinction between normal and pathological processes in hearing and in vision. We want to be careful not to blend this distinction and thereby define and characterize aging as an exclusively pathological expression. Rather, from a humanistic perspective we hold that aging is a process of becoming, of discovering new inner resources, and in finding deeper meaning in our relationships and life experiences.

Letting Go of Ego

Another entrapment of aging is our ego. To escape this entrapment of aging and move toward self-actualization is to let go of one's sense of self-importance – in effect, to let go of one's ego. Gayla Mills in her book *Making Music for Life: Rediscovering Your Musical Passion* offers how to approach music as an older musician. She relates how when young it is easier to take risks, to endure multiple music sets, to travel long distances, to stay up all night, to sleep on the floor, to have better hair (we add, to be thinner) without any apparent physical ill effects. In youth there is a confidence that one will succeed regardless of any barriers put before them. Her advice to older musicians is "You're past all that. Let it go."[8] Indeed, as Carl Jung has noted, it is unhealthy to "carry the psychology of the youthful phase over the threshold of the so-called years of discretion."[9] Thus, to cling to the standards of youth in later life, according to Jung, is a "shrinking back from the unknown in the world and in human existence ... and from the second half of life."[10]

As we become older, and perhaps wiser, we find a different way to express our passions – what to keep and what to let go. Thus, we find a way to live much more completely and with a renewed sense of wonder. Relatedly, Emily Remler, a renowned jazz guitarist, who tragically passed away at the age of thirty-two, expresses an old-soul approach to playing music.[11] She has taught us in her brief life that we are important as individuals and have the right to express ourselves in an authentic way – in effect, to let go of our ego. Once we do, we move beyond the restraints of ego and onto the way of becoming and achieving our greatest potential.

The leaving behind of one's ego speaks to a higher understanding of surrendering. The process of surrendering such as leaving jobs or careers, surrendering the loss of loved ones, the surrendering of physical and intellectual powers and capacities, surrendering the feeling of being important, and the surrendering of the ego means to move beyond the entrapments of aging. In Buddhism, to peel away layers of ego is to move toward finding the Eternal Self within. In Hinduism, in our spiritual journey we may move from the perspective of getting to that of giving as we seek greater enlightenment. In the Abrahamic traditions (Judaism, Christianity, Islam), it is in our self-less service to others and self-sacrifice for family and community. In faiths and traditions of First Nation peoples, it is in the awareness of our dependency on the earth, our relationship to all life forms, and the importance of our collective and communal orienta- tion. In all these faith traditions, going beyond ego reflects the humble understanding of the person's human needs, as well as one's limitations in conceiving of an Ultimate Power so great as to be able to create heavens and earths, and in realizing one's "smallness" in relation to a creation beyond our conception. These examples from a variety of faiths and philosophies imply the idea that aging is a spiritual journey. That is, while the physical body and the intellect may decline, our spiritual nature ascends to new points of awareness and leads us to a deeper understanding of our existence.

The Search for Meaning

Music can help us escape the entrapments of aging. We can escape the dialog of disability and decline. One way is to stop comparing ourselves to the octogenarian superwoman or superman and instead look for that which affirms our life and connects us to others. Music gives us that affirmation and the opportunity to stay involved. As we have presented, singing, playing an instrument, or listening keeps us connected to others and provides us a way to face everyday challenges. One of the authors, in an earlier chapter, related seeing and hearing Maestro Andres Segovia, who was then in his late eighties, perform. As the great Maestro came on stage, appearing fragile and deliberate in his steps, he was carefully escorted to his chair and handed his guitar. But when he began playing, the author described, it was the most energetic and wonderfully robust music to be heard. In a related instance, one of the authors recalls a friend who was in his eighties and was experiencing advanced cognitive decline. He would come to rehearsal or concerts but forget where his section was and had to be guided to his seat. One of the other players took him under her wing and made sure his music was in front of him and that he remembered to put his horn back in the case. He had left his instrument at a concert because he had forgotten to take it with him. However, he never missed a note when playing and in many instances was still able to play the music from memory. Both examples illustrate the duality or paradox of aging.

As presented in Chapter 8, we can consider this duality as a liminal space – that we are in a transition between different moments and times in our life. Examples of liminal space are the transition between health and illness, connection with others and loneliness, being young and being old, and living and dying. In the liminal space of health and illness, we can experience growth and at the same time decline, ambiguity, and uncertainty. We can be engaged, healthy, and content, and at the same time be dealing with medical conditions, worries, and anxieties. The fundamental question is how can we approach this liminal space as another way to overcome the entrapments of aging and regain a sense of hope? Perhaps, a first step is to understand this liminal space as a figure–ground experience; that is, that both states exist at the same time, but we place more emphasis on one than the other. To become involved in the process of self-actualization means to seek to understand this paradox. A potential outcome is that we may rise like a phoenix from the figure–ground contrast of decline and growth. Thus, as inspired by the pastel "Todavia Sueno de Mariposas" (I still dream of butterflies) by Chicana artist Judithe Hernadez, we may move beyond a duality of life and death in that one becomes transformed, changed, different.[12] It is this metamorphic resiliency that allows us to rebuild and renew ourselves when confronted with life's challenges.

When we begin to search for meaning in later life, we can begin to understand our connections to the past, present, and future, and the transitions and transformations of being and becoming that occur throughout the life course. Old age can provide us the insight and courage to look at the past and to address and redress our mistakes and transgressions. We begin to see relationships in a way that were hidden to us when younger. It is often related that one's relationships with parents are different when older. These relationships for some take on the added dimension of friendship. Perhaps this change in perception is borne from the insights one gains particularly when dealing with one's own children, careers, and daily finances. We may also experience a role reversal where we are now taking care of our parents. Maybe we begin to see ourselves in our parents and come to understand their struggles. One act of letting go of ego is to see ourselves in others.

It becomes clear that the standards we hold at a younger age change as we get older. We learn to adapt, compensate, and discover new ways to meet the challenges of getting older. For the musician, it might be learning to posture themselves in a way to reduce stress of holding an instrument for a long period of time, changing playing technique, rewriting a musical piece to a more simplified, easier-to-play form, or even changing the type of instrument one plays.[13]

In addition, our sense of wellness is likely to be attained with the help of others.[14] For example, interpersonal and communal connections afforded by later life musical involvements allow us to discover new ways of being and becoming, to increase our understanding of our existence and life experiences, and to offer a chance to connect to each other across generations. As we have related in an earlier chapter, older adults may provide guidance and instruction as well as inspiration to younger people – and vice versa. Maybe this means listening to new music for the older person or in recognizing and appreciating older music by the younger person. In another fashion, seeing our lives as a process of unfolding and becoming, in later life we may realize in a new way that the instructions from our teachers early in life (parents, mentors, conductors, music teachers, etc.) continue to resonate with us in many ways. In later life we may find new interpretations of and meaning in our earlier experiences.

Music affords us a conduit to lifelong learning. One of the authors recalls a discussion with his college piano teacher, Dr. Marion Lampe, in one of their last lessons together. As they worked on a piano piece by Felix Mendelssohn, she said, "You can continue to learn and be involved in mastering these pieces the rest of your life."[15] Again, recognizing this intergenerational exchange, the songs played and sung by older adults can offer insight to how the young might view old age. Through interactions with older adults, young people may come to see the subtleties and challenges of aging but also the ability to see their future with confidence. Music is such an important connection to us that we make necessary changes to keep that connection. We also change in how we view the world and our place in it. According to Tornstam, as we get older we "shift from a materialistic and rational view of the world to a more cosmic and transcendent one, normally accompanied by an increase in life satisfaction."[16] As part of this shift, music allows us to explore where we have been, where we are, and also what comes next.

Cosmic Musicians

Music involves the mind's cognitive, analytical, and emotional components. It also includes a conscious and unconscious connection to and engagement of personal experience. Any meaning in music is dependent upon the listener's own perception, but these perceptions can be non-representational; that is, they may not necessarily connect to a specific precept, structure, category, or thought but are felt at some cosmic, metaphysical level.

As we have proposed throughout this book, music is a holistic experience that often cannot be articulated. It also contains the breath of the cosmic. For example, Pythagoras proposed that the rotation and motion of celestial bodies and planets are musical in nature. A neo-Platonist view of the cosmos links music to a world soul.[17] Cosmologists are beginning to understand that we, indeed, came from the stars. We are children of the cosmos grounded on this Earth. Music is the conduit that connects us to both. It allows us to escape the weight of gravity and to touch an existence that is beyond our ability to articulate it.

In 1977, NASA launched the Voyager missions. Two space crafts, Voyager I and Voyager II, were tasked to explore the outer solar system. On each craft was affixed a gold-coated copper record – known as "The Golden Record"– containing recorded messages, photographs, greetings, and music. Just some of the 90 minutes of music included on The Golden Record is Bach's Brandenburg Concerto, No. 2 in F, First Movement, Gamelan orchestral music, Senegal percussion, Johnny B. Goode by Chuck Berry, Azerbaijan bagpipes, and an Indian raga "Jaat Kahan Ho." Astoundingly, 42 years later, Voyager I is more than 13 billion miles and Voyager II is 11 billion miles from Earth. Both have now reached interstellar space. In 38,200 years from now, Voyager I will come within 1.7 light years from a star in Ursa Minor called AC+ 79 3888. Voyager II in 40,000 years will come within 1.7 light years of the star called Ross 248 in the constellation Andromeda.[18] It is clear that those who envisioned this enterprise will be long dead, but this mission illustrates that we as a species strive for something beyond our immediate experience, in many ways to touch the stars from which we came. Indeed, it is believed that these space craft have the capacity to last a billion years or more.[19] If ever picked up by anyone, it is possible that they may be experiencing the only evidence of the existence of humans on this planet Earth.

And the Band Played On

We believe there is no one path or direction to follow in later life, no one definition of how "successful aging" may be realized for each person, or how our living and continued growth might be celebrated. Further, the process of continued growth and self-actualization involves looking closely at our lives and finding the courage to make adjustments as we travel along the way in our life journey. This process of making adjustments includes confronting ways we have viewed ourselves, held ourselves back through negative thoughts or feelings, or viewed the world and others in negative and demeaning ways. The process of self-actualization can include being courageous and creative in confronting our personal and societal forms of racism, sexism, and pessimism directed toward others, thus allowing us to become more compassionate, insightful, slow to judge or to condemn, and generous in the sharing of our resources with others. This is also a process of conversion and renewal, where we may seek reconciliation, grant forgiveness, and gain an intuition of a transcendental reality. As Carl Jung notes, a reality that makes aware "the transformation of what is mortal within me into what is immortal."[20]

What it means to live in a "well" society means to seek a deeper sense of care and compassion, understanding, acceptance, and appreciation of others. For the individual, the effect of music is to overcome our senses, neurological circuitry, emotions, and inspire us to action. We recognize that a well society embraces the whole person and works for social justice. A central message of our book is that there are countless possibilities in later life. That later life is a time of new discovery and ways of being and of becoming.

Presented here were the stories of those who represent these countless possibilities and ways of living. Each person's story illustrates a process of becoming, self-actualization, and authenticity. These stories represent distinct tiles that inlay and intersect in the mosaic of music, wellness, and aging. Further, they portray music as a way of directing, defining, and celebrating life. As poet and social justice activist Muriel Rukeyser states, "The Universe is made up of stories, not atoms."[21] Indeed, it is the stories we tell of those we have known and that others tell about us that define our humanity.

The life of each person is a story; each story is a song. It is first heard in the sounding rhythms of the infant's heartbeat. It is in the historical recording of each person's past, their challenges and successes, and the hopes that lie ahead as they endeavor into the future. Thus, the songs we sing, the musical works we play, and the sounds of music we hear herald old age to be a time where we may pass beyond our earlier youthful uncertainties to a moment of greater conviction and deeper trust. So, as we encounter the dynamic physical and intellectual changes that overtake us as we move closer to the end-of-life, we work toward letting go of what we earlier in life held and felt so important and consider what hope the legacy our lives will leave for those we love and the world at large. In this work of letting go, perhaps we can ultimately learn to accept who we are.

The Journey Continues

Our lives are a journey. We are always in transition. We do not recall who said that a life well spent makes for a happy death, but we believe that we know little about what makes up either. How do we know that we have spent our lives well? Maybe we are where we are meant to be – not to be blamed for our shortcomings and faults nor praised for our accomplishments, but more to the existential state of our being. We are where we are – and we try to make the best of it. But in trying to make the best of it, we know that there is more to our living and we strive for it. Music helps us do that. Music also links us to each other. Through music we become connected to others, we break down barriers that separate us and allow us to see that which is common to us all. Music is a metaphor for a deeper experience and, at whatever level of involvement, connects to a deeper sense of the life we hold and the transcendental experience we have. To paraphrase Shakespeare, maybe there is more than can ever be dreamt of in our philosophy. In our attempt to understand the intersection of music, wellness, and aging and how these come to define, direct, and celebrate our life, we conclude that we are still on that journey and that there is more to be "dreamt of." Perhaps we are always in transition; in a state of flux; residing in that liminal space – that threshold of where we are and where we will be; who we are and who we will become. But we know music will be there.

Notes

Program Notes

1. Fedric E. Rabinowitz, Glenn Good, and Liza Cozad, "Rollo May: A man of meaning and myth," *Journal of Counseling & Development* 67, no. 8 (1989), p. 96.

2. Erik J. Erikson, Joan M. Erikson, and Helen Q. Kivnick, *Vital Involvement in Old Age* (New York, NY: WW Norton & Company, 1994); C. G. Jung, "The Structure and Dynamics of the Psyche," *Collected Works of C. G. Jung*, 8 (Princeton, NJ: Princeton University Press, 1970); Abraham Maslow, *Motivation and Personality* (New York: Harper & Row, Publishers, 1954); Abraham Maslow, *Toward a Psychology of Being* (New York: Simon and Schuster, 2013); Rollo May, *The Courage to Create* (New York: WW Norton & Company, 1994); Rollo May, Ernst Angel, and Henri F. Ellenberger (eds.). *Existence* (New York: Jason Aronson, 1994); Carl R. Rogers, *A Way of Being* (Boston: Houghton Mifflin Company, 1980); Carl R. Rogers, *On Becoming a Person* (Boston: Houghton Mifflin Company, 1961); Tripathi, Nishi, "A valuation of Abraham Maslow's theory of self-actualization for the enhancement of quality of life," *Indian Journal of Health and Wellbeing* 9, no. 3 (2018), pp. 499–504.

3. R. May et al., *Existence*, 1994; A. Maslow, *Motivation and Personality*, 1954; N. Tripathi, "A valuation of Abraham Maslow's theory of self-actualization for the enhancement of quality of life," 2018, pp. 499–504.

4. F. E. Rabinowitz et al., "Rollo May: A man of meaning and myth,"1989, p. 96.

5. John David Kapusta, *American Music in the Culture of Self-Actualization: Performance and Composition in the Long 1970s.* eScholarship, University of California, 2017), p. 1.

6. Annabella S. K. Fung, "Music enables the holistic development and discovery of self: A phenomenological study of two Christian musicians," *Psychology of Music* 45, no. 3 (2017), pp. 400–416.

7. Daryl Bem, as cited in J. M. Darley, M. P. Zanna, and H. L. Roediger III (eds.). *The Complete Academic: A Practical Guide for the Beginning Social Scientist*, 2nd ed. (Washington, DC: American Psychological Association, 2003).

8. The Nielsen Company (2017). *Nielsen Music 360 2017.* Available through www.nielsen.com.

9. Clemence Michallon, "Rita Wilson shares quarantine playlist as she and Tom Hanks remain in coronavirus isolation," *The Independent*, March 13, 2020. www.independent.co.uk/arts-entertainment/music/news/tom-hanks-coronavirus; Mayukh Saha, "Idris Elba releases song about self-quarantine, positive coronavirus diagnosis," *The Union Journal*, March 20, 2020. https://theunionjournal.com/idris-elba-releases-song-about-self-quarantine-positive-coronavirus-diagnosis.

10. Vanessa Thorpe, "Italians sing patriotic songs from their balconies during coronavirus lockdown," *The Guardian*, March 14, 2020. www.theguardian.com/world/2020/mar/14/italians-sing-patriotic-songs-from-their-balconies-during-coronavirus-lockdown; Grace Hauck, "Chicagoans spread hope with a city-wide sing-along of Bon Jovi's 'Livin' on a Prayer," *The Naple News*, March 22, 2020. www.naplesnews.com/story/news/nation/2020/03/22/chicago-coronavirus-stay-at-home-order-sing-bon-jovi-livin-on-a-prayer/2892528001.

11. Douglas Perry, "Coronavirus comfort music: Lin-Manuel Miranda, Yo-Yo Ma post free music online to help people adjust to staying at home," *The Oregonian*, March 16, 2020. www.oregonlive.com/entertainment/2020/03/coronavirus-comfort-music-lin-manuel-miranda-yo-yo-ma-post-free-music-online-to-help-people-adjust-to-staying-at-home.html.

12. Mark Swec, "Commentary: El Sistema uses glorious Mahler to extol hope as the coronavirus attacks Venezuela," *Los Angeles Times*, March 21, 2020. www.latimes.com/entertainment-arts/story/2020–03-21/el-sistema-mahler-streaming-concert-coronavirus-venezuela.

13. Elizabeth Aubrey, "Keedron Bryant, 12, Signs Warner Record Deal for Black Lives Matter Protest Song," June 2020, *NME*. www.nme.com/news/music/keedron-bryant-12-signs-warner-records-deal-for-black-lives-matter-protest-song-2691817; Andrea Castillo, "How two Black women in LA helped build Black Lives Matter from hashtag to global movement," *Los Angeles Times*, June 21, 2020. www.latimes.com/california/story/2020–06-21/black-lives-matter-los-angeles-patrisse-cullors-melina-abdullah; Mark Savage, "Beyoncé releases surprise new song, Black Parade, on Juneteenth," *BBC News*, June 20, 2020. www.bbc.com/news/entertainment-arts-53119767; Brianne Tracy, "Celebrate Black Music Month with all the songs to come out of the protests," *People*, June 10, 2020. https://people.com/music/black-music-month-songs-black-lives-matter-protests.

14. BWW News Desk, "Music for Life International presents BEETHOVEN FOR THE ROHINGYA at Carnegie Hall," *Broadway World*, January10, 2019. www.broadwayworld.com/article/Music-For-Life-International-Presents-BEETHOVEN-FOR-THE-ROHINGYA-At-Carnegie-Hall-20190110; Diana Diaz, "At a Christmas concert in Panama, refugees are the guests of honour," *UNHCR, The UN Refugee Agency*, December 24, 2019. www.unhcr.org/en-us/news/stories/2019/12/5dfd3ecd4/christmas-concert-panama-refugees-guests-honour.html; Dalal Mawad, "US producer helps Syrian singer give voice to her dreams," *UNHCR, The UN Refugee Agency*, December6, 2019. www.unhcr.org/news/stories/2019/12/5de9083e4/producer-helps-syrian-singer-give-voice-dreams.html.

15. Natalie Rogers, Keith Tudor, Louise Embleton Tudor, and Keemar Keemar. "Person-centered expressive arts therapy: A theoretical encounter." *Person-Centered & Experiential Psychotherapies* 11, no. 1 (2012), pp. 31–47.

16. N. Rogers et al., "Person-centered expressive arts therapy: A theoretical encounter," 2012, p. 43.

1 Overture

1. Richard Rejino, "Kalie: Music Is My Healing Place," *What Music Means to Me*, December 4, 2016, used with permission. http://whatmusicmeanstome.org/?p=1273.

2. Flora R. Levin, *Greek Reflections on the Nature of Music* (New York, NY: Cambridge University Press, 2009), ix.

3. Levin, *Greek Reflections on the Nature of Music*, p. xii.

4. Stephen Joseph, "7 qualities of truly authentic people," *Psychology Today*, August 29, 2016. www.psychologytoday.com/us/blog/what-doesnt-kill-us/201608/7-qualities-truly-authentic-people (accessed May 20, 2018).

5. United Nations, *Constitution of the World Health Organization* (New York: United Nations, 1948). www.who.int/governance/eb/who_constitution_en.pdf (accessed May 5, 2018).

6. Daisy Fancourt and Saoiese Finn, "What Is the Evidence on the Role of the Arts in Improving Health and Well-Being? A Scoping Review." Copenhagen: WHO Regional Office of Europe, 2019. Health Evidence Network (HEN) Synthesis Report 67, 2.

7. See orienting works such as Alfred Adler and Heinz Ludwig Ansbacher, *The Individual Psychology of Alfred Adler: A Systematic Presentation in Selections from His Writings* (New York, NY: HarperPerennial, 1964); Gordon W. Allport, *Personality: A Psychological Interpretation* (New York, NY: Henry Holt and Company, 1937), pp. 22–23; Carl G. Jung, *The Undiscovered Self* (New York, NY: New American Library of World Literature, Inc., 1957), pp. 55–82; Abraham Maslow, "A theory of human motivation," *Psychological Review 50* (1943): 370–396; Carl R. Rogers, "Significant aspects of client-centered therapy," *American Psychologist 1* (1946): pp. 415–422.

8. Carl R. Rogers, *On Becoming a Person: A Therapist's View of Psychotherapy* (Boston, MA: Houghton Mifflin Company, 1961).

9. Harris M. Berger, *Metal, Rock, and Jazz: Perception and Phenomenology of Musical Experience (Music/Culture)* (London: Wesleyan University Press, 1999).

10. Kenneth LeFave, *The Sound of Ontology: Music as a Model of Metaphysics* (New York, NY: Lexington Books, 2017).

11. Edmund Husserl, *Ideas: General Introduction to Pure Phenomenology*, trans. W. R. Boyce Gibson (New York, NY: Collier Books, 1962), p. 7.

12. Carl G. Jung, *Man and His Symbols* (New York, NY: Dell, 1964).

13. Mark Cartwright, "Yin and Yang," *Ancient History Encyclopedia*, www.ancient.eu/Yin_and_Yang (updated May 16, 2018; accessed June 10, 2018).

14. Andrea Creech, Susan Hallam, Hilary McQueen, and Maria Varvarigou, "The power of music in the lives of older adults," *Research Studies in Music Education 35* (2013), pp. 87–102.

15. Quote from Dr. Martin Luther King Jr. on health care injustice, *PNHP Resources*, www.pnhp.org/news/2014/october/dr-martin-luther-king-on-heal th-care-injustice (accessed December 12, 2017).

16. Although we provide examples from other countries and historical perspectives, we focus primarily on unwellness in the United States of America in this chapter.

17. World Health Organization, *The World Health Report. Health Systems: Improving Performance* (World Health Organization: Geneva, Switzerland, 2000).

18. Centers for Medicare and Medicaid Services (CMS.gov.). www.cms.gov/ Research-Statistics-Data-and-Systems/Statistics-Trends-and Reports/Natio nalHealthExpendData/NationalHealthAccountsHistorical.html (accessed February 1, 2018).

19. Prepared by the Bureau of Labor Education, *The US Health-Care System: Best in the World, or Just the Most Expensive?* (Orono, Maine: University of Maine, 2001).

20. Philadelphia Musician's Union, Local 77, AFM (2016–2017). Wage scale.

21. Affordable Care Act (2010). www.healthcare.gov/glossary/affordable-care-a ct (accessed January 5, 2016).

22. August Brown, "Musicians rally to defend the Affordable Care Act," *Los Angeles Times*, January 11, 2017. www.latimes.com/entertainment/music/ la-et-musicians-hhs-20170111-story.html (accessed February 1, 2017).

23. Fancourt and Finn, "What Is the Evidence on the Role of the Arts in Improving Health and Well-Being? A Scoping Review."

24. Andrew J. Horton, "The forgotten avant garde: Soviet composers crushed by Stalin," *Central Europe Review 1* (June 28, 1999). www.ce-review.org/99/1/ music1_horton.html (accessed March 4, 2017).

25. Martin Lucke, "Vilified, venerated, forbidden: Jazz in the Stalinist era," trans. Anita Ip. *Music and Politics* (Summer 2007), pp. 1–9.

26. Solomon Volkov, *Testimony: The Memoirs of Dmitry Shostakovich.* In Solomon Volkov (ed.), trans. Antonina W. Bouis (New York, NY: Harper Colphon Books, Harper and Row, 1979).

27. Volkov, *Testimony: The Memoirs of Dmitry Shostakovich.*

28. Aida Huseinova, "Politically correct music: Stalin era and the struggle of Azerbaijani composers," *Azerbaijani International*, Summer 2006, pp. 56–65. www.azer.com/aiweb/categories/magazine/ai142_folder/142_articles/142_ai da_repression_music.html (accessed March 4, 2017).

29. The rubab is a lute-like instrument carved out of wood, with three main strings, two or three drone strings, and up to fifteen sympathetic strings strung across a membrane. Its tone projects much like the sound of a banjo or resonator guitar and allows for expression of penetrating single-string notes accompanied by rich harmonic overtone textures.

30. Simon Broughton, Mark Ellingham, James McConnachie, and Orla Duane (eds.), "Afghanistan: Red light at the crossroads," *World Music: Volume 2:*

Latin & North America, Caribbean, India, Asia, and Pacific: A Rough Guide (London England: Rough Guides Ltd., 2000), 4–5.

31. Tom Barnes, "Native American musicians stand up to stereotypes in new season of documentary," *MIC*, May 25, 2015. https://mic.com/articles/117 758/mtv-just-gave-these-artists-a-huge-platform-to-bring-attention-to-indi genous-rights#.6TU9qBcPE (accessed April 1, 2017).

32. Michelle A. Marzullo and Alyn J. Libman, *Research Overview: Hate Crimes and Violence Against Lesbian, Gay, Bisexual, and Transgender People*, Che Juan Gonzalez Ruddell-Tabisola (ed.) (Washington, DC: Human Rights Campaign Foundation, 2009), 1–24.

33. Melissa Quinn, "Supreme Court rules federal civil rights law protects LGBTQ workers," CBS News, June 15, 2020. www.cbsnews.com/news/supreme-cou rt-lgbt-rights-discrimination-rules-title-vii (accessed July 5, 2020).

34. Centers for Disease Control and Prevention, "Covid_19 in Racial and Ethnic Minority Groups, Centers for Disease Control and Prevention," *Corona Virus Disease 2019 (COVID-19)*. www.cdc.gov/coronavirus/2019-ncov/need-extr a-precautions/racial-ethnic-minorities.html (accessed May 1, 2020).

35. For more information, visit the website: www.history.com/topics/immigra tion/immigration-united-states-timeline.

36. For more information, see Office of the Historian, "The Immigration Act of 1924" (The Johnson-Reed Act). https://history.state.gov/milestones/1921–1936/immigration-act.

37. The Trump administration. www.aclu-wa.org/pages/timeline-muslim-ban (accessed December 15, 2020).

38. For more information, see Population Reference Bureau: www.prb.org.

39. Erik Erikson, *Childhood and Society*, 2nd ed. (New York, NY: Norton, 1963). Erik Erikson, *Identity: Youth and Crisis* (New York, NY: Norton, 1968).

40. Carl G. Jung, "The Stages of Life," *Volume 8 of the Collected Works of C. G. Jung*, 2nd ed. (Princeton, NJ: Princeton University Press, 1969), pp. 387–403.

41. For example, see reports by Paul T. Costa Jr., Robert R. McCrae, and Corinna E. Löckenhoff, "Personality across the life span," *Annual Review of Psychology 70* (2019), pp. 423–448; Paul T. Costa and Robert R. McCrae, "The NEO inventories as instruments of psychological theory," *The Oxford Handbook of the Five Factor Model* (2017), pp. 11–37.

42. Dorothy H. Eichorn, "The Berkeley Longitudinal Studies: Continuities and correlates of behaviour," *Canadian Journal of Behavioural Science 5*, no. 4 (1973), pp. 297–320.

43. Constance Jones, Harvey Peskin, Christian Wandeler, and David Woods, "Culturally gendered personality traits across the adult lifespan: Longitudinal findings from two cohorts of the intergenerational studies," *Psychology and Aging 34*, no. 8 (2019), pp. 1124–1133.

44. Alice Verstaen, Claudia M. Haase, Sandy J. Lwi, and Robert W. Levenson, "Age-related changes in emotional behavior: Evidence from a 13-year longi-tudinal study of long-term married couples," *Emotion 20*, no. 2 (2020), pp. 149–163.

45. Mohsen Naghavi, Amanuel Alemu Abajobir, Cristiana Abbafati, Kaja M. Abbas, Foad Abd-Allah, Semaw Ferede Abera, Victor Aboyans, et al., "Global, regional, and national age-sex specific mortality for 264 causes of death, 1980–2016: A systematic analysis for the Global Burden of Disease Study 2016," *The Lancet 390*, no. 10100 (2017), pp. 1151–1210.

46. Carl G. Jung, "The Stages of Life." Bernice L. Neugarten, "Continuities and discontinuities of psychological issues into adult life." In D. A. Neugarten (ed.). *The Meanings of Age: Selected Papers of Bernice L. Neugarten* (Chicago: The University of Chicago Press, 1996), pp. 88–95.

47. Lars Tornstam, "Maturing into geotranscendence," *Journal of Transpersonal Psychology 43*, no. 2 (2011) p. 166.

48. Tornstam, "Maturing into geotranscendence," p. 173.

49. Tornstam, "Maturing into geotranscendence," p. 176.

50. For example, see works by Lauren L. Carstensen, Helen H. Fung, and Susan T. Charles, "Socioemotional selectivity theory and the regulation of emotion in the second half of life," *Motivation and Emotion 27* (June 2003), pp. 103–123; Carol D. Ryff and Cory Lee M. Keyes, "The structure of psychological well-being revisited," *Journal of Personality and Social Psychology 69*, no. 4 (1995), pp. 719–727.

51. Lao Tzu, *Tao Te Ching*, Chapter 41, trans. Gia-fu Feng and Jane English. www.wussu.com/laotzu/laotzu41.html.

52. Jacob Needleman, "Questions of the heart: Inner empiricism as way to a science of consciousness," *Noetic Sciences Review* (Summer 1993), pp. 4–9.

53. For example, see articles by John Bond, "The medicalization of dementia," *Journal of Aging Studies 6*, no. 4 (1992), pp. 397–403; Caroll L. Estes and Elizabeth A. Binney, "The biomedicalization of aging: Dangers and dilemmas," *The Gerontologist 29*, no. 5 (1989), pp. 587–596. Stephen Katz and Toni Calasanti, "Critical perspectives on successful aging: Does it 'appeal more than it illuminates'?" *The Gerontologist 55*, no. 1 (2015), pp. 26–33; Marty Martinson and Clara Berridge, "Successful aging and its discontents: A systematic review of the social gerontology literature," *The Gerontologist 55*, no. 1 (2015), pp. 58–69; Irving Kenneth Zola, G. Albrecht, and J. Levy, "The medicalization of aging and disability." In Martin Lyon Levine (ed.). *The Elderly: Legal and Ethical Issues in Healthcare Policy* (New York, NY, 2016), pp. 299–315.

54. We recognize that for some, music may not be important in their lives. Some may not even like music. Others may have conditions that, when they hear music, all they hear is noise or they may find it extremely painful. For a discussion of neurological-related music disorders, see Oliver Sacks, *Musicophilia: Tales of Music and the Brain* (New York, NY: Alfred A. Knopf, 2007).

2 In Search of a Perfect Harmony: Music and Wellness in Later Life

1. Ralph W. Emerson, *Journals of Ralph Waldo Emerson, with Annotations*, v.5 (1838–41) (This work is in the public domain), p. 121.

2. Paul Tillich, P. *The Courage to Be* (New Haven, CT: Yale University Press, 2000).
3. Carl G. Jung, "The Structure and Dynamics of the Psyche," *Volume 8 of the Collected Works of C. G. Jung*, 2nd ed. (Princeton, NJ: Princeton University Press, 1969); Lewis Rowell, *Thinking about Music: An Introduction to the Philosophy of Music* (Ann Arbor, MI: University of Massachusetts Press, 1984).
4. Rowell, *Thinking about Music*, p. 57.
5. Michael Gallope, *Deep Refrains: Music, Philosophy, and the Ineffable (Chicago IL*: University of Chicago Press, 2017), p. 15.
6. Gallope, *Deep Refrains*, p. 87.
7. Ward Cannel and Fred Marx, *How to Play the Piano Despite Years of Lessons: What Music Is and How to Make It at Home* (New York, NY: Crown & Bridge, Publishers, 1976), p. 10.
8. Gallope, *Deep Refrains*, pp. 218–254.
9. See works by Francine V. Garlin and Katherine Owen, "Setting the tone with the tune: A meta-analytic review of the effects of background music in retail settings," *Journal of Business Research 59*, no. 6 (2006), pp. 755–764; John T. Lang, "Music and consumer experience," *The Wiley Blackwell Encyclopedia of Consumption and Consumer Studies* (2015), pp. 1–3.
10. See reports by Rui Zhu and Joan Meyers-Levy, "Distinguishing between the meanings of music: When background music affects product perceptions," *Journal of Marketing Research 42*, no. 3 (2005), pp. 333–345; Mark I. Alpert, Judy I. Alpert, and Elliot N. Maltz, "Purchase occasion influence on the role of music in advertising," *Journal of Business Research 58*, no. 3 (2005), pp. 369–376; Annika Beer and Tobias Greitemeyer, "The effects of background music on tipping behavior in a restaurant: A field study," *Psychology of Music 47*, no. 3 (2019), pp. 444–450.
11. For example, see discussions by Helen Lindquist Bonny, "Music and healing," *Music Therapy 6*, no. 1 (1986), pp. 3–12; Stephen Clift, Rebekah Gilbert, and T.R.I.S.H. Vella-Burrows, *A Choir in Every Care Home: A Review of Research on the Value of Singing for Older People* (London: The Baring Foundation, 2016); Rick Docksai, "The sounds of wellness," *The Futurist 45*, no. 5 (2011), p. 13.
12. Teppo Särkämö, Mari Tervaniemi, Sari Laitinen, Anita Forsblom, Seppo Soinila, Mikko Mikkonen, Taina Autti, et al., "Music listening enhances cognitive recovery and mood after middle cerebral artery stroke," *Brain 131*, no. 3 (2008), pp. 866–876; Sabine Schneider, Paul W. Schönle, Eckart Altenmüller, and Thomas F. Münte, "Using musical instruments to improve motor skill recovery following a stroke," *Journal of Neurology 254*, no. 10 (2007), pp. 1339–1346.
13. See reports by Maria J. Núñez, Paula Mañá, David Linares, María P. Riveiro, José Balboa, Juan Suárez-Quintanilla, Mónica Maracchi, Manuel Rey Méndez, José M. López, and Manuel Freire-Garabal, "Music, immunity and cancer," *Life Sciences 71*, no. 9 (2002), pp. 1047–1057; M. Uchiyama, X. Jin, Q. Zhang, A. Amano, T. Watanabe, and M. Niimi, "Music exposure induced prolongation of cardiac allograft survival and

generated regulatory CD4+ cells in mice," *Transplantation Proceedings 44*, no. 4 (2012), pp. 1076–1079.

14. See the research of Andrea Creech, Susan Hallam, Hilary McQueen, and Maria Varvarigou, "The power of music in the lives of 0lder adults," *Research Studies in Music Education 35*, no. 1 (2013), pp. 87–102; Andrew Sixsmith and Grant Gibson, "Music and the wellbeing of people with dementia," *Ageing & Society 27*, no. 1 (2007), pp. 127–145.

15. Daisy Fancourt, Adam Ockelford, and Abi Belai, "The psychoneuroimmunological effects of music: A systematic review and a new model," *Brain, Behavior, and Immunity 36* (2014), pp. 15–26.

16. Cathy H. McKinney, Frederick C. Tims, Adarsh M. Kumar, and Mahendra Kumar, "The effect of selected classical music and spontaneous imagery on plasma β-endorphin," *Journal of Behavioral Medicine 20*, no. 1 (1997), pp. 85–99.

17. Daisy Fancourt, Aaron Williamon, Livia A. Carvalho, Andrew Steptoe, Rosie Dow, and Ian Lewis, "Singing modulates mood, stress, cortisol, cytokine, and neuropeptide activity in cancer patients and carers." *ecancermedicalscience 10* (2016), p. 631. https://doi.org.10.3332/ecancer. 2016.631 (accessed February 16, 2018).

18. Kaoru Okada, Akira Kurita, Bonpei Takase, Toshiaki Otsuka, Eitaro Kodani, Yoshiki Kusama, Hirotsugu Atarashi, and Kyoichi Mizuno, "Effects of music therapy on autonomic nervous system activity, incidence of heart failure events, and plasma cytokine and catecholamine levels in elderly patients with cerebrovascular disease and dementia," *International Heart Journal 50*, no. 1 (2009), pp. 95–110.

19. See Stegan Koelsch, "Towards a neural basis of music-evoked emotions," *Trends in Cognitive Sciences 14*, no. 3 (2010), pp. 131–137; Patrick Vuilleumier and Wiebke Trost, "Music and emotions: From enchantment to entrainment," *Annals of the New York Academy of Sciences 1337*, no. 1 (2015), pp. 212–222.

20. Valorie Salimpoor, Mitchel Benovoy, Kevin Larcher, Alain Dagher, and Robert J. Zatorre, "Anatomically distinct dopamine release during anticipation and experience of peak emotion to music," *Nature Neuroscience 14*, no. 2 (2011), pp. 257–264.

21. Alan S. Cowen, Xia Fang, Disa Sauter, and Dacher Keltner. "What music makes us feel: At least 13 dimensions organize subjective experiences associated with music across different cultures," *Proceedings of the National Academy of Sciences* (2020).

22. Paul Byers, "Biological rhythms as information channels in interpersonal communication behavior," *Perspectives in Ethology* (Boston, MA: Springer, 1976), pp. 135–164; Ian Daly, James Hallowell, Faustina Hwang, Alexis Kirke, Asad Malik, Etienne Roesch, James Weaver, Duncan Williams, Eduardo Miranda, and Slawomir J. Nasuto, "Changes in music tempo entrain movement related brain activity." In *2014 36th Annual International Conference of the IEEE Engineering in Medicine and Biology Society* (2014), pp. 4595–4598; Wiebke J. Trost, Carolina Labbé,

and Didier Grandjean, "Rhythmic entrainment as a musical affect induction mechanism," *Neuropsychologia 96* (2017), pp. 96–110.

23. Patrick Gomez and Brigitta Danuser, "Relationships between musical structure and psychophysiological measures of emotion," *Emotion 7*, no. 2 (2007), pp. 377–387.

24. Bias Boshel, arranged by Richard Hewson, recorded by The Kiki Dee Band, "I've Got The Music In Me" (London, UK: The Rocket Record Company/ Universal Music Group), PIG -12.

25. Hajime Fukui, "Music and testosterone," *Annals of the New York Academy of Sciences 930*, no. 1 (2001), pp. 448–451.

26. Quiroga C. Murcia, Stephan Bongard, and Gunter Kreutz, "Emotional and neurohumoral responses to dancing tango argentino: The effects of music and partner," *Music and Medicine 1*, no. 1 (2009), pp. 14–21.

27. Fancourt et al., "Singing Modulates Mood, Stress, Cortisol, Cytokine and Neuropeptide Activity in Cancer Patients and Carers," 2016.

28. Sylvie Hébert, Renée Béland, Odrée Dionne-Fournelle, Martine Crête, and Sonia J. Lupien, "Physiological stress response to video-game playing: The contribution of built-in music," *Life Sciences 76*, no. 20 (2005), pp. 2371–2380.

29. See reports by Robert S. Bahadori and Barbara A. Bohne, "Adverse effects of noise on hearing," *American Family Physician 47*, no. 5 (1993), pp. 1219–1231; Robert Plutchik, "The effects of high intensity intermittent sound on performance, feeling and physiology," *Psychological Bulletin 56*, no. 2 (1959), pp. 133–151.

30. Juliette Volcler, *Extremely Loud: Sound as a Weapon* (New York, NY: The New Press, 2013).

31. Brigitta Berglund, Peter Hassmen, and R. F. Soames Job, "Sources and effects of low-frequency noise," *The Journal of the Acoustical Society of America 99*, no. 5 (1996), pp. 2985–3002.

32. See reports by Nick Broner, "The effects of low frequency noise on people – A review," *Journal of Sound and Vibration 58*, no. 4 (1978), pp. 483–500; Reiko Yagi, Emi Nishina, and Tsutomu Oohashi, "A method for behavioral evaluation of the 'hypersonic effect,'" *Acoustical Science and Technology 24*, no. 4 (2003), pp. 197–200.

33. Timothy G. Leighton, "Ultrasound in air – Guidelines, applications, public exposures, and claims of attacks in Cuba and China," *The Journal of the Acoustical Society of America 144*, no. 4 (2018), pp. 2473–2489.

34. William W. Clark and Barbara A. Bohne, "Effects of noise on hearing." *Journal of the American Medical Association 281*, no. 17 (1999), pp. 1658–1659.

35. See reports by Christos Baliatsas, Irene van Kamp, Ric van Poll, and Joris Yzermans, "Health effects from low-frequency noise and infrasound in the general population: Is it time to listen? A systematic review of observational studies," *Science of the Total Environment 557* (2016), pp. 163–169; Sahar Geravandi, Afshin Takdastan, Elahe Zallaghi, Mehdi Vousoghi Niri, Mohammad Javad Mohammadi, Hamed Saki, and Abolfazl Naiemabadi,

"Noise pollution and health effects," *Jundishapur Journal of Health Sciences* 7, no. 1 (2015), p. e63012.

36. Mette Sørensen, Matthias Ketzel, Kim Overvad, Anne Tjønneland, and Ole Raaschou-Nielsen, "Exposure to road traffic and railway noise and postmenopausal breast cancer: A cohort study," *International Journal of Cancer 134*, no. 11 (2014), pp. 2691–2698.

37. Mettie Sørensen, Zorana J. Andersen, Rikke B. Nordsborg, Thomas Becker, Anne Tjønneland, Kim Overvad, and Ole Raaschou-Nielsen, "Long-term exposure to road traffic noise and incident diabetes: A cohort study," *Environmental Health Perspectives 121*, no. 2 (2012), pp. 217–222.

38. See reports by Wolfgang Babisch, "Stress hormones in the research on cardiovascular effects of noise," *Noise and Health 5*, no. 18 (2003), pp. 1–11; Ramazan Mirzaei, Alireza Ansari-Mogaddam, Mahdi Mohammadi, Fatemeh Rakhshani, and Maryam Salmanpor, "Noise pollution in Zahedan and residents' knowledge about noise pollution," *Journal Health Scope 1*, no. 1 (2012), pp. 3–6; E. Powazka, K. Pawlas, B. Zahorska-Markiewicz, and Jan E. Zejda, "A cross-sectional study of occupational noise exposure and blood pressure in steelworkers," *Noise and Health 5*, no. 17 (2002), pp. 15–22.

39. Suzanne G. Cusick, "Musicology, torture, repair," *Radical Musicology 3*, no. 1 (2008), pp. 1–9.

40. James E. Birren, "A contribution to the theory of the psychology of aging: As a counterpart of development." In James E. Birren and Vern L. Bengtson (eds.). *Emergent Theories of Aging* (New York, NY: Springer Publishing Co., 1988), pp. 153–176.

41. Maurice Merleau-Ponty, *Phenomenology of Perception* (New York, NY: Routledge, 2013).

42. For example, see Vern L. Bengtson, "The generation gap: A review and typology of social-psychological perspectives," *Youth & Society 2*, no. 1 (1970), pp. 7–32; Brett Laursen and W. Andrew Collins, "Interpersonal conflict during adolescence," *Psychological Bulletin 115*, no. 2 (1994), pp. 197–209; Elliot Turiel and Cecilia Wainryb, "Social life in cultures: Judgments, conflict, and subversion," *Child Development 71*, no. 1 (2000), pp. 250–256.

43. Sabrina Koepke and Jaap J. A. Denissen, "Dynamics of identity develop-ment and separation–individuation in parent–child relationships during adolescence and emerging adulthood – A conceptual integration," *Developmental Review 32*, no. 1 (2012), pp. 67–88.

44. The Who, "My Generation," *The Who – My Generation* (London, UK: Brunswick Records, 1965).

45. Dave Marsh, *Before I Get Old: The Story of The Who* (New York: St. Martin's Press, 1983).

46. J. Sarwer-Foner Gerald, "Denial of death and the unconscious longing for indestructability and immortality in the terminal phase of adolescence," *Canadian Psychiatric Association Journal 17*, no. 6 supp 12 (1972), pp. 51–57; Rebecca Jones, "Imagining old age." In Jeanne Katz, Sheila Peace, and Sue Spurr (eds.). *Adult Lives: A Life Course Perspective*

(Bristol, UK: Policy Press, 2011), pp. 18–26; Heather P. Lacey, Dylan M. Smith, and Peter A. Ubel, "Hope I die before I get old: Mispredicting happiness across the adult lifespan," *Journal of Happiness Studies* 7, no. 2 (2006), pp. 167–182.

47. Pete Townshend, *Pete Townshend: Who I Am* (London: HarperCollins, 2012); Ruth Schmidt Neven, *Emotional Milestones: From Birth to Adulthood, a Psychodynamic Approach* (London: Jessica Kingsley Publishers, 1997); Debra S., Rosenblum, Peter Daniolos, Neal Kass, and Andres Martin, "Adolescents and popular culture: A psychodynamic overview," *The Psychoanalytic Study of the Child* 54, no. 1 (1999), pp. 319–338.

48. Lars Tornstam, *Gerotranscendence: A Developmental Theory of Positive Aging* (New York, NY: Springer Publishing Company, 2005).

49. See also Shayne Ann Vitemb, "'Talkin' 'bout my generation': Existentialism, aging, and newly emerging issues in group therapy," *International Journal of Group Psychotherapy* 68, no. 3 (2018), pp. 337–351.

50. Dan P. McAdams, "Life story: The encyclopedia of adulthood and aging," *Handbook of Personality* (2008), pp. 242–262.

51. Dan P. McAdams, "The psychology of life stories," *Review of General Psychology* 5, no. 2 (2001), pp. 100–122; Dan P. McAdams, E. D. de St Aubin, and R. L. Logan, "Generativity among young, midlife, and older adults," *Psychology and Aging* 8, no. 2 (1993), pp. 221–230; Michael W. Pratt, J. E. Norris, M. L. Arnold, M. L., and R. Filyer, "Generativity and moral development as predictors of value-socialization narratives for young persons across the adult life span: From lessons learned to stories shared," *Psychology and Aging* 14, no. 3 (1999), pp. 414–426; David Gutmann, *Reclaimed Powers: Men and Women in Later Life* (Chicago, IL: Northwestern University Press, 1994); David Gutmann, *The Human Elder in Nature, Culture, and Society* (New York: Routledge, 2019).

52. Stephen G. Post and Robert H. Binstock (eds.). *The Fountain of Youth: Cultural, Scientific, and Ethical Perspectives on a Biomedical Goal* (Oxford: Oxford University Press, 2004).

53. Farnáz Ma'súmián, *Life after Death: A Study of the Afterlife in World Religions* (Los Angeles, CA: Kalimat Press, 2002).

54. Kunlin Jin, "Modern biological theories of aging," *Aging and Disease 1*, no. 2 (2010), pp. 72–74.

55. Jay S. Olshansky, "Aging of US presidents," *JAMA 306*, no. 21 (2011), pp. 2328–2329.

56. Frederick B. Churchill, *August Weismann* (Boston, MA: Harvard University Press, 2015).

57. US Census Bureau, *65+ in the United States: 2010* (Washington, DC: US Government Printing Office, 2014), pp. P23–212.

58. M. Thönnes and N. R. Jakoby, "Where do people die? On the question of dying in institutions," *Zeitschrift fur Gerontologie und Geriatrie* 44, no. 5 (2011), pp. 336–339.

59. Lars Tornstam, "Gerotranscendence: The contemplative dimension of aging," *Journal of Aging Studies 11*, no. 2 (1997), pp. 143–154.

60. Mike Featherstone and Mike Hepworth, "Ageing, the lifecourse and the sociology of embodiment." In Graham Scambler and Paul Higgs (eds.). *Modernity, Medicine and Health* (New York: Routledge, 2005), pp. 165–194; Bernice L. Neugarten (ed.). *Middle Age and Aging: A Reader in Social Psychology* (Chicago, IL: University of Chicago Press, 1968).

61. Laura Marczak, Kevin O'Rourke, and Dawn Shepard, "When and why people die in the United States, 1990–2013," *Journal of the American Medical Association 315*, no. 3 (2016), pp. 241–241.

62. Stephanie Studenski, Subashan Perera, Kushang Patel, Caterina Rosano, Kimberly Faulkner, Marco Inzitari, Jennifer Brach, et al., "Gait speed and survival in older adults," *Journal of the American Medical Association 305*, no. 1 (2011), pp. 50–58.

63. Howard S. Friedman and Leslie R. Martin, *The Longevity Project: Surprising Discoveries for Health and Long Life from the Landmark Eight Decade Study* (Carlsbad, CA: Hay House, Inc, 2011).

64. P. O. Astrand, "Exercise physiology and its role in disease prevention and in rehabilitation," *Archives of Physical Medicine and Rehabilitation 68*, no. 5, pt. 1 (1987), pp. 305–309.

65. Rick Docksai, "The sounds of wellness," *The Futurist 45*, no. 5 (2011), pp. 13–14.

66. Candace B. Pert, *Molecules of Emotion: The Science behind Mind-Body Medicine* (New York, NY: Simon and Schuster, 2010).

67. Candace B. Pert, Henry E. Dreher, and Michael R. Ruff, "The psychosomatic network: Foundations of mind-body medicine," *Alternative Therapies in Health and Medicine 4*, no. 4 (1998), pp. 30–41; S. L. Parker and A. Balasubramaniam, "Neuropeptide Y Y2 receptor in health and disease," *British Journal of Pharmacology 153*, no. 3 (2008), pp. 420–431.

68. Jeffery A. Dusek and Herbert Benson, "Mind-body medicine: A model of the comparative clinical impact of the acute stress and relaxation responses," *Minnesota Medicine 92*, no. 5 (2009), pp. 47–50.

69. John A. Astin, Shauna L. Shapiro, David M. Eisenberg, and Kelly L. Forys, "Mind-body medicine: State of the science, implications for practice," *The Journal of the American Board of Family Practice 16*, no. 2 (2003), pp. 131–147; Michelle L. Dossett, Gregory L. Fricchione, and Herbert Benson, "A new era for mind-body medicine," *New England Journal of Medicine 382*, no. 15 (2020), pp. 1390–1391.

70. Don D. Coffman, "Music and quality of life in older adults," *Psychomusicology: A Journal of Research in Music Cognition 18*, no. 1–2 (2002), pp. 76–88.

71. Stefan Koelsch and Lutz Jäncke, "Music and the heart," *European Heart Journal 36*, no. 44 (2015), pp. 3043–3049.

72. Sharon M. Parr, "The effects of graduated exercise at the piano on the pianist's cardiac output, forearm blood flow, heart rate, and blood pressure," *Dissertation Abstracts International 46*(06), 1436A (University Microfilms No. AAT85-18673), 1985.

73. Stephen Clift and Grenville Hancox, "The perceived benefits of singing: Findings from preliminary surveys of a university college choral society," *The Journal of the Royal Society for the Promotion of Health 121*, no. 4 (2001), pp. 248–256.

74. Lars Olov Bygren, Boinkum Benson Konlaan, and Sven-Erik Johansson, "Attendance at cultural events, reading books or periodicals, and making music or singing in a choir as determinants for survival: Swedish interview survey of living conditions," *British Medical Journal 313*, no. 7072 (1996), pp. 1577–1580.

75. Gene Cohen, "New theories and research findings on the positive influence of music and art on health with ageing," *Arts & Health 1*, no. 1 (2009), pp. 48–62.

76. Gene D. Cohen, Susan Perlstein, Jeff Chapline, Jeanne Kelly, Kimberly M. Firth, and Samuel Simmens, "The impact of professionally conducted cultural programs on the physical health, mental health, and social functioning of older adults," *The Gerontologist 46*, no. 6 (2006), pp. 726–734.

77. Gary Johnson, David Otto, and Alicia Ann Clair, "The effect of instrumental and vocal music on adherence to a physical rehabilitation exercise program with persons who are elderly," *Journal of Music Therapy 38*, no. 2 (2001), pp. 82–96.

78. Costas I. Karageorghis, Peter C. Terry, and Andrew M. Lane, "Development and initial validation of an instrument to assess the motivational qualities of music in exercise and sport: The Brunel Music Rating Inventory," *Journal of Sports Sciences 17*, no. 9 (1999), pp. 713–724.

79. Bram van der Vlist, Christoph Bartneck, and Sebastian Mäueler, "moBeat: Using interactive music to guide and motivate users during aerobic exercising," *Applied Psychophysiology and Biofeedback 36*, no. 2 (2011), pp. 135–145.

80. Peter C. Terry and Costas I. Karageorghis, "Psychophysical effects of music in sport and exercise: An update on theory, research and application," *Proceedings of the 2006 Joint Conference of the Australian Psychological Society and New Zealand Psychological Society* (Melbourne, Victoria, Australia: Australian Psychological Society, 2006), pp. 415–419.

81. Jeannette A. Sorrell and Jeanne M. Sorrell, "Music as a healing art for older adults," *Journal of Psychosocial Nursing and Mental Health Services 46*, no. 3 (2008), pp. 21–24.

82. Saint Thomas More and Paul Turner, *Utopia. Translated with an Introduction by Paul Turner* (New York, NY: Penguin, 1965).

83. Nancy Sandars (ed.). *The Epic of Gilgamesh* (New York, NY: Penguin, 1972).

84. John Huston Finley, *Homer's Odyssey* (Cambridge, MA: Harvard University Press, 1978).

85. More and Turner, *Utopia*, pp. 7–23.

86. Edward Bellamy, *Looking Backward: 2000–1887* (Peterborough, ON: Broadview Press, 2003).

87. More and Turner, *Utopia*, p. 93.

88. More and Turner, *Utopia*, p. 96.

89. Carl G. Jung, *Synchronicity: An Acausal Connecting Principle, Volume 8 of the Collected Works of C. G. Jung*, 2nd ed. (Princeton, NJ: Princeton University Press, 1969), pp. 417–531; Carl Rogers, *A Way of Being* (Boston, MA: Houghton Mifflin Company, 1980).

90. For example, Helen C. Boucher and Tammy English, "The yin-yang of personality: Implications of naïve dialecticism for social cognition, the self-concept, and well-being." In A. T. Church (ed.). *The Praeger Handbook of Personality across Cultures: Evolutionary, Ecological, and Cultural Contexts of Personality* (Santa Barbara, CA: Praeger/ABC-CLIO, 2017), pp. 179–206; Paul Downes, "Concentric and diametric structures in yin/yang and the mandala symbol: A new wave of Eastern frames for psychology," *Psychology and Developing Societies 23*, no. 1 (2011), pp. 121–153; Edward Murguia and Kim Díaz, "The philosophical foundations of cognitive behavioral therapy: Stoicism, Buddhism, Taoism, and Existentialism," *Journal of Evidence-Based Psychotherapies 15*, no. 1 (2015); Roger Walsh and Shauna L. Shapiro, "The meeting of meditative disciplines and Western psychology: A mutually enriching dialogue," *American Psychologist 61*, no. 3 (2006), p. 227.

91. Louise Sundararajan, "The Chinese notions of harmony, with special focus on implications for cross-cultural and global psychology," *The Humanistic Psychologist 41*, no. 1 (2013), pp. 25–34.

92. Joel Y. Wong and Tao Liu, "Dialecticism and mental health: Toward a yin-yang vision of well-being." In J. Spencer-Rodgers and K. Peng (eds.). *Psychological and Cultural Foundations of Dialectical Thinking* (New York, NY: Oxford University Press, 2018), pp. 547–572.

93. Shuiyuan Xiao, "The concept of body-mind relationship in the context of Chinese culture." In Hoyle Leigh (ed.). *Global Psychosomatic Medicine and Consultation-Liaison Psychiatry* (San Francisco, CA: Springer, 2019), pp. 117–128; Qing Yan, "Stress and systemic inflammation: Yin-yang dynamics in health and diseases." In Qing Yan (ed.). *Psychoneuroimmunology – Methods in Molecular Biology*, vol. 1781 (New York, NY: Humana Press, 2018), pp. 3–20; Qing Yan, "Neuroimmune imbalances and yin-yang dynamics in stress, anxiety, and depression." In Qing Yan (ed.). *Psychoneuroimmunology – Methods in Molecular Biology*, vol. 1781 (New York, NY: Humana Press, 2018), pp. 77–85.

94. Lau Tzu, Gia-Fu Feng, and Jane English, trans. *Tao Te Ching* (New York, NY: Random House, 2012).

95. Dean D. VonDras and Herman T. Blumenthal, "Biological, social-environmental, and psychological dialecticism: An integrated model of aging," *Basic and Applied Social Psychology 22*, no. 3 (2000), pp. 199–212.

96. Jerome S. Bruner, *Acts of Meaning* (Cambridge, MA: Harvard University Press, 1990); Timothy Onosahwo Iyendo, Patrick Chukwuemeke Uwajeh, and Ezennia Stephen Ikenna, "The therapeutic impacts of environmental design interventions on wellness in clinical settings: A narrative review," *Complementary Therapies in Clinical Practice 24* (2016), pp. 174–188; Matilda van den Bosch and Å. Ode Sang, "Urban natural environments

as nature-based solutions for improved public health – A systematic review of reviews," *Environmental Research 158* (2017), pp. 373–384.

97. Bellamy, *Looking Backward: 2000–1887*.

98. Ellen J. Langer and Judith Rodin, "The effects of choice and enhanced personal responsibility for the aged: A field experiment in an institutional setting," *Journal of Personality and Social Psychology 34*, no. 2 (1976), pp. 191–198; Judith Rodin and Ellen J. Langer. "Long-term effects of a control-relevant intervention with the institutionalized aged," *Journal of Personality and Social Psychology 35*, no. 12 (1977), pp. 897–902; Melanie H. Mallers, Maria Claver, and Lisa A. Lares, "Perceived control in the lives of older adults: The influence of Langer and Rodin's work on gerontological theory, policy, and practice," *The Gerontologist 54*, no. 1 (2013), pp. 67–74.

99. Terrence Hays, "Well-being in later life through music," *Australasian Journal on Ageing 24*, no. 1 (2005), pp. 28–32.

100. Hays, "Well-being in later life through music," p. 29.

101. Hays, "Well-being in later life through music," p. 30.

102. Hays, "Well-being in later life through music," p. 30.

103. Hays, "Well-being in later life through music," p. 31.

104. Darina V. Petrovsky, Justine S. Sefcik, and Pamela Z. Cacchione, "A qualitative exploration of choral singing in community-dwelling older adults," *Western Journal of Nursing Research 42*, no. 5 (2020), pp. 340–347.

105. Julene K. Johnson, Anita L. Stewart, Michael Acree, Anna M. Nápoles, Jason D. Flatt, Wendy B. Max, and Steven E. Gregorich, "A community choir intervention to promote well-being among diverse older adults: Results from the Community of Voices Trial," *The Journals of Gerontology: Series B 75*, no. 3 (2020), pp. 549–559.

106. Jane Southcott and Rohan Nethsinghe, "Resilient senior Russian-Australian voices: 'We live to sing and sing to live,'" *Applied Research in Quality of Life 14*, no. 1 (2019), pp. 39–58.

107. Jane Southcott and Sicong Li, "'Something to live for': Weekly singing classes at a Chinese university for retirees," *International Journal of Music Education 36*, no. 2 (2018), pp. 283–296.

108. R. Covington, "The aria never ends in the opera that's Casa Verdi," *Smithsonian 26*, no. 9 (1995), pp. 92–99; Karl D. Davis and Eugene Cannava, "The meaning of retirement for communally living retired performing artists," *Nursing Science Quarterly 8*, no. 1 (1995), pp. 8–16; Daniel Snowman, *Giuseppe Verdi: Composer* (New York, NY: Cavendish Square Publishing, 2016). www.casaverdi.it.

109. George Whitney Martin, *Verdi: His Music, Life, and Times* (Milwaukee, WI: Hal Leonard Corporation, 1992); Michael Steen, *The Lives and Times of the Great Composers* (London: Icon Books Ltd, 2011).

110. Christian Wernerand and Sandra K. Linke, "The German project called 'Triangel Partnerschaften'(Triangle Partnerships): Can music bridge the intergenerational gap?" *Gifted and Talented International 28* (2013), pp. 239–248. www.triangel-partnerschaften.de/english.

111. The George Center website: www.thegeorgecenter.com.

112. Danial Thomas and Vicky Abad (eds.). "Caring for clients, colleagues, commissioners and cash-flow." In *The Economics of Therapy* (London: Jessica Kingsley Publishers, 2017), pp. 24–37.

3 Hearing the Muse's Message: Changes in Sensory–Perceptual and Cognitive Processes

1. Ludwig van Beethoven, G. Wallace, trans., "To the Elector of Cologne, Frederick Maximilian," *Beethoven's Letters (1790–1826) from the Collection of Dr. Ludwig Nohl: Also His Letters to the Archduke Rudolph, Cardinal-Archbishop of Olmütz, KW, from the Collection of Dr. Ludwig Ritter Von Kochel, vol. 1* (This text is in the public domain), pp. 32–33.

2. Ray Jackendoff and Fred Lerdahl, "The capacity for music: What is it, and what's special about it?" *Cognition 100*, no. 1 (2006), pp. 33–72; Aniruddh D. Patel, "Language, music, syntax and the brain," *Nature Neuroscience 6*, no. 7 (2003), pp. 674–681.

3. Mary Priestley, "Music and the shadow," *Music Therapy 6*, no. 2 (1987), pp. 20–27.

4. Jason Martineau, *The Elements of Music: Melody, Rhythm, and Harmony* (New York, NY: Bloomsbury Publishing USA, 2008); Peter Jason Rentfrow and Andrew J. Oxenham, *Foundations in Music Psychology: Theory and Research* (Cambridge, MA: MIT Press, 2019).

5. Ludwig van Beethoven, G. Wallace, trans., "Letter to Wegeler," *Beethoven's Letters (1790–1826) from the Collection of Dr. Ludwig Nohl: Also His Letters to the Archduke Rudolph, Cardinal-Archbishop of Olmütz, KW, from the Collection of Dr. Ludwig Ritter Von Kochel, vol. 1*, pp. 65–68.

6. Avraham Z. Cooper, Sunil S. Nair, and Joseph M. Tremaglio, "Diagnosing Beethoven: A new take on an old patient," *The American Journal of Medicine 129*, no. 1 (2016), pp. 126–127; Brian F. McCabe, "XV Beethoven's deafness," *Annals of Otology, Rhinology & Laryngology 67*, no. 1 (1958), pp. 192–206; Stanley J. Oiseth, "Beethoven's autopsy revisited: A pathologist sounds a final note," *Journal of Medical Biography 25*, no. 3 (2017), pp. 139–147.

7. P. Harrison, "The effects of deafness on musical composition," *Journal of the Royal Society of Medicine 81*, no. 10 (1988), pp. 598–601.

8. Harrison, "The effects of deafness on musical composition," p. 598.

9. Martin Cooper and Edward Larkin, *The Last Decade 1817–1827* (Oxford, UK: Oxford University Press, 1970); Edoardo Saccenti, Age K. Smilde, and Wim H. M. Saris, "Beethoven's deafness and his three styles," *British Medical Journal 343* (2011), p. d7589.

10. Derek Clements-Croome (ed.). *Creating the Productive Workplace* (London: Taylor & Francis, 2006), p. xxvii.

11. Jayant M. Pinto, David W. Kern, Kristen E. Wroblewski, Rachel C. Chen, L. Philip Schumm, and Martha K. McClintock, "Sensory function: Insights from Wave 2 of the National Social Life, Health, and Aging Project," *Journals of Gerontology Series B: Psychological Sciences and Social Sciences 69*, no. 2 (2014), pp. S144–S153.

12. James L. Fozard and Sandra Gordon-Salant, "Changes in vision and hearing with aging." In James E. Birren, K. Warner Schaie, Ronald P. Abeles, Margaret Gatz, and Timothy A. Salthouse (eds.). *Handbook of the Psychology of Aging, vol. 2* (Oxford, UK: Gulf Professional Publishing, 2001), pp. 241–266.

13. H. J. Beckers, M. A. van Kooten-Noordzij, R. M. De Crom, J. S. Schouten, and C. A. Webers, "Visual complaints and eye problems in orchestral musicians," *Medical Problems of Performing Artists 31*, no. 3 (2016), pp. 140–144; Eddie F. Kadrmas, John A. Dyer, and George B. Bartley, "Visual problems of the aging musician," *Survey of Ophthalmology 40*, no. 4 (1996), pp. 338–341; Debbie Rohwer, "Health and wellness issues for adult band musicians," *Medical Problems of Performing Artists 23*, no. 2 (2008), pp. 54–58.

14. Stephen R. Lord, "Visual risk factors for falls in older people," *Age and Ageing 35*, no. 2 (2006), pp. ii42–ii45; Rebecca Q. Ivers Boptom, Robert G. Cumming, Paul Mitchell, and Karin Attebo, "Visual impairment and falls in older adults: The Blue Mountains Eye Study," *Journal of the American Geriatrics Society 46*, no. 1 (1998), pp. 58–64.

15. Linda Weaver Moore, Rose E. Constantino, and Marion Allen, "Severe visual impairment in older women," *Western Journal of Nursing Research 22*, no. 5 (2000), pp. 571–595.

16. Mary E. Fischer, Karen J. Cruickshanks, Barbara E. K. Klein, Ronald Klein, Carla R. Schubert, and Terry L. Wiley, "Multiple sensory impairment and quality of life," *Ophthalmic Epidemiology 16*, no. 6 (2009), pp. 346–353.

17. Pinto et al., "Sensory function: Insights from Wave 2 of the National Social Life, Health, and Aging Project," pp. S144-S153.

18. Larry J. Brant and James L. Fozard, "Age changes in pure-tone hearing thresholds in a longitudinal study of normal human aging," *The Journal of the Acoustical Society of America 88*, no. 2 (1990), pp. 813–820; George A. Gates and John H. Mills, "Presbycusis," *The Lancet 366*, no. 9491 (2005), pp. 1111–1120.

19. Bacterial infection of the middle ear may cause inflammation that damages the air pockets of the skull bone adjacent to the ear (i.e., mastoiditis), or the ossicles of the middle ear, and resultantly cause hearing impairment. Similarly, traumatic brain injury caused by explosion or concussion may injure the ear drum, middle ear, and inner ear structures, as well as the auditory pathway and centralized processing areas of the brain, producing loss of hearing or deafness. Further, damage to the cochlea of the inner ear or auditory centers of the brain may also occur due to stroke and neurological illnesses such as Huntington's disease and Parkinson's disease.

20. Don D. Coffman, "Music and quality of life in older adults," *Psychomusicology: A Journal of Research in Music Cognition 18*, no. 1–2 (2002), pp. 76–88; Ee-Munn Chia, Jie Jin Wang, Elena Rochtchina, Robert R. Cumming, Philip Newall, and Paul Mitchell, "Hearing impairment and health-related quality of life: The Blue Mountains Hearing Study," *Ear and Hearing 28*, no. 2 (2007), pp. 187–195; Dayna S. Dalton, Karen

J. Cruickshanks, Barbara E. K. Klein, Ronald Klein, Terry L. Wiley, and David M. Nondahl, "The impact of hearing loss on quality of life in older adults," *The Gerontologist 43*, no. 5 (2003), pp. 661–668.

21. Frank R. Lin, Roland Thorpe, Sandra Gordon-Salant, and Luigi Ferrucci, "Hearing loss prevalence and risk factors among older adults in the United States," *Journals of Gerontology Series A: Biomedical Sciences and Medical Sciences 66*, no. 5 (2011), pp. 582–590.

22. J. M. Ordy, K. R. Brizzee, T. Beavers, and P. Medart, "Age differences in the functional and structural organization of the auditory system in man," *Sensory Systems and Communication in the Elderly, Aging 10* (1979), pp. 153–166.

23. Andrew J. Oxenham, "How we hear: The perception and neural coding of sound," *Annual Review of Psychology 69* (2018), pp. 27–50.

24. Lin et al., "Hearing loss prevalence and risk factors among older adults in the United States," pp. 582–590.

25. Samuel Rosen, Moe Bergman, Dietrich Plester, Aly El-Mofty, and Mohamed Hamad Satti, "LXII presbycusis study of a relatively noise-free population in the Sudan," *Annals of Otology, Rhinology & Laryngology 71*, no. 3 (1962), pp. 727–743.

26. Paul B. Baltes, Hayne W. Reese, and John R. Nesselroade, *Life-Span Developmental Psychology: Introduction to Research Methods* (New York, NY: Psychology Press, 2014).

27. Gretchen Stevens, Seth Flaxman, Emma Brunskill, Maya Mascarenhas, Colin D. Mathers, and Mariel Finucane, "Global and regional hearing impairment prevalence: An analysis of 42 studies in 29 countries," *The European Journal of Public Health 23*, no. 1 (2011), pp. 146–152.

28. Heli Laitinen, "Factors affecting the use of hearing protectors among classical music players," *Noise and Health 7*, no. 26 (2005), pp. 21–29.

29. Pouryaghoub Gholamreza, Ramin Mehrdad, and Saeed Pourhosein, "Noise-induced hearing loss among professional musicians," *Journal of Occupational Health 16*–0217 (2016), pp. 33–37.

30. R. R. A. Coles, M. E. Lutman, and J. T. Buffin, "Guidelines on the diagnosis of noise-induced hearing loss for medicolegal purposes," *Clinical Otolaryngology & Allied Sciences 25*, no. 4 (2000), pp. 264–273.

31. Gholamreza et al., "Noise-induced hearing loss among professional musicians," pp. 33–37.

32. Fei Zhao, Vinaya K. C. Manchaiah, David French, and Sharon M. Price, "Music exposure and hearing disorders: An overview," *International Journal of Audiology 49*, no. 1 (2010), pp. 54–64.

33. William E. Daniell, Susan S. Swan, Mary M. McDaniel, Janice E. Camp, Martin A. Cohen, and John G. Stebbins, "Noise exposure and hearing loss prevention programmes after 20 years of regulations in the United States," *Occupational and Environmental Medicine 63*, no. 5 (2006), pp. 343–351; Sally Lechlitner Lusk, David L. Ronis, and Leslie Martel Baer, "A comparison of multiple indicators: Observations, supervisor report, and self-report as measures of workers' hearing protection use," *Evaluation & The Health Professions 18*, no. 1 (1995), pp. 51–63.

34. Laitinen, "Factors affecting the use of hearing protectors among classical music players," pp. 21–29.

35. Nicolas Schmuziger, Jochen Patscheke, and Rudolf Probst, "Hearing in nonprofessional pop/rock musicians," *Ear and Hearing 27*, no. 4 (2006), pp. 321–330.

36. Richard L. Doty and Vidyulata Kamathm, "The influences of age on olfaction: A review," *Frontiers in Psychology 5* (2014), p. 20; Annika Brämerson, Leif Johansson, Lars Ek, Steven Nordin, and Mats Bende, "Prevalence of olfactory dysfunction: The Skövde population-based study," *The Laryngoscope 114*, no. 4 (2004), pp. 733–737.

37. Richard L. Doty, Paul Shaman, Steven L. Applebaum, Ronita Giberson, Lenore Siksorski, and Lysa Rosenberg, "Smell identification ability: Changes with age," *Science 226*, no. 4681 (1984), pp. 1441–1443.

38. Joseph C. Stevens, L. Alberto Cruz, Julianne M. Hoffman, and Matthew Q. Patterson, "Taste sensitivity and aging: High incidence of decline revealed by repeated threshold measures," *Chemical Senses 20*, no. 4 (1995), pp. 451–459.

39. Jos Mojet, Elly Christ-Hazelhof, and Johannes Heidema, "Taste perception with age: Generic or specific losses in threshold sensitivity to the five basic tastes?" *Chemical Senses 26*, no. 7 (2001), pp. 845–860.

40. Richard L. Doty, "Clinical studies of olfaction," *Chemical Senses 30*, no. 1 (2005), pp. i207–i209; Karl-Bernd Hüttenbrink, Thomas Hummel, Daniela Berg, Thomas Gasser, and Antje Hähner, "Olfactory dysfunction: Common in later life and early warning of neurodegenerative disease," *Deutsches Ärzteblatt International 110*, nos. 1–2 (2013), pp. 1–7.

41. Carl M. Philpott and Duncan Boak, "The impact of olfactory disorders in the United Kingdom," *Chemical Senses 39*, no. 8 (2014), pp. 711–718; Marion Rochet, Wissam El-Hage, Sami Richa, François Kazour, and Boriana Atanasova, "Depression, olfaction, and quality of life: A mutual relationship," *Brain Sciences 8*, no. 5 (2018), p. 80.

42. Jayant M. Pinto, Kristen E. Wroblewski, David W. Kern, L. Philip Schumm, and Martha K. McClintock, "Olfactory dysfunction predicts 5-year mortality in older adults," *PLOS One 9*, no. 10 (2014), p. e107541; Robert S. Wilson, Lei Yu, and David A. Bennett, "Odor identification and mortality in old age," *Chemical Senses 36*, no. 1 (2010), pp. 63–67.

43. Doty and Kamathm, "The influences of age on olfaction: A review," p. 20.

44. Katrin Markovic, Udo Reulbach, Agapi Vassiliadu, Jens Lunkenheimer, Birgit Lunkenheimer, Rita Spannenberger, and Norbert Thuerauf, "Good news for elderly persons: Olfactory pleasure increases at later stages of the life span," *The Journals of Gerontology Series A: Biological Sciences and Medical Sciences 62*, no. 11 (2007), pp. 1287–1293.

45. Anthony Remaud, Cécile Thuong-Cong, and Martin Bilodeau, "Age-related changes in dynamic postural control and attentional demands are minimally affected by local muscle fatigue," *Frontiers in Aging Neuroscience 7* (2016), p. 257.

46. Matthiue P. Boisgontier, Isabelle Olivier, Olivier Chenu, and Vincent Nougier, "Presbypropria: The effects of physiological ageing on proprioceptive control," *Age 34*, no. 5 (2012), pp. 1179–1194.

47. Marie-Louise Bird, Jane Pittaway, Isobel Cuisick, Megan Rattray, and Kiran Ahuja, "Age-related changes in physical fall risk factors: Results from a 3-year follow-up of community dwelling older adults in Tasmania, Australia," *International Journal of Environmental Research and Public Health 10*, no. 11 (2013), pp. 5989–5997; Horst R. Konrad, Marian Girardi, and Robert Helfert, "Balance and aging," *The Laryngoscope 109*, no. 9 (1999), pp. 1454–1460.

48. Alice C. Scheffer, Marieke J. Schuurmans, Nynke Van Dijk, Truus Van Der Hooft, and Sophia E. De Rooij, "Fear of falling: Measurement strategy, prevalence, risk factors and consequences among older persons," *Age and Ageing 37*, no. 1 (2008), pp. 19–24.

49. Mizue Suzuki, Naomi Ohyama, Kiyomi Yamada, and Masao Kanamori, "The relationship between fear of falling, activities of daily living and quality of life among elderly individuals," *Nursing & Health Sciences 4*, no. 4 (2002), pp. 155–161; G. Salkeld, Shanthi N. Ameratunga, I. D. Cameron, R. G. Cumming, S. Easter, J. Seymour, S. E. Kurrle, S. Quine, and Paul M. Brown, "Quality of life related to fear of falling and hip fracture in older women: A time trade off study commentary: Older people's perspectives on life after hip fractures," *British Medical Journal 320*, no. 7231 (2000), pp. 341–346.

50. Steven L. Wolf, Huiman X. Barnhart, Nancy G. Kutner, Elizabeth McNeely, Carol Coogler, Tingsen Xu, and Atlanta FICSIT Group, "Reducing frailty and falls in older persons: An investigation of Tai Chi and computerized balance training," *Journal of the American Geriatrics Society 44*, no. 5 (1996), pp. 489–497.

51. Florence Everett Goold, "The Eurhythmics of Jacques-Dalcroze," *American Physical Education Review 20*, no. 1 (1915), pp. 35–37.

52. Andrea Trombetti, Mélany Hars, François R. Herrmann, Reto W. Kressig, Serge Ferrari, and René Rizzoli, "Effect of music-based multitask training on gait, balance, and fall risk in elderly people: A randomized controlled trial," *Archives of Internal Medicine 171*, no. 6 (2011), pp. 525–533.

53. Patricia T. Alpert, Sally K. Miller, Harvey Wallmann, Richard Havey, Chad Cross, Theresa Chevalia, Carrie B. Gillis, and Keshavan Kodandapari, "The effect of modified jazz dance on balance, cognition, and mood in older adults," *Journal of the American Academy of Nurse Practitioners 21*, no. 2 (2009), pp. 108–115.

54. Sibel Eyigor, Hale Karapolat, Berrin Durmaz, Ugur Ibisoglu, and Serap Cakir, "A randomized controlled trial of Turkish folklore dance on the physical performance, balance, depression and quality of life in older women," *Archives of Gerontology and Geriatrics 48*, no. 1 (2009), pp. 84–88.

55. Ryosuke Shigematsu, Milan Chang, Noriko Yabushita, Tomoaki Sakai, Masaki Nakagaichi, Hosung Nho, and Kiyoji Tanaka, "Dance-based aerobic exercise may improve indices of falling risk in older women," *Age and Ageing 31*, no. 4 (2002), pp. 261–266.

56. Giorgos Sofianidis, Vassilia Hatzitaki, Stella Douka, and Giorgos Grouios, "Effect of a 10-week traditional dance program on static and dynamic balance control in elderly adults," *Journal of Aging and Physical Activity 17*, no. 2 (2009), pp. 167–180.

57. D. R. Kenshalo, "Age changes in touch, vibration, temperature, kinesthesis and pain sensitivity." In James E. Birren and K. Warner Schaie (eds.). *Handbook of the Psychology of Aging* (1977), pp. 562–579; Stefan Lautenbacher, Jan H. Peters, Michael Heesen, Jennifer Scheel, and Miriam Kunz, "Age changes in pain perception: A systematic review and meta-analysis of age effects on pain and tolerance thresholds," *Neuroscience & Biobehavioral Reviews 75* (2017), pp. 104–113; Ronalid T. Verrillo, *Sensory Research: Multimodal Perspectives* (London: Psychology Press, 2014).

58. Jeffrey Berko, Deborah D. Ingram, Shubhayu Saha, and Jennifer D. Parker, "Deaths attributed to heat, cold, and other weather events in the United States, 2006–2010," *National Health Statistics Reports*, no. 76 (Hyattsville, MD: National Center for Health Statistics, 2014), pp. 1–16.

59. Sylvia M. Gustin, Lucinda A. Burke, Chris C. Peck, Greg M. Murray, and Luke A. Henderson, "Pain and personality: Do individuals with different forms of chronic pain exhibit a mutual personality?" *Pain Practice 16*, no. 4 (2016), pp. 486–494.

60. H. El Tumi, M. I. Johnson, P. B. F. Dantas, M. J. Maynard, and O. A. Tashani, "Age-related changes in pain sensitivity in healthy humans: A systematic review with meta-analysis," *European Journal of Pain 21*, no. 6 (2017), pp. 955–964.

61. Gustin et al., "Pain and personality: Do individuals with different forms of chronic pain exhibit a mutual personality?" pp. 486–494.

62. Inge E. Lamé, Madelon L. Peters, Johan W. S. Vlaeyen, Maarten V. Kleef, and Jacob Patijn, "Quality of life in chronic pain is more associated with beliefs about pain, than with pain intensity," *European Journal of Pain 9*, no. 1 (2005), pp. 15–24.

63. Matthew J. Bair, Rebecca L. Robinson, Wayne Katon, and Kurt Kroenke, "Depression and pain comorbidity: A literature review," *Archives of Internal Medicine 163*, no. 20 (2003), pp. 2433–2445; Kate L. Lapane, Brian J. Quilliam, Wing Chow, and Myoung Kim, "The association between pain and measures of well-being among nursing home residents," *Journal of the American Medical Directors Association 13*, no. 4 (2012), pp. 344–349; David Niv and Shulamith Kreitler, "Pain and quality of life," *Pain Practice 1*, no. 2 (2001), pp. 150–161; Adley Tsang, Michael Von Korff, Sing Lee, Jordi Alonso, Elie Karam, Matthias C. Angermeyer, Guilherme Luiz Guimaraes Borges, et al., "Common chronic pain conditions in developed and developing countries: Gender and age differences and comorbidity with depression-anxiety disorders," *The Journal of Pain 9*, no. 10 (2008), pp. 883–891.

64. Ruth McCaffrey and Edward Freeman, "Effect of music on chronic osteoarthritis pain in older people," *Journal of Advanced Nursing 44*, no. 5 (2003), pp. 517–524; Sandra L. Siedliecki and Marion Good, "Effect of music on

power, pain, depression and disability," *Journal of Advanced Nursing 54*, no. 5 (2006), pp. 553–562.

65. Colleen M. Zelazny, "Therapeutic instrumental music playing in hand rehabilitation for older adults with osteoarthritis: Four case studies," *Journal of Music Therapy 38*, no. 2 (2001), pp. 97–113.

66. M. S. Cepeda, D. B. Carr, J. Lau, and H. Alvarez, "Music for pain relief (Cochrane Review)," *The Cochrane Library 2*, no. 2 (New York, NY: John Wiley & Sons, 2006).

67. Petr Janata, Jeffrey L. Birk, Barbara Tillmann, and Jamshed J. Bharucha, "Online detection of tonal pop-out in modulating contexts," *Music Perception: An Interdisciplinary Journal 20*, no. 3 (2003), pp. 283–305.

68. Paul Verhaeghen and John Cerella, "Aging, executive control, and attention: A review of meta-analyses," *Neuroscience & Biobehavioral Reviews 26*, no. 7 (2002), pp. 849–857.

69. Celine Maes, Jolien Gooijers, Jean-Jacques Orban de Xivry, Stephan P. Swinnen, and Matthieu P. Boisgontier, "Two hands, one brain, and aging," *Neuroscience & Biobehavioral Reviews 75* (2017), pp. 234–256; Joan M. McDowd and Raymond J. Shaw, "Attention and aging: A functional perspective." In F. I. M. Craik and T. A. Salthouse (eds.). *The Handbook of Aging and Cognition* 2nd ed. (Mahwah, NJ: Erlbaum, 2000), pp. 221–292.

70. Karlene Ball and George Rebok, "Evaluating the driving ability of older adults," *Journal of Applied Gerontology 13*, no. 1 (1994), pp. 20–38.

71. Yung-Ching Liu, "Comparative study of the effects of auditory, visual and multimodality displays on drivers' performance in advanced traveller information systems," *Ergonomics 44*, no. 4 (2001), pp. 425–442.

72. Dana L. Strait, Nina Kraus, Alexandra Parbery-Clark, and Richard Ashley, "Musical experience shapes top-down auditory mechanisms: Evidence from masking and auditory attention performance," *Hearing Research 261*, nos. 1–2 (2010), pp. 22–29.

73. Dana L. Strait and Nina Kraus, "Can you hear me now? Musical training shapes functional brain networks for selective auditory attention and hearing speech in noise," *Frontiers in Psychology 2* (2011), p. 113.

74. Brenda Hanna-Pladdy and Alicia MacKay, "The relation between instrumental musical activity and cognitive aging," *Neuropsychology 25*, no. 3 (2011), p. 378.

75. James E. Birren and Laurel M. Fisher, "Aging and speed of behavior: Possible consequences for psychological functioning," *Annual Review of Psychology 46*, no. 1 (1995), pp. 329–353; Timothy A. Salthouse, "The processing-speed theory of adult age differences in cognition," *Psychological Review 103*, no. 3 (1996), pp. 403–428.

76. James H. Cole and Katja Franke, "Predicting age using neuroimaging: Innovative brain ageing biomarkers," *Trends in Neurosciences 40*, no. 12 (2017), pp. 681–690; Stephen M. Smith, Lloyd T. Elliott, Fidel Alfaro-Almagro, Paul McCarthy, Thomas E. Nichols, Gwenaëlle Douaud, and Karla L. Miller, "Brain aging comprises many modes of structural and

functional change with distinct genetic and biophysical Associations," *BioRxiv* (2020), p. 802686.

77. Sian L. Beilock, Bennett I. Bertenthal, Annette M. McCoy, and Thomas H. Carr, "Haste does not always make waste: Expertise, direction of attention, and speed versus accuracy in performing sensorimotor skills," *Psychonomic Bulletin & Review 11*, no. 2 (2004), pp. 373–379.

78. Robert A. Duke, Carla Davis Cash, and Sarah E. Allen, "Focus of attention affects performance of motor skills in music," *Journal of Research in Music Education 59*, no. 1 (2011), pp. 44–55.

79. Timothy A. Salthouse, "Effects of age and skill in typing," *Journal of Experimental Psychology: General 113*, no. 3 (1984), pp. 345–371.

80. Carolyn Drake and Caroline Palmer, "Skill acquisition in music performance: Relations between planning and temporal control," *Cognition 74*, no. 1 (2000), pp. 1–32; Christine L. MacKenzie, Judith A. Nelson-Schultz, and Barry L. Wills, "A preliminary investigation of motor programming in piano performance as a function of skill level." In *The Acquisition of Symbolic Skills* (Springer, Boston, MA, 1983), pp. 283–292; Caroline Palmer and Carolyn Drake, "Monitoring and planning capacities in the acquisition of music performance skills," *Canadian Journal of Experimental Psychology/ Revue Canadienne de Psychologie Expérimentale 51*, no. 4 (1997), p. 369.

81. Frances H. Rauscher, "Can music instruction affect children's cognitive development?" *ERIC Digest* (2003); Frances H. Rauscher, Gordon L. Shaw, and Katherine N. Ky, "Listening to Mozart enhances spatial-temporal reasoning: Towards a neurophysiological basis," *Neuroscience Letters 185*, no. 1 (1995), pp. 44–47.

82. Sara Bottiroli, Alessia Rosi, Riccardo Russo, Tomaso Vecchi, and Elena Cavallini, "The cognitive effects of listening to background music on older adults: Processing speed improves with upbeat music, while memory seems to benefit from both upbeat and downbeat music," *Frontiers in Aging Neuroscience 6* (2014), p. 284; Nicola Mammarella, Beth Fairfield, and Cesare Cornoldi, "Does music enhance cognitive performance in healthy older adults? The Vivaldi Effect," *Aging Clinical and Experimental Research 19*, no. 5 (2007), pp. 394–399.

83. Caterina Padulo, Nicola Mammarella, Alfredo Brancucci, Mario Altamura, and Beth Fairfield, "The effects of music on spatial reasoning," *Psychological Research* (2019), pp. 1–6.

84. Juliane Kämpfe, Peter Sedlmeier, and Frank Renkewitz, "The impact of background music on adult listeners: A meta-analysis," *Psychology of Music 39*, no. 4 (2011), pp. 424–448.

85. Daniel L. Schacter and Donna Rose Addis, "The cognitive neuroscience of constructive memory: Remembering the past and imagining the future," *Philosophical Transactions of the Royal Society B: Biological Sciences 362*, no. 1481 (2007), pp. 773–786.

86. Kenneth A. Norman and Daniel L. Schacter, "False recognition in younger and older adults: Exploring the characteristics of illusory memories," *Memory & Cognition 25*, no. 6 (1997), pp. 838–848.

87. Andrea R. Halpern and James C. Bartlett, "Aging and memory for music: A review," *Psychomusicology: A Journal of Research in Music Cognition 18*, nos. 1–2 (2002), pp. 10–27.

88. Mikko Sams, Riitta Hari, Josi Rif, and Jukka Knuutila, "The human auditory sensory memory trace persists about 10 sec: Neuromagnetic evidence," *Journal of Cognitive Neuroscience 5*, no. 3 (1993), pp. 363–370.

89. Stefan Koelsch, Thomas C. Gunter, Matthias Wittfoth, and Daniela Sammler, "Interaction between syntax processing in language and in music: An ERP study," *Journal of Cognitive Neuroscience 17*, no. 10 (2005), pp. 1565–1577.

90. Stefan Koelsch, Thomas Fritz, Katrin Schulze, David Alsop, and Gottfried Schlaug, "Adults and children processing music: An fMRI study," *Neuroimage 25*, no. 4 (2005), pp. 1068–1076.

91. Jordan Smith, "Does Music Become More Emotional as You Get Older?" *CMUSE*, April 1, 2016. www.cmuse.org/does-music-become-more-emotional-as-you-get-older (accessed September 18, 2018).

92. Jenny M. Groarke and Michael J. Hogan, "Enhancing wellbeing: An emerging model of the adaptive," *Journal of Theory and Research 9*, no. 2 (2015), pp. 95–115.

93. Nash Unsworth and Randall W. Engle, "On the division of short-term and working memory: An examination of simple and complex span and their relation to higher order abilities," *Psychological Bulletin 133*, no. 6 (2007), pp. 1038–1066.

94. Susan E. Gathercol and Alan D. Baddeley, *Working Memory and Language* (New York, NY: Psychology Press, 2014); Robert H. Logie, *Visuo-Spatial Working Memory* (New York, NY: Psychology Press, 2014).

95. Timothy A. Salthouse, *Theoretical Perspectives on Cognitive Aging* (Hillsdale, NJ: Erlbaum, 1991).

96. Yana Fandakova, Myriam C. Sander, Markus Werkle-Bergner, and Yee Lee Shing, "Age differences in short-term memory binding are related to working memory performance across the lifespan," *Psychology and Aging 29*, no. 1 (2014), pp. 140–149.

97. Elizabeth L. Glisky, "Changes in cognitive function in human aging." In David R. Riddle (ed.). *Brain Aging: Models, Methods, and Mechanisms* (New York, NY: Taylor and Francis, 2007), pp. 3–20; Cheryl L. Grady and Fergus I. M. Craik, "Changes in memory processing with age," *Current Opinion in Neurobiology 10*, no. 2 (2000), pp. 224–231; Salthouse, *Theoretical Perspectives on Cognitive Aging*.

98. Rossana De Beni and Paola Palladino, "Decline in working memory updating through ageing: Intrusion error analyses," *Memory 12*, no. 1 (2004), pp. 75–89; Monica Fabiani, Benjamin Zimmerman, and Gabriele Gratton, "Working memory and aging: A review." In Pierre Jolicoeur, Christine Lefebvre, and Julio Martinez-Trujillo (eds.). *Mechanisms of Sensory Working Memory: Attention and Performance XXV* (New York, NY: Academic Press, 2015), pp. 131–149.

99. Elliot M. Tucker-Drob, "Neurocognitive functions and everyday functions change together in old age," *Neuropsychology 25*, no. 3 (2011), pp. 368–377.

100. Patrick Rabbitt, "Mild hearing loss can cause apparent memory failures which increase with age and reduce with IQ," *Acta Oto-Laryngologica 111*, no. 476 (1991), pp. 167–176.

101. Bob Snyder and Robert Snyder, *Music and Memory: An Introduction* (Cambridge, MA: MIT Press, 2000).

102. Larry R. Squire, "Memory systems of the brain: A brief history and current perspective," *Neurobiology of Learning and Memory 82*, no. 3 (2004), pp. 171–177.

103. Nichole Lighthall, Lindsay Conner, and Kelly S. Giovanello, "Learning and memory in the aging brain: The function of declarative and nondeclarative memory over the life span," *PsyArXiv*, August 1 (2018). https://doi.org/10 .31234/osf.io/eqym4; Emma V. Ward and David R. Shanks, "Implicit memory and cognitive aging." In *Oxford Research Encyclopedia of Psychology* (2018).

104. Nils C. J. Müller, Lisa Genzel, Boris N. Konrad, Marcel Pawlowski, David Neville, Guillén Fernández, Axel Steiger, and Martin Dresler, "Motor skills enhance procedural memory formation and protect against age-related decline," *PLOS One 11*, no. 6 (2016).

105. Lars Bäckman, "Recognition memory across the adult life span: The role of prior knowledge," *Memory & Cognition 19*, no. 1 (1991), pp. 63–71.

106. Sherrie L. Parks and Stephanie Clancy Dollinger, "The positivity effect and auditory recognition memory for musical excerpts in young, middle-aged, and older adults," *Psychomusicology: Music, Mind, and Brain 24*, no. 4 (2014), p. 298.

107. Harry P. Bahrick, Phyllis O. Bahrick, and Roy P. Wittlinger, "Fifty years of memory for names and faces: A cross-sectional approach," *Journal of Experimental Psychology: General 104*, no. 1 (1975), pp. 54–75.

108. Joseph M. Fitzgerald, "Autobiographical memory and social cognition: Development of the remembered self in adulthood." In T. M. Hess and F. Blanchard-Fields (eds.). *Social Cognition and Aging* (San Diego, CA: Academic Press, 1999), pp. 143–171; Peggy L. St. Jacques and Brian Levine, "Ageing and autobiographical memory for emotional and neutral events," *Memory 15*, no. 2 (2007), pp. 129–144.

109. Hervé Platel, Jean-Claude Baron, Béatrice Desgranges, Frédéric Bernard, and Francis Eustache, "Semantic and episodic memory of music are subserved by distinct neural networks," *Neuroimage 20*, no. 1 (2003), pp. 244–256.

110. Lars Bäckman and Lars-Göran Nilsson, "Semantic memory functioning across the adult life span," *European Psychologist 1*, no. 1 (1996), pp. 27–33; Amee Baird and Séverine Samson, "Music and dementia," *Progress in Brain Research 217* (2015), pp. 207–235; Ashley D. Vanstone, Ritu Sikka, Leila Tangness, Rosalind Sham, Angeles Garcia, and Lola L. Cuddy, "Episodic and semantic memory for melodies in Alzheimer's disease," *Music Perception: An Interdisciplinary Journal 29*, no. 5 (2012), pp. 501–507.

111. James D. Churchill, Jessica J. Stanis, Cyrus Press, Michael Kushelev, and William T. Greenough, "Is procedural memory relatively spared from age effects?" *Neurobiology of Aging 24*, no. 6 (2003), pp. 883–892.

112. A. Baird and S. Samson, "Music and dementia" (2015), pp. 207–235.

113. Luc P. De Vreese, Mirco Neri, Mario Fioravanti, Luciano Belloi, and Orazio Zanetti, "Memory rehabilitation in Alzheimer's disease: A review of progress," *International Journal of Geriatric Psychiatry 16*, no. 8 (2001), pp. 794–809; Orazio Zanetti, Gabriele Zanieri, Giuseppina Di Giovanni, Luc Pietre De Vreese, Alessandra Pezzini, Tiziana Metitieri, and Marco Trabucchi, "Effectiveness of procedural memory stimulation in mild Alzheimer's disease patients: A controlled study," *Neuropsychological Rehabilitation 11*, nos. 3–4 (2001), pp. 263–272.

114. B. Hermelin, N. O'Connor, S. Lee, and D. Treffert. "Intelligence and musical improvisation," *Psychological Medicine 19*, no. 2 (1989), pp. 447–457.

115. Ken Kamoche, Miguel Pina, E. Cunha, and Joao Vieira da Cunha, "Towards a theory of organizational improvisation: Looking beyond the jazz metaphor," *Journal of Management Studies 40*, no. 8 (2003), pp. 2023–2051.

116. Patricia Shehan Campbell, "Learning to improvise music, improvising to learn music." In Gabriel Solis and Bruno Nettl (eds.). *Musical Improvisation: Art, Education, and Society* (Champaign, IL: University of Illinois Press, 2009), pp. 119–142; Phillip N. Johnson-Laird, "How jazz musicians improvise," *Music Perception: An Interdisciplinary Journal 19*, no. 3 (2002), pp. 415–442.

117. William L. Berz, "Working memory in music: A theoretical model," *Music Perception: An Interdisciplinary Journal 12*, no. 3 (1995), pp. 353–364; Robert B. Glassman, "Hypothesized neural dynamics of working memory: Several chunks might be marked simultaneously by harmonic frequencies within an octave band of brain waves," *Brain Research Bulletin 50*, no. 2 (1999), pp. 77–93; Petr Janata, Barbara Tillmann, and Jamshed J. Bharucha, "Listening to polyphonic music recruits domain: General attention and working memory circuits," *Cognitive, Affective, & Behavioral Neuroscience 2*, no. 2 (2002), pp. 121–140; Adam Ockelford, "A music module in working memory? Evidence from the performance of a prodigious musical savant," *Musicae Scientiae 11*, no. 2 (2007), pp. 5–36.

118. Stefan Koelsch, Thomas C. Gunter, Matthias Wittfoth, and Daniela Sammler, "Interaction between syntax processing in language and in music: An ERP study," *Journal of Cognitive Neuroscience 17*, no. 10 (2005), pp. 1565–1577; Aniruddh D. Patel, "Language, music, syntax and the brain," *Nature Neuroscience 6*, no. 7 (2003), pp. 674–681; Lindsey M. Thompson and Marjorie J. Yankeelov, "Music and the phonological loop." In C. E. Cambouropoulos, C. Tsougras, P. Mavromatis, and K. Pastiadis (eds.). *Proceedings of the 12th International Conference on Music Perception and Cognition and the 8th Triennial Conference of the European Society for the Cognitive Sciences of Music* (2012), pp. 980–986; Robert J. Zatorre and Andrea R. Halpern, "Mental concerts: Musical imagery and auditory cortex," *Neuron 47*, no. 1 (2005), pp. 9–12.

119. Andrea Halpern and Robert J. Zatorre, "When that tune runs through your head: A PET investigation of auditory imagery for familiar melodies,"

Cerebral Cortex 9, no. 7 (1999), pp. 697–704; Johnson-Laird, "How jazz musicians improvise" (2002), pp. 415–442; Snyder and Snyder, *Music and Memory: An Introduction.*

120. Rosemary Mountain, "Composers and imagery: Myths and realities." In R. I. Godøy and H. Jörgensen (eds.). *Musical Imagery* (Lisse, Netherlands: Swets & Zeitlinger, 2001), pp. 271–288; Zatorre and Halpern, "When that tune runs through your head: A PET investigation of auditory imagery for familiar melodies," pp. 9–12.

121. Ludwig van Beethoven, G. Wallace, trans., "To Pastor Amenda," *Beethoven's Letters (1790–1826) from the Collection of Dr. Ludwig Nohl: Also His Letters to the Archduke Rudolph, Cardinal-Archbishop of Olmütz, KW, from the Collection of Dr. Ludwig Ritter Von Kochel 1*, pp. 59–60.

122. Nicolas Farrugia, Kelly Jakubowski, Rhodri Cusack, and Lauren Stewart, "Tunes stuck in your brain: The frequency and affective evaluation of involuntary musical imagery correlate with cortical structure," *Consciousness and Cognition 35* (2015), pp. 66–77.

123. Mildred P. Dacog, "Remembering my roots, interrogating the present, envisioning my future," *Educational Insights 8*, no. 2 (2003).

4 Sing a New Song! Therapeutic Interventions with Music

1. US Congress, Hearing before the Special Committee on Aging, *Forever Young: Music and Aging*, 101st Congress, Session 1, August 1, 1991, Serial No. 102-9 (Washington DC: US Government Printing Office, 1992), p. 98.

2. World Health Organization, "Dementia," *Newsroom Fact Sheets*, May 14, 2019. www.who.int/en/news-room/fact-sheets/detail/dementia (accessed May 20, 2019).

3. Fiona E. Matthews, Antony Arthur, Linda E. Barnes, John Bond, Carol Jagger, Louise Robinson, Carol Brayne, and Medical Research Council Cognitive Function and Ageing Collaboration, "A two-decade comparison of prevalence of dementia in individuals aged 65 years and older from three geographical areas of England: Results of the cognitive function and ageing study I and II," *The Lancet 382*, no. 9902 (2013), pp. 1405–1412.

4. Miriam L. Haaksma, Lara R. Vilela, Alessandra Marengoni, Amaia Calderón-Larrañaga, Jeannie-Marie S. Leoutsakos, Marcel G. M. Olde Rikkert, and René J. F. Melis, "Comorbidity and progression of late onset Alzheimer's disease: A systematic review," *PlOS One 12*, no. 5 (2017), p. e0177044; Gill Livingston, Andrew Sommerlad, Vasiliki Orgeta, Sergi G. Costafreda, Jonathan Huntley, David Ames, Clive Ballard, et al., "Dementia prevention, intervention, and care," *The Lancet 390*, no. 10113 (2017), pp. 2673–2734; Linda Teri, Louise E. Ferretti, Laura E. Gibbons, Rebecca G. Logsdon, Susan M. McCurry, Walter A. Kukull, Wayne C. McCormick, James D. Bowen, and Eric B. Larson, "Anxiety in Alzheimer's disease: Prevalence and comorbidity,"

Journals of Gerontology Series A: Biomedical Sciences and Medical Sciences 54, no. 7 (1999), pp. M348–M352.

5. Helen C. Kales, Laura N. Gitlin, and Constantine G. Lyketsos, "Assessment and management of behavioral and psychological symptoms of dementia," *British Medical Journal 350* (2015), p. h369; Livingston et al., "Dementia prevention, intervention, and care," pp. 2673–2734.

6. Julian Hughes, C. Julian, Stephen J. Louw, and Steven R. Sabat (eds.). *Dementia: Mind, Meaning, and the Person* (OUP: Oxford, 2006); Kathryn G. Kietzman, "Using a "person-centered" approach to improve care coordination: Opportunities emerging from the Affordable Care Act," *Journal of Geriatric Care Management Journal 22*, no. 2 (2012), pp. 13–19; Janice Penrod, Fang Yu, Ann Kolanowski, Donna M. Fick, Susan J. Loeb, and Judith E. Hupcey, "Reframing person-centered nursing care for persons with dementia," *Research and Theory for Nursing Practice 21*, no. 1 (2007), pp. 57–72.

7. Jan Baars, Joseph Dohmen, Amanda Grenier, and Chris Phillipson (eds.). *Ageing, Meaning and Social Structure: Connecting Critical and Humanistic Gerontology* (Chicago IL: Policy Press, 2013).

8. Carl G. Jung, "The archetypes and the collective unconscious," *Volume 9, I, of the Collected Works of C. G. Jung*, 2nd ed. (Princeton, NJ: Princeton University Press, 1969), pp. 4–5.

9. Jung, *Volume 9, I, of the Collected Works of C. G. Jung*, 2nd ed., pp. 3–53.

10. Jung, *Volume 9, I, of the Collected Works of C. G. Jung*, 2nd ed., p. 219.

11. Thomas R. Cole and Michelle Sierpina, "Humanistic gerontology and the meaning(s) of aging." In Janet M. Wilmoth and Kenneth F. Ferraro (eds.). *Gerontology: Perspectives and Issues, 3rd ed.* (New York, NY: Spring, 2007), pp. 245–263.

12. Emily LaBarge, Dean VonDras, and Cheryl Wingbermuehl, "An analysis of themes and feelings from a support group for people with Alzheimer's disease," *Psychotherapy: Theory, Research, Practice, Training 35*, no. 4 (1998), pp. 537–544.

13. Susan McCurry, *When a Family Member Has Dementia: Steps to Becoming a Resilient Caregiver* (Santa Barbara, CA: Greenwood Publishing Group, 2006), p. xii.

14. G. P. Mulley, "Differential diagnosis of dementia," *British Medical Journal (Clinical Research ed.) 292*, no. 6533 (1986), pp. 1416–1418.

15. Kristan Arp, "Old age in existentialist perspective." In Geoffrey Scarre (ed.). *The Palgrave Handbook of the Philosophy of Aging* (London: Palgrave Macmillan, 2016), pp. 135–148.

16. Correne A. DeCarlo, Holly A. Tuokko, Dorothy Williams, Roger A. Dixon, and Stuart W. S. MacDonald, "BioAge: Toward a multi-determined, mechanistic account of cognitive aging," *Ageing Research Reviews 18* (2014), pp. 95–105; Cheryl L. Grady, "Functional brain imaging and age-related changes in cognition," *Biological Psychology 54*, nos. 1–3 (2000), pp. 259–281; Goran Papenburg, Ulman Lindenberger, and Lars Backman, "Genetic and the cognitive science of aging." In Roberto Cabeza, Lars Nyberg, and Denise C. Park (eds.). *Cognitive*

Neuroscience of Aging: Linking Cognitive and Cerebral Aging (Oxford, UK: Oxford University Press, 2016), pp. 414–438.

17. Timothy A. Salthouse, "The processing-speed theory of adult age differences in cognition," *Psychological Review 103*, no. 3 (1996), pp. 403–428.

18. Robert G. Crowder, "The interference theory of forgetting in long-term memory." In *Principles of Learning and Memory* (New York, NY: Psychology Press, 2014), pp. 234–279.

19. Robert Snyder, *Music and Memory: An Introduction* (Boston, MA: MIT Press, 2000).

20. Karl M. Healey, Lynn Hasher, and Karen L. Campbell, "The role of suppression in resolving interference: Evidence for an age-related deficit," *Psychology and Aging 28*, no. 3 (2013), pp. 721–728; Authur P. Shimamura and Paul J. Jurica, "Memory interference effects and aging: Findings from a test of frontal lobe function," *Neuropsychology 8*, no. 3 (1994), pp. 408–412.

21. Robert A. Bjork and Elizabeth Ligon Bjork, "A new theory of disuse and an old theory of stimulus fluctuation." In Alice F. Healy, Stephen M. Kosslyn, and Richard M. Shiffrin (eds.). *From Learning Processes to Cognitive Processes: Essays in Honor of William K. Estes*, vol. II (1992), pp. 35–67.

22. David Carr, "The stories of our lives: Aging and narrative." In Geoffrey Scarre (ed.). *The Palgrave Handbook of the Philosophy of Aging* (London: Palgrave Macmillan, 2016), pp. 171–185.

23. Mary Margaret McCabe, "Virtue, ageing and failing." In *The Palgrave Handbook of the Philosophy of Aging* (London: Palgrave Macmillan, 2016), pp. 437–438.

24. Lisa S. Caddell and Linda Clare, "I'm still the same person: The impact of early-stage dementia on identity," *Dementia 10*, no. 3 (2011), pp. 379–398; Lisa S. Caddell and Linda Clare, "The impact of dementia on self and identity: A systematic review," *Clinical Psychology Review 30*, no. 1 (2010), pp. 113–126.

25. Caddell and Clare, "I'm still the same person: The impact of early-stage dementia on identity," 2011, p. 385.

26. Michael Ignatieff, Michael Andre Bernstein, and Robert Alter, "Berlin in autumn: The philosopher in old age," *Occasional Papers of the Doreen B. Townsend Center for the Humanities*, no. 16 (Berkley, CA: The Regents of the University of California and the Doreen B. Townsend Center for the Humanities, 1999), pp. 19–20.

27. James Rupert Fletcher, "A symbolic interactionism of dementia: A tangle in 'the Alzheimer donundrum,'" *Social Theory & Health 16*, no. 2 (2018), pp. 172–187.

28. John C. Hughes, Stephen J. Louw, and Steven R. Sabat, "Seeing whole." In J. C. Hughes, S. J. Louw, and S. R. Sabat (eds.). *Dementia: Mind, Meaning, and the Person* (Oxford England: Oxford University Press, 2006), pp. 1–39.

29. Howard Chertkow, "Mild cognitive impairment," *Current Opinion in Neurology 15*, no. 4 (2002), pp. 401–407.

30. Ronald C. Petersen, "Mild cognitive impairment," *New England Journal of Medicine 364*, no. 23 (2011), pp. 2227–2234.

31. Joseph T. Coyle, Donald L. Price, and Mahlon R. Delong, "Alzheimer's disease: A disorder of cortical cholinergic innervation," *Science 219*, no. 4589 (1983), pp. 1184–1190; Bruno Dubois, Howard H. Feldman, Claudia Jacova, Jeffrey L. Cummings, Steven T. DeKosky, Pascale Barberger-Gateau, André Delacourte, et al., "Revising the definition of Alzheimer's disease: A new lexicon," *The Lancet Neurology 9*, no. 11 (2010), pp. 1118–1127; Angela L. Guillozet, Sandra Weintraub, Deborah C. Mash, and M. Marsel Mesulam, "Neurofibrillary tangles, amyloid, and memory in aging and mild cognitive impairment," *Archives of Neurology 60*, no. 5 (2003), pp. 729–736.

32. Antonio Terracciano and Angelina R. Sutin, "Personality and Alzheimer's disease: An integrative review," *Personality Disorders: Theory, Research, and Treatment 10*, no. 1 (2019), pp. 4–12.

33. Victor Alexander and David Anand, "Awareness of dementia," *Pharmacology, Toxicology and Biomedical Reports 4*, no. 2 (2018), pp. 10–14; Sytze P. Rensma, Thomas T. van Sloten, Lenore J. Launer, and Coen D. A. Stehouwer, "Cerebral small vessel disease and risk of incident stroke, dementia and depression, and all-cause mortality: A systematic review and meta-analysis," *Neuroscience & Biobehavioral Reviews 90* (2018), pp. 164–173.

34. Maria Grazia Spillantini, R. Anthony Crowther, Ross Jakes, Masato Hasegawa, and Michel Goedert, "α-Synuclein in filamentous inclusions of Lewy bodies from Parkinson's disease and dementia with Lewy bodies," *Proceedings of the National Academy of Sciences 95*, no. 11 (1998), pp. 6469–6473; Kay Seidel, Josefine Mahlke, Sonny Siswanto, Reijko Krüger, Helmut Heinsen, Georg Auburger, Mohamed Bouzrou, et al., "The brainstem pathologies of Parkinson's disease and dementia with Lewy bodies," *Brain Pathology 25*, no. 2 (2015), pp. 121–135; Zuzana Walker, Katherine L. Possin, Bradley F. Boeve, and Dag Aarsland, "Lewy body dementias," *The Lancet 386*, no. 10004 (2015), pp. 1683–1697.

35. Jon Palfreman, *Brain Storms: The Race to Unlock the Mysteries of Parkinson's Disease* (New York, NY: Macmillan, 2015).

36. Sara Garcia-Ptacek and Milica G. Kramberger, "Parkinson disease and dementia," *Journal of Geriatric Psychiatry and Neurology 29*, no. 5 (2016), pp. 261–270; Seidel et al., "The brainstem pathologies of Parkinson's disease and dementia with Lewy bodies," pp. 121–135.

37. Raj N. Kalaria, Rufus Akinyemi, and Masafumi Ihara, "Stroke injury, cognitive impairment and vascular dementia," *Biochimica et Biophysica Acta (BBA)-Molecular Basis of Disease 1862*, no. 5 (2016), pp. 915–925.

38. Priscila Corraini, Victor W. Henderson, Anne G. Ording, Lars Pedersen, Erzsébet Horváth-Puhó, and Henrik T. Sørensen, "Long-term risk of dementia among survivors of ischemic or hemorrhagic stroke," *Stroke 48*, no. 1 (2017), pp. 180–186; Xinxin Guo, Svante Östling, Silke Kern, Lena Johansson, and Ingmar Skoog, "Increased risk for dementia both before and after stroke: A population-based study in women followed over 44 years," *Alzheimer's & Dementia 14*, no. 10 (2018), pp. 1253–1260;

Kalaria et al., "Stroke injury, cognitive impairment and vascular dementia," pp. 915–925.

39. Lieke L. Smits, Argonde C. van Harten, Yolande A. L. Pijnenburg, Esther L. G. E. Koedam, Femke H. Bouwman, Nicole Sistermans, Ilona E. W. Reuling et al., "Trajectories of cognitive decline in different types of dementia," *Psychological Medicine 45*, no. 5 (2015), pp. 1051–1059.

40. David M. Erlanger, Kenneth C. Kutner, Jeffrey T. Barth, and Ronnie Barnes, "Forum neuropsychology of sports-related head injury: Dementia pugilistica to post concussion syndrome," *The Clinical Neuropsychologist 13*, no. 2 (1999), pp. 193–209.

41. Leonardo Caixeta, Iron Dangoni Filho, Rafael Dias de Sousa, Pedro Paulo Dias Soares, and Andreia Costa Rabelo Mendonça, "Extending the range of differential diagnosis of chronic traumatic encephalopathy of the boxer: Insights from a case report," *Dementia & Neuropsychologia 12*, no. 1 (2018), pp. 92–96; Erlanger et al., "Forum neuropsychology of sports-related head injury: Dementia pugilistica to post concussion syndrome," pp. 193–209; Matthew Saint, "Chronic traumatic encephalopathy: Confronting repetitive head injury in contact sports," *The INSPIRE Experience: A New Student Research Journal, for Students and by Students* (2017), pp. 8–9.

42. Robert C. Cantu, "Head injuries in sport," *British Journal of Sports Medicine 30*, no. 4 (1996), pp. 289–296; Patrick R. Hof, Constantin Bouras, L. Buee, A. Delacourte, D. P. Perl, and J. H. Morrison, "Differential distribution of neurofibrillary tangles in the cerebral cortex of dementia pugilistica and Alzheimer's disease cases," *Acta Neuropathologica 85*, no. 1 (1992), pp. 23–30; Michael A. Kiraly, and Stephen J. Kiraly, "Traumatic brain injury and delayed sequelae: A review - Traumatic brain injury and mild traumatic brain injury (concussion) are precursors to later-onset brain disorders, including early-onset dementia," *The Scientific World Journal 7* (2007), pp. 1768–1776.
Also note that retroactive amnesia refers to a loss of memory for events preceding the concussion or injury, in contrast to anterograde amnesia, which refers to an inability to remember or learn any new information following concussion or injury to the brain.

43. Hai Kang, Fengqing Zhao, Llbo You, and Cinzia Giorgetta, "Pseudo-dementia: A neuropsychological review," *Annals of Indian Academy of Neurology 17*, no. 2 (2014), pp. 147–154; S. Srikanth and A. V. Nagaraja, "A prospective study of reversible dementias: Frequency, causes, clinical profile and results of treatment," *Neurology India 53*, no. 3, pp. 291–294; Victor Maurice, Raymond D. Adams, and George H. Collins, "The Wernicke-Korsakoff syndrome. A clinical and pathological study of 245 patients, 82 with post-mortem examinations," *Contemporary Neurology Series 7* (1971), pp. 1–206.

44. M. Vandewoude, P. Barberger-Gateau, Tommy Cederholm, P. Mecocci, A. Salvà, G. Sergi, E. Topinkova, and D. Van Asselt, "Healthy brain ageing and cognition: Nutritional factors," *European Geriatric Medicine 7*, no. 1 (2016), pp. 77–85.

45. Srikanth and Nagaraja, "A prospective study of reversible dementias: Frequency, causes, clinical profile and results of treatment," pp. 291–294.
46. Martin Sarter, John P. Bruno, and Vinay Parikh, "Abnormal neurotransmitter release underlying behavioral and cognitive disorders: Toward concepts of dynamic and function-specific dysregulation," *Neuropsychopharmacology 32*, no. 7 (2007), pp. 1452–1461; Fabrizio Vecchio, Francesca Miraglia, Giuseppe Curcio, Riccardo Altavilla, Federica Scrascia, Federica Giambattistelli, Carlo Cosimo Quattrocchi, Placido Bramanti, Fabrizio Vernieri, and Paolo Maria Rossini, "Cortical brain connectivity evaluated by graph theory in dementia: A correlation study between functional and structural data," *Journal of Alzheimer's Disease 45*, no. 3 (2015), pp. 745–756.
47. Bruce S. McEwen, "The neurobiology of stress: From serendipity to clinical relevance," *Brain Research 886*, nos. 1–2 (2000), pp. 172–189; Bruce S. McEwen and Robert M. Sapolsky, "Stress and cognitive function," *Current Opinion in Neurobiology 5*, no. 2 (1995), pp. 205–216.
48. Arne Dietrich, "Functional neuroanatomy of altered states of consciousness: The transient hypofrontality hypothesis," *Consciousness and Cognition 12*, no. 2 (2003), pp. 231–256; Robert L. Kahn, Steven H. Zarit, Nancy M. Hilbert, and George Niederehe, "Memory complaint and impairment in the aged: The effect of depression and altered brain function," *Archives of General Psychiatry 32*, no. 12 (1975), pp. 1569–1573.
49. Ming Hung Hsu, Rosamund Flowerdew, Michael Parker, Jörg Fachner, and Helen Odell-Miller, "Individual music therapy for managing neuropsychiatric symptoms for people with dementia and their carers: A cluster randomised controlled feasibility study," *BMC Geriatrics 15*, no. 1 (2015), p. 84; Sara Eldirdiry Osman, Victoria Tischler, and Justine Schneider, "'Singing for the brain': A qualitative study exploring the health and well-being benefits of singing for people with dementia and their carers," *Dementia 15*, no. 6 (2016), pp. 1326–1339.
50. Diana Deutsch (ed.). *Psychology of Music* (New York, NY: Elsevier, 2013); Marc D. Hauser and Josh McDermott, "The evolution of the music faculty: A comparative perspective," *Nature Neuroscience 6*, no. 7 (2003), pp. 663–668; David Hargreaves and Adrian North, *The Social and Applied Psychology of Music* (Oxford, UK: Oxford University Press, 2008).
51. Laura Fusar-Poli, Łucja Bieleninik, Natascia Brondino, Xi-Jing Chen, and Christian Gold, "The effect of music therapy on cognitive functions in patients with dementia: A systematic review and meta-analysis," *Aging & Mental Health 22*, no. 9 (2018), pp. 1103–1112; Maureen Le Danseur, April D. Crow, Sonja E. Stutzman, Marcos D. Villarreal, and DaiWai M. Olson, "Music as a therapy to alleviate anxiety during inpatient rehabilitation for stroke," *Rehabilitation Nursing Journal 44*, no. 1 (2019), pp. 29–34; Hilary Moss, "The use of music in the chronic pain experience: An investigation into the use of music and music therapy by patients and staff at a hospital outpatient pain clinic," *Music and Medicine 11*, no. 1 (2019), pp. 6–22; Teppo Särkämö and David Soto, "Music listening after stroke: Beneficial effects and potential neural mechanisms," *Annals of the New York*

Academy of Sciences 1252, no. 1 (2012), pp. 266–281; Nina Schaffert, Thenille Braun Janzen, Klaus Mattes, and Michael H. Thaut, "A review on the relationship between sound and movement in sports and rehabilitation," *Frontiers in Psychology 10* (2019), p. 244.

52. Lars Ole Bonde and Tony Wigram, *A Comprehensive Guide to Music Therapy: Theory, Clinical Practice, Research and Training* (London, UK: Jessica Kingsley Publishers, 2002); Jane Edwards (ed.). *The Oxford Handbook of Music Therapy* (Oxford, United Kingdom: Oxford University Press, 2016); Gary McPherson and Graham F. Welch (eds.), *Special Needs, Community Music, and Adult Learning: An Oxford Handbook of Music Education*, vol. 4 (Oxford, UK: Oxford University Press, 2018).

53. Leslie Bunt, *Music Therapy: An Art beyond Words* (New York, NY: Routledge, 2003); Meredith Faith Hamons, *Musically Engaged Seniors: 40 Session Plans and Resources for a Vibrant Music Therapy Program* (Online: Whelk and Waters Publishing, 2013).

54. Shawn C. Green and Daphne Bavelier, "Exercising your brain: A review of human brain plasticity and training-induced learning," *Psychology and Aging 23*, no. 4 (2008), pp. 692–701.

55. Frances H. Rauscher, Gordon L. Shaw, and Catherine N. Ky, "Music and spatial task performance," *Nature 365*, no. 6447 (1993), p. 611.

56. John R. Hughes, Yaman Daaboul, John J. Fino, and Gordon L. Shaw, "The 'Mozart Effect' on epileptiform activity," *Clinical Electroencephalography 29*, no. 3 (1998), pp. 109–119; Johannes Sarnthein, Astrid VonStein, Peter Rappelsberger, Hellmuth Petsche, Frances Rauscher, and Gordon Shaw, "Persistent patterns of brain activity: An EEG coherence study of the positive effect of music on spatial-temporal reasoning," *Neurological Research 19*, no. 2 (1997), pp. 107–116; Walter Verrusio, Evaristo Ettorre, Edoardo Vicenzini, Nicola Vanacore, Mauro Cacciafesta, and Oriano Mecarelli, "The Mozart effect: A quantitative EEG study," *Consciousness and Cognition 35* (2015), pp. 150–155.

57. Kenneth M. Steele, Karen E. Bass, and Melissa D. Croo, "The mystery of the Mozart effect: Failure to replicate," *Psychological Science 10*, no. 4 (1999), pp. 366–369; William Forde Thompson, E. Glenn Schellenberg, and Gabriela Husain, "Arousal, mood, and the Mozart effect," *Psychological science 12*, no. 3 (2001), pp. 248–251.

58. Kristin M. Nantais and E. Glenn Schellenberg, "The Mozart effect: An artifact of preference," *Psychological Science 10*, no. 4 (1999), pp. 370–373; E. Glenn Schellenberg, Takayuki Nakata, Patrick G. Hunter, and Sachiko Tamoto, "Exposure to music and cognitive performance: Tests of children and adults," *Psychology of Music 35*, no. 1 (2007), pp. 5–19.

59. Sylvain Moreno, "Can music influence language and cognition?" *Contemporary Music Review 28*, no. 3 (2009), pp. 329–345.

60. Teppo Särkämö, Mari Tervaniemi, Sari Laitinen, Ava Numminen, Merja Kurki, Julene K. Johnson, and Pekka Rantanen, "Cognitive, emotional, and social benefits of regular musical activities in early dementia: Randomized controlled study," *The Gerontologist 54*, no. 4 (2014), pp. 634–650.

61. Vinoo Alluri, Petri Toiviainen, Iiro P. Jääskeläinen, Enrico Glerean, Mikko Sams, and Elvira Brattico, "Large-scale brain networks emerge from dynamic processing of musical timbre, key and rhythm," *Neuroimage* 59, no.4 (2012), pp. 3677–3689.
62. Jeffrey R. Binder, Julie A. Frost, Thomas A. Hammeke, Robert W. Cox, Stephen M. Rao, and Thomas Prieto, "Human brain language areas identified by functional magnetic resonance imaging," *Journal of Neuroscience 17*, no. 1 (1997), pp. 353–362.
63. Alluri et al., "Large-scale brain networks emerge from dynamic processing of musical timbre, key and rhythm," pp. 3677–3689.
64. Siri Leknes and Irene Tracey, "A Common neurobiology for pain and pleasure," *Nature Reviews Neuroscience 9*, no. 4 (2008), p. 314; Edita Navratilova, Christopher W. Atcherley, and Frank Porreca, "Brain circuits encoding reward from pain relief," *Trends in Neurosciences 38*, no. 11 (2015), pp. 741–750.
65. Petr Janata and Scott T. Grafton, "Swinging in the brain: Shared neural substrates for behaviors related to sequencing and music," *Nature Neuroscience 6*, no. 7 (2003), p. 682; Petr Janata, Barbara Tillmann, and Jamshed J. Bharucha, "Listening to polyphonic music recruits domain-general attention and working memory circuits," *Cognitive, Affective, & Behavioral Neuroscience 2*, no. 2 (2002), pp. 121–140; Petr Janata, Stefan T. Tomic, and Jason M. Haberman, "Sensorimotor coupling in music and the psychology of the groove," *Journal of Experimental Psychology: General 141*, no. 1 (2012), pp. 54–75; Daniel J. Levitin, Jessica A. Grahn, and Justin London, "The psychology of music: Rhythm and movement," *Annual Review of Psychology 69* (2018), pp. 51–75; Michael H. Thaut, Gerald C. McIntosh, and Volker Hoemberg, "Neurobiological foundations of neurologic music therapy: Rhythmic entrainment and the motor system," *Frontiers in Psychology 5* (2015), p. 1185.
66. Jiancheng Hou, Bei Song, Andrew C. N. Chen, Changan Sun, Jiaxian Zhou, Haidong Zhu, and Theodore P. Beauchaine, "Review on neural correlates of emotion regulation and music: Implications for emotion dysregulation," *Frontiers in Psychology 8* (2017), p. 501; Petr Janata, "The neural architecture of music-evoked autobiographical memories," *Cerebral Cortex 19*, no. 11 (2009), pp. 2579–2594; Petr Janata, Stefan T. Tomic, and Sonja K. Rakowski, "Characterisation of music-evoked autobiographical memories," *Memory 15*, no. 8 (2007), pp. 845–860; Christof Karmonik, Anthony Brandt, Jeff R. Anderson, Forrest Brooks, Julie Lytle, Elliott Silverman, and Jefferson Todd Frazier, "Music listening modulates functional connectivity and information flow in the human brain," *Brain Connectivity 6*, no. 8 (2016), pp. 632–641; Stephan Koelsch, "Towards a neural basis of music-evoked emotions," *Trends in Cognitive Sciences 14*, no. 3 (2010), pp. 131–137; Stefan Koelsch, "Music and the brain." In P. J. Rentfrow and D. J. Levitin (eds.). *Foundations in Music Psychology: Theory and Research* (Cambridge, MA: MIT Press, 2019), pp. 407–458; Stefan Koelsch and Walter A. Siebel, "Towards a neural basis of music

perception," *Trends in Cognitive Sciences 9*, no. 12 (2005), pp. 578–584; Alfredo Raglio, Lapo Attardo, Giulia Gontero, Silvia Rollino, Elisabetta Groppo, and Enrico Granieri, "Effects of music and music therapy on mood in neurological patients," *World Journal of Psychiatry 5*, no. 1 (2015), pp. 68–78; Shankha Sanyal, Sayan Nag, Archi Banerjee, Ranjan Sengupta, and Dipak Ghosh, "Music of brain and music on brain: A novel EEG sonification approach," *Cognitive Neurodynamics 13*, no. 1 (2019), pp. 13–31.

67. Ken-ichi Tabei, Masayuki Satoh, Jun-ichi Ogawa, Tomoko Tokita, Noriko Nakaguchi, Koji Nakao, Hirotaka Kida, and Hidekazu Tomimoto, "Physical exercise with music reduces gray and white matter loss in the frontal cortex of elderly people: The Mihama-Kiho scan project," *Frontiers in Aging Neuroscience 9* (2017), pp. 174–189.

68. Margarita Alexomanolaki, Catherine Loveday, and Chris Kennett, "Music and memory in advertising: Music as a device of implicit learning and recall," *Music, Sound, and the Moving Image 1*, no. 1 (2007), pp. 51–71; Brigitte Bogert, Taru Numminen-Kontti, Benjamin Gold, Mikko Sams, Jussi Numminen, Iballa Burunat, Jouko Lampinen, and Elvira Brattico, "Hidden sources of joy, fear, and sadness: Explicit versus implicit neural processing of musical emotions," *Neuropsychologia 89* (2016), pp. 393–402; Lutz Jäncke, "Music, memory and emotion," *Journal of Biology 7*, no. 6 (2008), p. 21; Martin Rohrmeier and Patrick Rebuschat, "Implicit learning and acquisition of music," *Topics in Cognitive Science 4*, no. 4 (2012), pp. 525–553.

69. Sylvain Moreno and Gavin M. Bidelman, "Examining neural plasticity and cognitive benefit through the unique lens of musical training," *Hearing Research 308* (2014), p. 84–97; Laurel J. Trainor, Antoine J. Shahin, and Larry E. Robertsa, "Understanding the benefits of musical training," *The Neurosciences and Music III: Disorders and Plasticity 1169* (2009), pp. 133–142.

70. Elżbieta Galińska, "Music therapy in neurological rehabilitation settings," *Psychiatria Polska 49*, no. 4 (2015), pp. 835–846; Teppo Särkämö, Eckart Altenmüller, Antoni Rodríguez-Fornells, and Isabelle Peretz, "Music, brain, and rehabilitation: Emerging therapeutic applications and potential neural mechanisms," *Frontiers in Human Neuroscience 10* (2016), p. 103; Aleksi J. Sihvonen, Teppo Saerkaemoe, Vera Leo, Mari Tervaniemi, Eckart Altenmüller, and Seppo Soinila, "Music-based interventions in neurological rehabilitation," *The Lancet Neurology 16*, no. 8 (2017), pp. 648–660.

71. Mark I. Alpert, Judy I. Alpert, and Elliot N. Maltz, "Purchase occasion influence on the role of music in advertising," *Journal of Business Research 58*, no. 3 (2005), pp. 369–376; Gordon C. Bruner, "Music, mood, and marketing," *Journal of Marketing 54*, no. 4 (1990), pp. 94–104.

72. Wanda Wallace, "Memory for music," *Journal of Experimental Psychology: Learning, Memory, and Cognition 20*, no. 6 (1994), pp. 1471–1485; R. F. Yalch, "Memory in a jingle jungle: Music as a mnemonic device in

communicating advertising slogans," *Journal of Applied Psychology 76*, no. 2 (1991), pp. 268–275.

73. Matthew D. Schulkind, Laura Kate Hennis, and David C. Rubin, "Music, emotion, and autobiographical memory: They're playing your song," *Memory & Cognition 27*, no. 6 (1999), pp. 948–955.

74. Nicola Mammarella, Beth Fairfield, and Cesare Cornoldi, "Does music enhance cognitive performance in healthy older adults? The Vivaldi effect," *Aging Clinical and Experimental Research 19*, no. 5 (2007), pp. 394–399.

75. Rebecca G. Thompson, C. J. A. Moulin, S. Hayre, and R. W. Jones, "Music enhances category fluency in healthy older adults and Alzheimer's disease patients," *Experimental Aging Research 31*, no. 1 (2005), pp. 91–99.

76. Sara Bottiroli, Alessia Rosi, Riccardo Russo, Tomaso Vecchi, and Elena Cavallini, "The cognitive effects of listening to background music on older adults: Processing speed improves with upbeat music, while memory seems to benefit from both upbeat and downbeat music," *Frontiers in Aging Neuroscience 6* (2014), p. 284.

77. Eri Hirokawa, "Effects of music listening and relaxation instructions on arousal changes and the working memory task in older adults," *Journal of Music Therapy 41*, no. 2 (2004), pp. 107–127.

78. Agnes S. Chan, Yim-Chi Ho, and Mei-Chun Cheung, "Music training improves verbal memory," *Nature 396*, no. 6707 (1998), p. 128.

79. Travis White-Schwoch, Kali Woodruff Carr, Samira Anderson, Dana L. Strait, and Nina Kraus, "Older adults benefit from music training early in life: Biological evidence for long-term training-driven plasticity," *Journal of Neuroscience 33*, no. 45 (2013), pp. 17667–17674.

80. Raif Th Krampe and K. Anders Ericsson, "Maintaining excellence: Deliberate practice and elite performance in young and older pianists," *Journal of Experimental Psychology: General 125*, no. 4 (1996), pp. 331–359.

81. Jennifer A. Bugos, William M. Perlstein, Christina S. McCrae, Timothy S. Brophy, and Purvis H. Bedenbaugh, "Individualized piano instruction enhances executive functioning and working memory in older adults," *Aging and Mental Health 11*, no. 4 (2007), pp. 464–471.

82. Dieke Mansens, D. J. H. Deeg, and H. C. Comijs, "The association between singing and/or playing a musical instrument and cognitive functions in older adults," *Aging & Mental Health 22*, no. 8 (2018), pp. 970–977.

83. Kim E. Innes, Terry Kit Selfe, Dharma Singh Khalsa, and Sahiti Kandati, "Meditation and music improve memory and cognitive function in adults with subjective cognitive decline: A pilot randomized controlled trial," *Journal of Alzheimer's Disease 56*, no. 3 (2017), pp. 899–916.

84. Teppo Särkämö, Sari Laitinen, Ava Numminen, Merja Kurki, and Pekka Rantanen, "The role of musical leisure activities in dementia care: Applicability and benefits perceived by caregivers," *Journal of Communications Research 5*, no. 3 (2013), pp. 331–352.

85. Rebecca G. Deason, Nicholas R. Simmons-Stern, Bruno S. Frustace, Brandon A. Ally, and Andrew E. Budson, "Music as a memory enhancer: Differences between healthy older adults and patients with Alzheimer's

disease," *Psychomusicology: Music, Mind, and Brain 22*, no. 2 (2012), pp. 175–179; Nicholas R. Simmons-Stern, Andrew E. Budson, and Brandon A. Ally, "Music as a memory enhancer in patients with Alzheimer's disease," *Neuropsychologia 48*, no. 10 (2010), pp. 3164–3167.

86. Fusar-Poli et al., "The effect of music therapy on cognitive functions in patients with dementia: A systematic review and meta-analysis," pp. 1103–1112.

87. Felicity A. Baker, Jeanette Tamplin, Nikki Rickard, Jennie Ponsford, Peter W. New, and Young-Eun C. Lee, "A therapeutic songwriting intervention to promote reconstruction of self-concept and enhance well-being following brain or spinal cord injury: Pilot randomized controlled trial," *Clinical Rehabilitation* (2019), 0269215519831417.

88. Stephane Guetin, F. Portet, M. C. Picot, C. Pommié, M. Messaoudi, L. Djabelkir, A. L. Olsen, M. M. Cano, E. Lecourt, and J. Touchon, "Effect of music therapy on anxiety and depression in patients with Alzheimer's type dementia: Randomised, controlled study," *Dementia and Geriatric Cognitive Disorders 28*, no. 1 (2009), pp. 36–46.

89. Sato Ashida, "The effect of reminiscence music therapy sessions on changes in depressive symptoms in elderly persons with dementia," *Journal of Music Therapy 37*, no. 3 (2000), pp. 170–182; Guetin et al., "Effect of music therapy on anxiety and depression in patients with Alzheimer's type dementia: Randomised, controlled study," pp. 36–46; Muireann Irish, Conal J. Cunningham, J. Bernard Walsh, Davis Coakley, Brian A. Lawlor, Ian H. Robertson, and Robert F. Coen, "Investigating the enhancing effect of music on autobiographical memory in mild Alzheimer's disease," *Dementia and Geriatric Cognitive Disorders 22*, no. 1 (2006), pp. 108–120; Orii McDermott, Nadia Crellin, Hanne Mette Ridder, and Martin Orrell, "Music therapy in dementia: A narrative synthesis systematic review," *International Journal of Geriatric Psychiatry 28*, no. 8 (2013), pp. 781–794; Séverine Samson, Sylvain Clément, Pauline Narme, Loris Schiaratura, and Nathalie Ehrlé, "Efficacy of musical interventions in dementia: Methodological requirements of nonpharmacological trials," *Annals of the New York Academy of Sciences 1337*, no. 1 (2015), pp. 249–255.

90. Mohamad El Haj, Luciano Fasotti, and Philippe Allain, "The involuntary nature of music-evoked autobiographical memories in Alzheimer's disease," *Consciousness and Cognition 21*, no. 1 (2012), pp. 238–246.

91. Lola L. Cuddy, Ritu Sikka, Kristen Silveira, Sean Bai, and Ashley Vanstone, "Music-evoked autobiographical memories (MEAMs) in Alzheimer's disease: Evidence for a positivity effect," *Cogent Psychology 4*, no. 1 (2017), 1277578.

92. Lola L. Cuddy, Ritu Sikka, and Ashley Vanstone, "Preservation of musical memory and engagement in healthy aging and Alzheimer's disease," *Annals of the New York Academy of Sciences 1337*, no. 1 (2015), pp. 223–231.

93. Katlyn J. Peck, Todd A. Girard, Frank A. Russo, and Alexandra J. Fiocco, "Music and memory in Alzheimer's disease and the potential underlying mechanisms," *Journal of Alzheimer's Disease 51*, no. 4 (2016), pp. 949–959.

94. McDermott et al., "Music therapy in dementia: A narrative synthesis systematic review," pp. 781–794.

95. Raglio et al., "Effects of music and music therapy on mood in neurological patients," pp. 68–78.

96. Aidin Ashoori, David M. Eagleman, and Joseph Jankovic, "Effects of auditory rhythm and music on gait disturbances in Parkinson's disease," *Frontiers in Neurology* 6 (2015), p. 234.

97. Frederik Styns, Leon van Noorden, Dirk Moelants, and Marc Leman, "Walking on music," *Human Movement Science* 26, no. 5 (2007), pp. 769–785.

98. Joanne E. Wittwer, Kate E. Webster, and Keith Hill, "Music and metronome cues produce different effects on gait spatiotemporal measures but not gait variability in healthy older adults," *Gait & Posture 37*, no. 2 (2013), pp. 219–222.

99. Cristina Nombela, Laura E. Hughes, Adrian M. Owen, and Jessica A. Grahn, "Into the groove: Can rhythm influence Parkinson's disease?" *Neuroscience & Biobehavioral Reviews* 37, no. 10 (2013), pp. 2564–2570.

100. Andrea Schiavi and Eckart Altenmüller, "Exploring music-based rehabilitation for Parkinsonism through embodied cognitive science," *Frontiers in Neurology* 6 (2015), p. 217.

101. Natalie de Bruin, Jon B. Doan, George Turnbull, Oksana Suchowersky, Stephan Bonfield, Bin Hu, and Lesley A. Brown, "Walking with music is a safe and viable tool for gait training in Parkinson's disease: The effect of a 13-week feasibility study on single and dual task walking," *Parkinson's Disease* (2010), 48530.

102. Michael H. Thaut, Regina Miltner, Herwig W. Lange, Corene P. Hurt, and Volker Hoemberg, "Velocity modulation and rhythmic synchronization of gait in Huntington's disease," *Movement Disorders: Official Journal of the Movement Disorder Society 14*, no. 5 (1999), pp. 808–819.

103. Mei-Ching Chen, Pei-Luen Tsai, Yu-Ting Huang, and Keh-chung Lin, "Pleasant music improves visual attention in patients with unilateral neglect after stroke," *Brain Injury 27*, no. 1 (2013), pp. 75–82; Le Danseur et al., "Music as a therapy to alleviate anxiety during inpatient rehabilitation for stroke," pp. 29–34; Särkämö and Soto, "Music listening after stroke: Beneficial effects and potential neural mechanisms," pp. 266–281.

104. Michael H. Thaut, Gerald C. McIntosh, and Ruth R. Rice, "Rhythmic facilitation of gait training in hemiparetic stroke rehabilitation," *Journal of the Neurological Sciences 151*, no. 2 (1997), pp. 207–212.

105. Eckhart Altenmuller, J. Marco-Pallares, T. F. Munte, and S. Schneider, "Neural reorganization underlies improvement in stroke-induced motor dysfunction by music-supported therapy," *Annals of the New York Academy of Sciences 1169*, no. 1 (2009), pp. 395–405; Yingshi Zhang, Jiayi Cai, Yaqiong Zhang, Tianshu Ren, Mingyi Zhao, and Qingchun Zhao, "Improvement in stroke-induced motor dysfunction by music-supported therapy: A systematic review and meta-analysis," *Scientific Reports 6* (2016), 38521.

106. Baker et al., "A therapeutic songwriting intervention to promote recon-struction of self-concept and enhance well-being following brain or spinal cord injury: Pilot randomized controlled trial," 0269215519831417.

107. Rita Formisano, Vincenzo Vinicola, Francesca Penta, Mariella Matteis, Stefano Brunelli, and Jurgen W. Weckel, "Active music therapy in the rehabilitation of severe brain injured patients during coma recovery," *Ann Ist Super Sanita 37*, no. 4 (2001), pp. 627–630.

108. Hanne Mette Ridder and David Aldridge, "Individual music therapy with persons with frontotemporal dementia: Singing dialogue," *Nordic Journal of Music Therapy 14*, no. 2 (2005), pp. 91–106.

109. Steve Hollaway, "Who is blind and who can see?" *Block Island Times*, March 28, 2017. www.blockislandtimes.com/affiliate-post/who-blind-an d-who-can-see/49052 (accessed December 22, 2020); Terre Johnson, "Hallelujah, amen!" *Choral Journal 58*, no. 11 (2018), p. 45; Ashley Jones, "Ken Medema, a blind musician, will be performing at Centenary United Methodist Church on Sunday," *Southeast Missourian*, January 13, 2012. www.semissourian.com/story/1804040.html (accessed December 22, 2020); Ken Medema, Beverly Vander Molen, Dave Vander Molen, Kurt Kaiser, Paula D'Arcy, Matt Greer, Amy Greer, et al., "Ken Medema at a glance" (2017). https://libraries.mercer.edu/ur sa/handle/10898/4846 (accessed December 22, 2020); Ken Medema, Elizabeth D. Hammond, and Rebecca Sandifer, "Ken Medema promo-tional video" (2017). https://libraries.mercer.edu/ursa/handle/10898/3789 (accessed December 22, 2020); *Shreveport Times*, "Noted author to speak about 'mending what is broken'," *Shreveport Times*, February 13, 2018. www.shreveporttimes.com/story/life/2018/02/13/noted-author-speak-men ding-what-broken/330478002 (accessed December 22, 2020).

110. Lisa Snyder, "Personhood and interpersonal communication in dementia." In Julian Hughes, C. Julian, Stephen J. Louw, and Steven R. Sabat (eds.). *Dementia: Mind, Meaning, and the Person* (OUP: Oxford, 2006), pp. 259–276.

111. F. Brian Allen and Peter G. Coleman, "Spiritual perspectives on the person with dementia: Identity and personhood." In Julian Hughes, C. Julian, Stephen J. Louw, and Steven R. Sabat (eds.). *Dementia: Mind, Meaning, and the Person* (OUP: Oxford, 2006), pp. 205–222; Pia C. Kontos, "Ethnographic reflections on selfhood, embodiment and Alzheimer's dis-ease," *Ageing & Society 24*, no. 6 (2004), pp. 829–849; Annette Leibing, "Divided gazes: Alzheimer's disease, the person within, and death in life." In Annette Leibing and Lawrence Cohen (eds.). *Thinking about Dementia* (Piscataway, NJ: Rutgers University Press, 2006), pp. 240–268.

5 Trio: Resilience, Recovery, and Growth

1. Mac Randall, "Given the gift of life: Interview with Frank Vignola," *JazzTimes 48*, no. 4 (May 2018), pp. 10–11. Used with permission.

2. Brian Abrams, "Humanistic approaches." In Barbara L. Wheeler (ed.). *Music Therapy Handbook* (New York, NY: The Gulford Press, 2015), p. 152.

3. Plato, *The Republic and Other Works*, trans. Benjamin Jowett (New York, NY: Anchor Books Doubleday, 1989), pp. 85–94.

4. Sarah Whitefield, "Music: Its expressive power and moral significance," *Musical Offerings 1*, no. 1 (Spring 2010), pp. 11–19.

5. Anne W. Lipe, "Beyond therapy: Music, spirituality, and health in human experience: A review of literature," *Journal of Music Therapy 3* (2002), pp. 209–240.

6. William B. Davis, Kate E. Gfeller, and Michael H. Thaut (eds.). *An Introduction to Music Therapy: Theory and Practice*, 3rd ed. (Silver Spring, MD: American Music Therapy Association, 2008).

7. John Sloboda, Alexandra Lamont, and Alinka Greasley, "Choosing to hear music: Motivation, process, and effect." In Susan Hallam, Ian Cross, and Michael Thaut (eds.). *Oxford Handbook of Music Psychology* (Oxford, UK: Oxford University Press, 2009), pp. 431–440.

8. Petri Laukka, "Use of music and psychological well-being among the elderly," *Journal of Happiness Studies 8* (2006), pp. 215–241.

9. Laukka, "Use of music and psychological well-being among the elderly," p. 225.

10. Sarah Oetken, Katharina D. Pauly, Ruben C. Gur, Frank Schneider, Ute Habel, and Anna Pohl, "Don't worry, be happy - Neural correlates of the influence of musically induced mood on self-evaluation," *Neuropsychologia 100* (2017), pp. 26–34.

11. Helen L. Bonny, *The Role of Taped Music Programs in GIM Process: GIM Monograph No. 2* (Salina, KS: The Bonny Foundation, 1978).

12. Debra S. Burns, "The effect of the Bonny Method of guided imagery and music on mood and life quality of cancer patients," *Journal of Music Therapy 38*, no. 1 (2001), pp. 51–85.

13. L. Toomey, "Literature review: The Bonny Method of guided imagery and music," *Journal of the Association for Music and Imagery 5* (1996), pp. 75–103.

14. Abrams, "Humanistic approaches," p. 153.

15. Abrams, "Humanistic approaches," p. 148.

16. Abrams, "Humanistic approaches," p. 153.

17. Abrams, "Humanistic approaches," p. 150.

18. John Sommers-Flannagan, "The development and evolution of person-centered expressive art therapy: A conversation with Natalie Rogers," *Journal of Counseling and Development 85* (Winter 2007), pp. 120–125.

19. Centers for Disease Control Diabetes Management. www.cdc.gov/diabetes/index.html (accessed May 20, 2020).

20. Craig Idlebrook and Martin Hensel, "Celebrating B.B. King's life with diabetes," *Type 2 Nation 1* (2015). www.type2nation.com/treatment/celebrating-b-b-kings-life-with-diabetes (accessed May 8 2020).

21. John Mulholland, "Joe Bonamassa, B. B. King Remembered," *The Guardian* (December 27, 2015). www.theguardian.com/music/2015/dec/27/bb-king-r

emembered-by-joe-bonamassa (accessed May 8, 2020). Quote used with permission.

22. Oscar Peterson/Clark Terry, *Oscar Peterson Trio +1-Clark Terry*-Versve, B0009652-02 [CD] (1964).

23. Clark Terry, *Clark: The Autobiography of Clark Terry* (Los Angeles, CA: University of California Press, 2011).

24. Insulin is a hormone made by the pancreas that helps glucose in the blood to enter the cells of the body. Insulin sensitivity is the degree to which cells can take up glucose from the blood. High sensitivity means that a smaller amount of insulin is needed to take up glucose. Low sensitivity means that more insulin is needed to take up glucose. Insulin resistance is when the cells in the body are unable to effectively take up glucose from the blood. The A1C test is the average blood glucose level measured over the past three months. www.niddk.nih.gov/health-information/diabetes/overview/what-is-diabetes/prediabetes-insulin-resistance (accessed May 8, 2020).

25. Kathryn E. Wellen and Gokhan S. Hotamisligil, "Inflammation, stress, and diabetes," *The Journal of Clinical Investigation 115*, no. 5 (2005), pp. 1111–1119.

26. Wellen and Hotamisligil, "Inflammation, stress, and diabetes," p. 1113.

27. Richard S. Surwitt, Mark S. Schneider, and Mark N. Feinglos, "Stress and diabetes mellitus," *Diabetes Care 15*, no. 10 (1992), p. 1420.

28. Alexandra Linnemann, Beate Ditzen, Jana Strahler, Johanna M. Doerr, and Urs M. Nater, "Music listening as means of stress reduction in daily life," *Psychoneuroendocrinology 60* (2015), pp. 80–90.

29. Alexandra Linnemann, Jana Strahler, and Urs M. Nater, "The stress-reducing impact of music listening varies depending on the social context," *Psychoneuroendocrinology 72* (2016), pp. 97–105.

30. Timothy Onosahwo Lyendo, "Exploring the effect of sound and music on health in hospital settings: A narrative review," *International Journal of Nursing Studies 63* (2016), pp. 82–100.

31. Jun Jiang, Linshu Zhou, Daphne Rickson, and Cunmei Jiang, "The effects of sedative and stimulative music on stress reduction depend on music preference," *The Arts in Psychotherapy 40* (2013), pp. 201–205.

32. C. Anjali Devi, "Impact of music on type 2 diabetes," *International Journal of Diabetes and Metabolic Disorders 1* (August 2016), pp. 1–2.

33. Susan E. Mandel, Beth A. Davis, and Michelle Secic, "Effects of music therapy and music-assisted relaxation and imagery on health-related outcomes in diabetes education: A feasibility study," *The Diabetes Educator 39* (July/August 2013), pp. 568–581.

34. Li Ji, Jiao-Jiao Bai, Jiao Sun, Yue Ming, and Li-Rong Chen, "Effect of combining music media therapy with lower extremity exercise on elderly patients with diabetes mellitus," *International Journal of Nursing Sciences 2*, no. 3 (2015), pp. 243–247.

35. Marc Wortmann, "World Alzheimer Report 2014: Dementia and risk reduction," *Alzheimer's & Dementia: The Journal of the Alzheimer's Association 11*, no. 7 (2015), p. P837.

36. Laura A. Pratt and Debra J. Brody, "Depression in the United States household population, 2005–2006," *NCHS Data Brief 7*, no. 7 (2008), pp. 1–8.

37. Sophia Bennett and Alan J. Thomas, "Depression and dementia: Cause, consequence or coincidence?" *Maturitas 79*, no. 2 (2014), pp. 184–190; Ranbir Singh, Nadeem Mazi-Kotwal, and Madhusudan Deepak Thalitaya, "Recognising and treating depression in the elderly," *Psychiatr Danub 27*, no. 1 (2015), pp. S231–234.

38. Joan Girgus, Kaite Yang, and Christine Ferri, "The gender difference in depression: Are elderly women at greater risk for depression than elderly men?" *Geriatrics 2*, no. 4 (2017), p. 35.

39. Keith Jongenelis, Anne Margriet Pot, Amy M. H. Eisses, Aaartjan T. F. Beekman, H. Kluiter, and M. W. Ribbe, "Prevalence and risk indicators of depression in elderly nursing home patients: The AGED study," *Journal of Affective Disorders 83*, nos. 2–3 (2004), pp. 135–142.

40. Fiona Costa, Adam Ockelford, and David J. Hargreaves, "The effect of regular listening to preferred music on pain, depression and anxiety in older care home residents," *Psychology of Music 46*, no. 2 (2018), pp. 174–191.

41. Orti de la Rubia Orti, Jose Enrique, Maria Pilar Garcia Pardo, Maria Benllochi, Eraci Drehmer, Jose Luis Platero, David Sancho, and Maria Mar Lopez Rodriguez, "Music therapy decreases sadness and increases happiness in Alzheimer's patients: A pilot study," *Neuropsychiatry Journal 9*, no. 1 (2019), pp. 2013–2020.

42. Moon Fai Chan, Engle Angela Chan, Esther Mok, and Fionca Yuk Kwan Tse, "Effect of music on depression levels and physiological responses in community-based older adults," *International Journal of Mental Health Nursing 18*, no. 4 (2009), pp. 285–294.

43. Kun Zhao, Zheng Gang Bai, Ai Bo, and Iris Chi, "A systematic review and meta-analysis of music therapy for the older adults with depression," *International Journal of Geriatric Psychiatry 31*, no. 11 (2016), pp. 1188–1198.

44. Iosief Abraha, Joseph M. Rimland, Fabiana Mirella Trotta, Giuseppina Dell'Aquila, Alfonso Cruz-Jentoft, Mirko Petrovic, Adalsteinn Gudmundsson, et al., "Systematic review of systematic reviews of non-pharmacological interventions to treat behavioural disturbances in older patients with dementia. The SENATOR-OnTop Series," *British Medical Journal Open 7*, no. 3 (2017), p. e012759.

45. Jasmin Werner, Thomas Wosch, and Christian Gold, "Effectiveness of group music therapy versus recreational group singing for depressive symptoms of elderly nursing home residents: Pragmatic trial," *Aging & Mental Health 21*, no. 2 (2017), pp. 147–155.

46. Kelvin K. F. Tsoi, Joyce Y. C. Chan, Yiu-Ming Ng, Mia M. Y. Lee, Timothy C. Y. Kwok, and Samuel Y. S. Wong, "Receptive music therapy is more effective than interactive music therapy to relieve behavioral and psychological symptoms of dementia: A systematic review and meta-analysis," *Journal of the American Medical Directors Association 19*, no. 7 (2018), pp. 568–576.

47. Catherine Carr, Patricia d'Ardenne, Ann Sloboda, Carleen Scott, Duolao Wang, and Stefan Priebe, "Group music therapy for patients with persistent post-traumatic stress disorder – An exploratory randomized

controlled trial with mixed methods evaluation," *Psychology and Psychotherapy: Theory, Research and Practice 85*, no. 2 (2012), pp. 179–202.

48. Carr, "Group music therapy for patients with persistent post-traumatic stress disorder – An exploratory randomized controlled trial with mixed methods evaluation," pp. 179–202.

49. Mary De Groot, Ryan Anderson, Kenneth E. Freedland, Ray E. Clouse, and Patrick J. Lustman, "Association of depression and diabetes complications: A meta-analysis," *Psychosomatic Medicine 63*, no. 4 (2001), pp. 619–630; Dean D. VonDras and Wemara Lichty, "Correlates of depression in diabetic adults," *Behavior, Health, & Aging 1*, no. 2 (1990), pp. 79–84.

50. Suvi Saarikallio, "Music as emotional self-regulation throughout adulthood," *Psychology of Music 39*, no. 3 (2011), pp. 307–327.

51. Ann Gold and Ajay Clare, "An exploration of music listening in chronic pain," *Psychology of Music 41*, no. 5 (2013), pp. 545–564.

52. Hillary Moss, "The use of music in the chronic pain experience: An investigation into the use of music and music therapy by patients and staff at a hospital outpatient pain clinic," *Music and Medicine 11*, no. 1 (2019), pp. 6–22.

53. Shih-Tzu Huang, Marion Good, and Jaclene A. Zauszniewski, "The effectiveness of music in relieving pain in cancer patients: A randomized controlled trial," *International Journal of Nursing Studies 47*, no. 11 (2010), pp. 1354–1362; Mohammad Tahan, Mahmoud Akherati Evari, and Elahe Ahangri, "The effect of music therapy on stress, anxiety, and depression in patients with cancer in Valiasr Hospital in Birjand, 2017," *Journal of Clinical Nursing and Midwifery 7*, no. 3 (2018), pp. 186–193.

54. Joke Bradt, Marisol Norris, Minjung Shim, Edward J. Gracely, and Patricia Gerrity, "Vocal music therapy for chronic pain management in inner-city African Americans: A mixed methods feasibility study," *Journal of Music Therapy 53*, no. 2 (2016), pp. 178–206. https://doi.org:10.1093/jmt/thw004.

55. On pain during surgery: Nimet Ovayolu, Ozlem Ucan, Seda Pehlivan, Yavuz Pehlivan, Hakan Buyukhatipoglu, M. Cemil Savas, and Murat T. Gulsen, "Listening to Turkish classical music decreases patients' anxiety, pain, dissatisfaction and the dose of sedative and analgesic drugs during colonoscopy: A prospective randomized controlled trial," *World Journal of Gastroenterology 12*, no. 46 (2006), p. 7532; on pain management for intensive care patients: Celine Gelinas, Caroline Arbour, Cecile Michaud, Lauren Robar, and José Côté, "Patients and ICU nurses' perspectives of non-pharmacological interventions for pain management," *Nursing in Critical Care 18*, no. 6 (2013), pp. 307–318; on pain during postsurgical recovery: Marion Good, Michael Stanton-Hicks, Jeffrey A. Grass, Gene Cranston Anderson, Hui-Ling Lai, Varunyupa Roykulcharoen, and Patricia A. Adler, "Relaxation and music to reduce postsurgical pain," *Journal of Advanced Nursing 33*, no. 2 (2001), pp. 208–215; on pain management for intensive care patients: Celine Gelinas, Caroline Arbour, Cecile Michaud, Lauren Robar, and José Côté, "Patients and ICU nurses'

perspectives of non-pharmacological interventions for pain management," *Nursing in Critical Care 18*, no. 6 (2013), pp. 307–318.

56. Mimi M. Y. Tse, M. F. Chan, and Iris F. F. Benzie, "The effect of music therapy on postoperative pain, heart rate, systolic blood pressure and analgesic use following nasal surgery," *Journal of Pain & Palliative Care Pharmacotherapy 19*, no. 3 (2005), pp. 21–29.

57. Lisa M. Gallagher, Vickie Gardner, Debbie Bates, Shelley Mason, Jeanine Nemecek, Jacquelyn Baker DiFiore, James Bena, Manshi Li, and Francois Bethoux, "Impact of music therapy on hospitalized patients post-elective orthopaedic surgery," *Orthopaedic Nursing 37*, no. 2 (2018), pp. 124–133.

58. Hakeem Leonard, "Live music therapy during rehabilitation after total knee arthroplasty: A randomized controlled trial," *Journal of Music Therapy 56*, no. 1 (2019), pp. 61–89.

59. Ciaran Grafton-Clarke, Laura Grace, and Amer Harky, "Music therapy following cardiac surgery – Is it an effective method to reduce pain and anxiety?" *Interactive Cardiovascular and Thoracic Surgery 28*, no. 5 (2018), pp. 722–727.

60. Elyas Soltani, Mahin Nomali, Shahrzad Ghiyasvandian, Anoushirvan Kazemnejad, and Masumeh Zakerimoghadam, "Effect of listening to preferred music on general comfort level among patients who underwent coronary artery bypass graft surgery: A randomized controlled trial," *The Journal of Medical Research 4*, no. 5 (2018), pp. 234–239.

61. Anne Kühlmann, A. de Rooij, Leonard Kroese, Menno V. van Dijk, Myriam Hunink, and Hans Jeekel, "Meta-analysis evaluating music interventions for anxiety and pain in surgery," *British Journal of Surgery 105*, no. 7 (2018), pp. 773–783.

62. Guenther Bernatzky, Michaela Presch, Mary Anderson, and Jaak Panksepp, "Emotional foundations of music as a non-pharmacological pain management tool in modern medicine," *Neuroscience & Biobehavioral Reviews 35*, no. 9 (2011), pp. 1989–1999.

63. Kevin Dinstell, "Just keep moving: How one man faces ankylosing spondylitis pain," *Health Stories Project*, April 27, 2017. https://healthstoriesproject.com/ankylosing-spondylitis-pain (accessed March 3, 2020).

64. Jim Weatherhead, "My surreal and deeply emotional day," *Spondylitis Plus*, January 1, 2016. www.spondylitis.org/Spondylitis-Plus/jim-weatherhead-surreal-emotional-story (accessed March 3, 2020).

65. Jim Weatherhead, "A blessed man's journey," *The Faces of Ankylosing Spondiylitis*, June 12, 2019. https://thefacesofankylosingspondylitis.com/anas-life-a-blessed-mans-journey (accessed March 3, 2020); maintained by Cookie Hopper.

66. Jim Weatherhead, "Personal communication to Dean D. VonDras," July 5, 2020.

67. Anne Y. R. Kühlmann, Jonathan R. G. Etnel, Jolien W. Roos-Hesselink, Johannes Jeekel, Ad J. J. C. Bogers, and Johanna J. M. Takkenberg, "Systematic review and meta-analysis of music interventions in hypertension treatment: A quest for answers," *BMC Cardiovascular Disorders 16*, no. 1

(2016), p. 69; Jian-Fei Niu, Xiao-Feng Zhao, Han-Tong Hu, Jia-Jie Wang, Yan-Ling Liu, and De-Hua Lu, "Should acupuncture, biofeedback, massage, Qi Gong, relaxation therapy, device-guided breathing, yoga and Tai Chi be used to reduce blood pressure? Recommendations based on high-quality systematic reviews," *Complementary Therapies in Medicine 42* (2019), pp. 322–331; X. F. Teng, M. Y. Wong, and Y. T. Zhang, "The effect of music on hypertensive patients." In *Conference Proceedings: Annual International Conference of the IEEE Engineering in Medicine and Biology Society. IEEE Engineering in Medicine and Biology Society* (2007), pp. 4649–4651.

68. Paula de Marchi Scarpin Hagemann, Luis Cuadrado Martin, and Carmen Maria Bueno Neme, "The effect of music therapy on hemodialysis patients' quality of life and depression symptoms," *Brazilian Journal of Nephrology 41*, no. 1 (2019), pp. 74–82.

69. Anna Zumbansen and Pascale Tremblay, "Music-based interventions for aphasia could act through a motor-speech mechanism: A systematic review and case–control analysis of published individual participant data," *Aphasiology 33*, no. 4 (2019), pp. 466–497.

70. Luc P. De Vreese, Mirco Neri, Mario Fioravanti, Luciano Belloi, and Orazio Zanetti, "Memory rehabilitation in Alzheimer's disease: A review of progress," *International Journal of Geriatric Psychiatry 16*, no. 8 (2001), pp. 794–809.

71. Ken-ichi Tabei, Masayuki Satoh, Jun-ichi Ogawa, Tomoko Tokita, Noriko Nakaguchi, Koji Nakao, Hirotaka Kida, and Hidekazu Tomimoto, "Physical exercise with music reduces gray and white matter loss in the frontal cortex of elderly people: The Mihama-Kiho scan project," *Frontiers in Aging Neuroscience 9* (2017), p. 174.

72. US War Department, "Music in reconditioning in AST convalescent and general hospitals," *Technical Bulletin 187*, TB MED 187, July 26, 1945 (Washington, DC, 1945), p. 1–10.

73. C. Anjali Devi, "Impact of music on type 2 diabetes," pp. 1–2; Jun Jiang et al., "The effects of sedative and stimulative music on stress reduction depend on music preference," pp. 201–205.

74. War Department, *Technical Bulletin 187*, pp. 1–10.

75. American Music Therapy Association, *Music Therapy and Military Populations: A Status Report and Recommendations on Music Therapy Treatment, Programs, Research, and Practice Policies* (Silver Spring, MD: American Music Therapy Association, 2014), pp. 1–43.

76. Benita Koeman, *Operations We Are Here: Resources for the Military Community and Military Supporters* (2008–2019). www.operationwearehere.com (accessed December 11, 2019).

77. *Guitars for Vets* (Milwaukee, WI: 2015–2018). http://guitars4vets.org (accessed December 11, 2019).

78. *Music for Veterans* (Erie, PA: 2018). www.music4veterans.org (accessed December 12, 2019).

79. Colette Hebert, *Operation Music Aid: Instruments for Wounded Veterans*. https://makingmusicmag.com/operation-music-aid (accessed December 12, 2019).

80. Julia LeDoux, "Musicians bring healing to wounded warriors," *US Army Military Human Interest News* (September 4, 2015). www.army.mil/article/1550 34/musicians_bring_healing_to_wounded_warriors (accessed December 12, 2019).

81. Mildred McNeill, "83 Year-old 'Atomic Veteran' Paid Back for a Lifetime of Suffering," (April 21, 2020). www.hartford.edu/unotes/2020/04/bolden-ato mic-vet-hartt.aspx (accessed August 8, 2020).

82. Anna Järvinen, Julie R. Korenberg, and Ursula Bellugi, "The social phenotype of Williams syndrome," *Current Opinion in Neurobiology 23*, no. 3 (2013), pp. 414–422; Williams Syndrome Association (2019). https://williams-syn drome.org (accessed August 1, 2019).

83. Rowena Ng, Phillip Lai, Daniel J. Levitin, and Ursula Bellugi, "Musical correlates with sociability and emotionality in Williams syndrome," *Journal of Mental Health Research in Intellectual Disabilities 6* (2013), pp. 268–279; Audrey J. Don, E. Glenn Schellenberg, and Byron P. Rourke, "Music and language skills of children with Williams syndrome," *Child Neuropsychology 5*, no. 3 (1999), pp. 154–170.

84. Oliver Sacks, G. Schlaug, L. Jancke, Y. Huang, and H. Steinmetz, "Musical ability," *Science-AAAS-Weekly Paper Edition 268*, no. 5211 (1995), p. 621.

85. M. Lense and E. Dykens, "Musical learning in children and adults with Williams syndrome," *Journal of Intellectual Disability Research 57*, no. 9 (2013), pp. 850–860.

86. Sally M. Reis, Robin Schader, Harry Milne, and Robert Stephens, "Music and minds: Using a talent development approach for young adults with Williams syndrome," *Exceptional Children 69*, no. 3 (2003), pp. 293–313.

87. Ewie Erasmus and Liesl van der Merwe, "An interpretative phenomenological analysis of the lived musical experiences of three Williams syndrome individuals," *Psychology of Music 45*, no. 6 (2017), pp. 781–794.

88. Elizabeth M. Cherniske, Thomas O. Carpenter, Cheryl Klaiman, Eytan Young, Joel Bergman, Karl Insogna, Robert T. Schultz, and Barbara R. Pober, "Multisystem study of 20 older adults with Williams syndrome," *American Journal of Genetics 131*, no. A (2004), pp. 255–264.

89. Elizabeth M. Dykens, "Aging in rare intellectual disability syndromes," *Developmental Disabilities Research Reviews 18* (2013), pp. 75–83.

90. Darlynne A. Devenny, Sharon J. Krinsky-McHale, Phyllis M. Kittler, Michael Flory, Edmund Jenkins, and W. Ted Brown, "Age associated memory changes in adults with Williams syndrome," *Developmental Neuropsychology 26* (2004), pp. 691–706.

91. Sarah Elison, Chris Stinton, and Patricia Howlin, "Health and social outcomes in adults with Williams syndrome: Findings from cross-sectional and longitudinal cohorts," *Research in Developmental Disabilities 31* (2010), pp. 587–599.

92. Teri Sforza with Howard and Sylvia Lenhoff, *The Strangest Song: One Father's Quest to Help His Daughter Find Her Voice* (Amherst, NY: Prometheus Books, 2006).

93. Lipe, "Beyond therapy: Music, spirituality, and health in human experience: A review of literature," pp. 209–240.

6 Tutti: Music in Relationships and Communities

1. Carolyn M. Clark and Marsha Rossiter, "Narrative learning in Adulthood," *New Directions for Adult and Continuing Education* no. 119 (2008), pp. 61–70; Ivor Goodson and Scherto Gill, *Narrative Pedagogy: Life History and Learning*, vol. 386 (New York, NY: Peter Lang, 2011); Bradford W. Mott, Charles B. Callaway, Luke S. Zettlemoyer, Seung Y. Lee, and James C. Lester, "Towards narrative-centered learning environments." In *Proceedings of the 1999 AAAI Fall Symposium on Narrative Intelligence* (1999), pp. 78–82.

2. Irwin G. Sarason (ed.). *Social Support: Theory, Research and Applications*, vol. 24 (New York: Springer Science & Business Media, 2013).

3. Evangelos Bebetsos, "Prediction of participation of undergraduate university students in a music and dance master's degree program," *International Journal of Instruction 8*, no. 2 (2015), pp. 165–176; Jennifer M. St. George, "The relationship of practice to continued participation in musical instrument learning." In *Proceedings of the XXVIIIth Annual Conference: 24–26 September 2006. Music Education, Standards and Practices*, p. 126. Australian Association for Research in Music Education, 2006.

4. Pachal Sheerhan and Sheina Orbell, "Using implementation intentions to increase attendance for cervical cancer screening," *Health Psychology 19*, no. 3 (2000), pp. 283–289.

5. Icek Ajzen, "The theory of planned behavior," *Organizational Behavior and Human Decision Processes 50* (1991), pp. 179–211.

6. Sheerhan and Orbell, "Using implementation intentions to increase attendance for cervical cancer screening," pp. 283–289.

7. Peter M. Gollwitzer, "Goal achievement: The role of intentions." In Wolfgang Stroebe and Miles Hewstone (eds.) *European Review of Social Psychology 4* (CITY: John Wiley & Sons, LTD, 1993), pp. 141–185.

8. Dean D. VonDras and Scott F. Madey, "The attainment of important health goals throughout adulthood: An integration of the theory of planned behavior and aspects of social support," *International Journal of Aging and Human Development 59*, no. 3 (2004), pp. 205–234.

9. Dean D. VonDras and Scott F. Madey, "Perceived spousal support and attainment of health goals in later-life," *International Journal of Personality Research 8*, no. 1 (2013), pp. 1–16.

10. Redford B. Williams, John C. Barefoot, Robert M. Califf, et al., "Prognosis of important social and economic resources among medically treated patients with angiographically documented coronary artery disease," *Journal of the American Medical Association* (JAMA) *267*, no. 4 (1992), pp. 520–524.

11. Sheerhan and Orbell, "Using implementation intentions to increase attendance for cervical cancer screening," pp. 283–289.

12. Harald Jørgensen, "Strategies for individual practice," *Musical Excellence: Strategies and Techniques to Enhance Performance* (2004), pp. 85–103; Jennifer Mary St. George, Allyson Patricia Holbrook, and Robert H. Cantwell, "Learning patterns in music practice: Links between disposition, practice strategies and outcomes," *Music Education Research 14*, no. 2 (2012), pp. 243–263.

13. Peggy A. Thoits, "Stress, coping, and social support processes: Where are we? What next?" *Journal of Health and Social Behavior Extra Issue* (1995), pp. 53–79.

14. Suzanne B. Hanser, "Music therapy and stress reduction research," *Journal of Music Therapy 22*, no. 4 (1985), pp. 193–206; Nechama Yehuda, "Music and stress," *Journal of Adult Development 18*, no. 2 (2011), pp. 85–94.

15. Susan Folkman, Richard S. Lazarus, Christine Dunkel-Schetter, Anita DeLongis, and Rand J. Gruen, "Dynamics of a stressful encounter: Cognitive appraisal, coping, and encounter outcomes," *Journal of Personality and Social Psychology 50*, no. 5 (1986), pp. 992–1003.

16. Charles S. Carver, Michael Scheier, and Jagdish Kumari Weintraub, "Assessing coping strategies: A theoretically based approach," *Journal of Personality and Social Psychology 56*, no. 2 (1989), pp. 267–283.

17. Elise Labbé, Nicholas Schmidt, Jonathan Babin, and Martha Pharr, "Coping with stress: The effectiveness of different types of music," *Applied Psychophysiology and Biofeedback 32*, no. 3-4 (2007), pp. 163–168; Scottie Blake Reynolds, "Biofeedback, relaxation training, and music: Homeostasis for coping with stress." *Biofeedback and Self-Regulation 9*, no. 2 (1984), pp. 169–179.

18. Veronica T. Fallon, Samantha Rubenstein, Rebecca Warfield, Hanna Ennerfelt, Brenna Hearn, and Echo Leaver, "Stress reduction from a musical intervention," *Psychomusicology: Music, Mind, and Brain 30*, no. 1 (2019), pp. 20–27.

19. Andrea Creech, Susan Hallam, Marcia Varvarigou, et al., "Active music making: A route to enhance subjective well-being among older people," *Perspectives in Public Health 133*, no. 1 (January 2013), pp. 36–43.

20. Creech, "Active music making: A route to enhance subjective well-being among older people," pp. 36–43.

21. Creech, "Active music making: A route to enhance subjective well-being among older people," pp. 36–43.

22. Joe Bozzi Band, "Joe's Coming Events" *JoeBozziBand.com* (2019). www.jo ebozziband.com/events.htm (accessed May 7, 2019); Steve Pick, "Trumpet Italiano," *St. Louis Magazine*, July 24, 2007. www.stlmag.com/Trumpet-Ita liano (accessed December 22, 2020).

23. "Henry Orland," *Prabook* (2019). https://prabook.com/web/henry.orland/4 65728 (accessed February 6, 2019).

24. Music at Michigan, "In memorium," *The University of Michigan School of Music 28*, no. 1 (1994), p. 38.

25. Creech, "Active music making: A route to enhance subjective well-being among older people," pp. 36–43.

26. Janice L. Chapman, *Singing and Teaching Singing: A Holistic Approach to Classical Voice* (London: Plural Publishing, 2016).

27. Carol Beynon and Jennifer Lang, "The more we get together, the more we learn: Focus on intergenerational and collaborative learning through singing," *Journal of Intergenerational Relationships 16*, nos. 1–2 (2018), pp. 45–63.

28. Brian Helman, personal communication, 2012.

29. We are offering our reflections on the photo Jazz Portrait – Harlem, New York, 1958 by Art Kane.
30. Don D. Coffman and Mary S. Adamek, "Perceived social support of New Horizons Band participants," *Contributions to Music Education* (2001), pp. 27–40; Christine Carucci, "An investigation of social support in adult recreational music ensembles," *International Journal of Community Music 5*, no. 3 (2012), pp. 237–252.
31. Beth Nemesh, "Family therapists' perspectives on implementing musical interventions in family therapy: A mixed-methods study," *Journal of Family Psychotherapy 28*, no. 2 (2017), pp. 118–133.
32. Jerry Fryrear, "Expressive Arts Therapy with Bereaved Families" (Doctoral dissertation, University of North Texas, 2001): 222.
33. Teresa Fernández de Jaun, "Music therapy for women survivors of intimate partner violence: An intercultural experience from a feminist perspective," *The Arts in Psychotherapy 48* (2016), pp. 19–27.
34. Alicia Ann Clair and Allison G. Ebberts, "The effects of music therapy on interactions between family caregivers and their care receivers with late stage dementia," *Journal of Music Therapy 34*, no. 3 (1997), pp. 148–164.
35. Alicia Ann Clair, "The effects of music therapy on engagement in family caregiver and care receiver couples with dementia," *American Journal of Alzheimer's Disease & Other Dementias® 17*, no. 5 (2002), pp. 286–290.
36. Meghan Hinman, "Our song: Music therapy with couples when one partner is medically hospitalized," *Music Therapy Perspectives 28*, no. 1 (2010), pp. 29–36.
37. Marco Aurelio Janaudis, Michelle Fleming, and Pablo González Blasco, "The sound of music: Transforming medical students into reflective practitioners," *Creative Education 4*, no. 6A (2013), p. 49.
38. Waldie E. Hanser, Tom F. M. ter Bogt, Annemieke J. M. Van den Tol, Ruth E. Mark, and Ad J. J. M. Vingerhoets, "Consolation through music: A survey study," *Musicae Scientiae 20*, no. 1 (2016), pp. 122–137.
39. Katrina Skewes McFerran and Daphne Rickson, "Community music therapy in schools: Realigning with the needs of contemporary students, staff and systems," *International Journal of Community Music 7*, no. 1 (2014), pp. 75–92.
40. S. Diamond, "Why we love music – and Freud despised it," *Psychology Today 10* (2012).
41. David Kozel, "Mythological archetype in music and principles of its interpretation," *International Review of the Aesthetics and Sociology of Music* (2016), pp. 3–15; David Kozel, "Repetition as a principle of mythological thinking and music of the twentieth century," *Musicologica Brunesia 52*, no. 2 (2017), pp. 157–167; Samuel Wilson (ed.). *Music – Psychoanalysis – Musicology* (New York: Routledge, 2017).
42. Şebnem Bilgiç and Rengin Acaroğlu, "Effects of listening to music on the comfort of chemotherapy patients," *Western Journal of Nursing Research 39*, no. 6 (2017), pp. 745–762.

43. Terrence Hays and Victor Minichiello, "The meaning of music in the lives of older people: A qualitative study," *Psychology of Music 33*, no. 4 (2005), pp. 437–451.

44. Ronald H. Aday and Benjaman S. Austin, "Images of aging in the lyrics of American country music," *Educational Gerontology 26*, no. 2 (2000), pp. 135–154.

45. Terrence Hays, Ruth Bright, and Victor Minichiello, "The contribution of music to positive aging: A review," *Journal of Aging and Identity 7*, no. 3 (2002), pp. 165–175; Jane E. Southcott, "And as I go, I love to sing: The Happy Wanderers, music and positive aging," *International Journal of Community Music 2*, nos. 2–3 (2009), pp. 143–156.

46. Creech, "Active music making: A route to enhance subjective well-being among older people," pp. 36–43.

47. "Music and Your Health," presented at a workshop given by Dr. Roy Ernst in April 2011 in Ohio. https://newhorizonsmusic.org/dr-roy-ernst.

48. "Music and Your Health."

49. New Horizons International Music Association, 2019. https://newhorizons music.org/new-horizons-groups.

50. Carl Sponenberg, personal correspondence, May 21, 2020.

51. Interview with Heather Gateau McEndree at Cumberland Valley School of Music, Wilson College, Chambersburg, PA, February 5, 2019.

52. Testimonials received February 5–9, 2019.

53. Paul Westermeyer, *Let Justice Sing: Hymnody and Justice* (Collegeville, Minnesota: Liturgical Press, 1998).

54. Woody Guthrie, *Bound for Glory* (New York, NY: Penguin Group (Plume) Publishing, 1943/1983); Pete Seeger, Rob Rosenthal, and Sam Rosenthal, *Pete Seeger in His Own Words* (New York: Routledge, 2015).

55. Joel Westheimer, "What did you learn in school today? Music education, democracy, and social justice," *The Oxford Handbook of Social Justice in Music Education* (2015), pp. 107–115.

56. David J. Hargreaves, Raymond MacDonald, and Dorothy Miell, "How do people communicate using music," *Musical Communication 1* (2005), pp. 1–26.

57. Peter J. Rentfrow, "The role of music in everyday life: Current directions in the social psychology of music," *Social and Personality Psychology Compass 6*, no. 5 (2012), pp. 402–416.

58. Minette Mans, *Music as Instrument of Diversity and Unity: Notes on a Namibian Landscape*, vol. 124 (Nordic Africa Institute, 2003), p. 49.

59. Natalie R. Sarrazin, *Music and the Child* (Geneseo, NY: Open SUNY Textbooks, 2016); Mans, *Music as Instrument of Diversity and Unity: Notes on a Namibian Landscape*, 2003; Natalei Sarrazin, "Exploring aesthetics focus on Native Americans: Using the example of Native American music, Natalie Sarrazin suggests ways of introducing the music of other cultures into the classroom," *Music Educators Journal 81*, no. 4 (1995), pp. 33–36.

60. Guylaine Vaillancourt, "Music therapy: A community approach to social justice," *The Arts in Psychotherapy 39*, no. 3 (2012), pp. 173–178.

61. UN General Assembly, "Universal Declaration of Human Rights," *UN General Assembly 302*, no. 2 (1948).

62. Julian Rappaport, *Community Psychology: Values, Research, and Action* (New York: Harcourt School, 1977).

63. Julian Rappaport, "Community psychology is (thank God) more than science," *American Journal of Community Psychology 35*, nos. 3–4 (2005), pp. 231–238.

64. Barbara Steinberg, "Open to all: How the Symphony of the New World made history," *Allegro 114*, no. 2 (2014). www.local802afm.org/allegro/articles/o pen-to-all (accessed June 16, 2019); Joan Peyser, "The Negro in Search of an Orchestra, Symphony of the New World Flyer, Used With Permission," *The New York Times*, November 26, 1967.

65. Mission Statement of the Symphony of the New World. http://barbaraanne shaircombblog.com/images/symphonyofthenewworld/symphonyofthenew world-missionstatement1964.jpg (accessed June 16, 2019).

66. "In Memory of Julius Miller," Greenidge Funeral Homes, Inc., November 24, 2017. https://greenidgefuneralhomes.com/tribute/details/131 6/Julius-Miller/obituary.html (accessed January 30, 2018).

67. Daniel Weinstein, Jacques Launay, Eiluned Pearce, Robin I. M. Dunbar, and Lauren Stewart, "Singing and social bonding: Changes in connectivity and pain threshold as a function of group size," *Evolution and Human Behavior 37*, no. 2 (2016), pp. 152–158.

68. Robin I. M. Dunbar, Kostas Kaskatis, Ian MacDonald, and Vinnie Barra, "Performance of music elevates pain threshold and positive affect: Implications for the evolutionary function of music," *Evolutionary Psychology 10*, no. 4 (2012), 147470491201000403.

69. Ryan Robert Luhrs, "Singing for Social Harmony: Choir Member Perceptions during Intergroup Contact" (Doctoral dissertation, The Florida State University, 2015).

70. Luhrs, "Singing for Social Harmony: Choir Member Perceptions during Intergroup Contact," 2015.

71. Idil Kokal, Annerose Engel, Sebastian Kirschner, and Christian Keysers, "Synchronized drumming enhances activity in the caudate and facilitates prosocial commitment – If the rhythm comes easily," *PLOS One 6*, no. 11 (2011), e27272.

72. Kozel, "Repetition as a principle of mythological thinking and music of the twentieth century," 2017.

73. Shannon S. Clark and S. Giacomantonio, "Music preferences and empathy: Toward predicting prosocial behavior," *Psychomusicology: Music, Mind, and Brain 23*, no. 3 (2013), p. 177.

74. Tobias Greitemeyer, "Effects of songs with prosocial lyrics on prosocial thoughts, affect, and behavior," *Journal of Experimental Social Psychology 45*, no. 1 (2009), pp. 186–190.

75. Tobias Greitemeyer, "Exposure to music with prosocial lyrics reduces aggression: First evidence and test of the underlying mechanism," *Journal of Experimental Social Psychology 47*, no. 1 (2011), pp. 28–36.

76. Tal-Chen Rabinowitch, Ian Cross, and Pamela Burnard, "Long-term musical group interaction has a positive influence on empathy in children," *Psychology of Music 41*, no. 4 (2013), pp. 484–498.

77. Hauke Egermann and Stephen McAdams, "Empathy and emotional contagion as a link between recognized and felt emotions in music listening," *Music Perception: An Interdisciplinary Journal 31*, no. 2 (2013), pp. 139–156.

78. Eric Clarke, Tia DeNora, and Jonna Vuoskoski, "Music, empathy and cultural understanding," *Physics of Life Reviews 15* (2015), pp. 61–88.

79. Stefan Koelsch, "Music-evoked emotions: Principles, brain correlates, and implications for therapy," *Annals of the New York Academy of Sciences 1337*, no. 1 (2015), pp. 193–201; Jonna K. Vuoskoski and Tuomas Eerola, "The pleasure evoked by sad music is mediated by feelings of being moved," *Frontiers in Psychology 8* (2017), pp. 439.

80. David Carr, "The significance of music for the moral and spiritual cultivation of virtue," *Philosophy of Music Education Review 14*, no. 2 (2006), pp. 103–117; Marcel Cobussen and Nanette Nielsen, *Music and Ethics* (New York: Routledge, 2016).

81. Klaus R. Scherer and Marcel R. Zentner, "Emotional effects of music: Production rules," *Music and Emotion: Theory and Research 16* (2001), pp. 361–392.

82. Luis-Manuel Garcia, *Can You Feel It, Too? Intimacy and Affect at Electronic Dance Music Events in Paris, Chicago, and Berlin* (The University of Chicago: UMI Dissertation Publishing, 2011), 3472580; Julie Taylor, "Tango," *Cultural Anthropology 2*, no. 4 (1987), pp. 481–493; Chrysalis L. Wright, "Family structure and music as a model of dyadic behavior," *Marriage & Family Review 49*, no. 4 (2013), pp. 309–329; Christine R. Yano, "Covering disclosures: Practices of intimacy, hierarchy, and authenticity in a Japanese popular music genre," *Popular Music and Society 28*, no. 2 (2005), pp. 193–205.

83. Ellen Laan, Walter Everaerd, Ricky Van Berlo, and Ludy Rijs, "Mood and sexual arousal in women," *Behaviour Research and Therapy 33*, no. 4 (1995), pp. 441–443; William B. Mitchell, Patricia Marten Dibartolo, Timothy A. Brown, and David H. Barlow, "Effects of positive and negative mood on sexual arousal in sexually functional males," *Archives of Sexual Behavior 27*, no. 2 (1998): 197–207; Cynthia Wan and Martin L. Lalumiere, "Can music cue sexual arousal?" *The Canadian Journal of Human Sexuality 26*, no. 3 (2017), pp. 238–248.

84. James L. May and Phyllis Ann Hamilton, "Effects of musically evoked affect on women's interpersonal attraction toward and perceptual judgments of physical attractiveness of men," *Motivation and Emotion 4*, no. 3 (1980), pp. 217–228; Christine Hall Hansen and Walter Krygowski, "Arousal-augmented priming effects: Rock music videos and sex object schemas," *Communication Research 21*, no. 1 (1994), pp. 24–47.

85. Christy Barongan and Gordon C. Nagayama Hall, "The influence of misogynous rap music on sexual aggression against women," *Psychology of Women Quarterly 19*, no. 2 (1995), pp. 195–207; Janet S. St. Lawrence and Doris J. Joyner, "The effects of sexually violent rock music on males'

acceptance of violence against women," *Psychology of Women Quarterly 15*, no. 1 (1991), pp. 49–63.

86. Jimmy McHugh, Dorothy Fields, and Johnny Warrington, *"I'm in the Mood for Love"* (Chicago IL: Robbins Music Corporation, 1935).

87. Carlos Gardel and Alfredo Le Pera, *"Por una Cabeza"* (Los Angeles, CA: Alfred Publishing, 1935).

88. Martin Brest, *Scent of a Woman (motion picture)* (Hollywood, CA: Universal Studios, 1992).

89. Terrance Hays, "Well-being in later life through music," *Australasian Journal on Ageing 24*, no. 1 (March 2005), pp. 28–32.

7 Rhythm and Blues: Work and Retirement

1. Walt Whitman, "A Song for Occupations," *Leaves of Grass* (public domain, 1881–1882), p. 169.

2. Merek Korczynski, Michael Pickering, and Emma Robertson, *Rhythms of Labour: Music at Work in Britain* (Cambridge: Cambridge University Press, 2013). Listen to examples of work songs in the Library of Congress, "Traditional Work Songs," *Digital Collections: The Library of Congress Celebrates the Songs of America.* www.loc.gov/collections/songs-of-america/art icles-and-essays/musical-styles/traditional-and-ethnic/traditional-work-songs.

3. Donald M. O'Neill, "Music to enhance the work environment," *Human Resource Management 5*, no. 3 (1966), pp. 17–23; Roy J. Shephard, "Perception of effort in the assessment of work capacity and the regulation of the intensity of effort," *International Journal of Industrial Ergonomics 13*, no. 1 (1994), pp. 67–80.

4. Stella Compton Dickinson, "7 ways music can enhance wellbeing," *Occupational Health & Wellbeing 70*, no. 2 (2018), pp. 20–21; Gordon Marc le Roux, "'Whistle while you work': A historical account of some associations among music, work, and health," *American Journal of Public Health 95*, no. 7 (2005), pp. 1106–1109.

5. Todd Rundgren, "Bang the Drum All Day," *The Ever Popular Tortured Artist Effect* (Bearsville, 1983), 66005.

6. Eli Ginzberg, Sol W. Ginsburg, Sidney Axelrad, and John L. Herma, *Occupational Choice: An Approach to a General Theory* (New York, Columbia University Press, 1951); Eli Ginzberg, "Toward a theory of occupational choice," *Occupations: The Vocational Guidance Journal 30*, no. 7 (1952), pp. 491–494.

7. Howie B and Robbie Robertson, "Dead End Kid," *Sinematic* (Santa Monica, CA: Universal Music Group, Inc., 2019).

8. Erik H. Erikson, *Childhood and Society* (New York, NY: W. W. Norton & Company, 1993); Erik H. Erikson *Identity and the Life Cycle* (New York, NY: W. W. Norton & Company, 1994); Erik H. Erikson, *Identity: Youth and Crisis* (New York, NY: W. W. Norton & Company, 1968).

9. Donald E. Super, "A theory of vocational development," *American Psychologist 8*, no. 5 (1953), pp. 185–190; Donald E. Super,

Reuben Starishevsky, Norman Matlin, and Jan Pieere Jordaan, *Career Development; Self-Concept Theory* (New York, NY: College Entrance Examination Board, 1963).

10. Karen Burland, "Becoming a Musician: A Longitudinal Study Investigating the Career Transitions of Undergraduate Music Students" (PhD dissertation, University of Sheffield, Sheffield, UK, 2005); Robert R. Faulkner, "Career concerns and mobility motivations of orchestra musicians," *The Sociological Quarterly 14*, no. 3 (1973), pp. 334–349; Charles Umney and Lefteris Kretsos, "'That's the experience' – Passion, work precarity, and life transitions among London jazz musicians," *Work and Occupations 42*, no. 3 (2015), pp. 313–334; Jonas Vaag, Fay Giæver, and Ottar Bjerkeset, "Specific demands and resources in the career of the Norwegian freelance musician," *Arts & Health 6*, no. 3 (2014), pp. 205–222.

11. Shoshona Dobrow Riza and Daniel Heller, "Follow your heart or your head? A longitudinal study of the facilitating role of calling and ability in the pursuit of a challenging career," *Journal of Applied Psychology 100*, no. 3 (2015), pp. 695–712; Richard Schulz and Jutta Heckhausen, "A life span model of successful aging," *American Psychologist 51*, no. 7 (1996), pp. 702–714.

12. Angus Young, Malcolm Young, and Ronald Belford Scott, "*It's a Long Way to the Top (If You Wanna Rock 'n' Roll)*" (Santa Monica, CA: Universal Music Publishing Group, 1975).

13. Carl G. Jung, "The Stages of Life," *Volume 8 of the Collected Works of C. G. Jung, 2nd ed.* (Princeton, NJ: Princeton University Press, 1969), pp. 387–403.

14. David Gutmann, *The Human Elder in Nature, Culture, and Society* (New York, NY: Routledge, 2019); David Gutmann, *Reclaimed Powers: Men and Women in Later Life* (Evanston, IL: Northwestern University Press, 1994); Bernice L. Neugarten (ed.). *Middle Age and Aging* (Chicago, IL: University of Chicago Press, 1968).

15. James W. Fowler, *Stages of Faith: The Psychology of Human Development and the Quest for Meaning* (New York, NY: HarperCollins, 1981).

16. Robert V. Wells, *Life Flows on in Endless Song: Folk Songs and American History* (Urbana, IL: University of Illinois Press, 2009).

17. John L. Holland, *Making Vocational Choices: A Theory of Vocational Personalities and Work Environments* (Odessa, FL: Psychological Assessment Resources, 1997).

18. Paul T. Costa, Robert R. McCrae, and John L. Holland, "Personality and vocational interests in an adult sample," *Journal of Applied Psychology 69*, no. 3 (1984), pp. 390–400.

19. Adrian Furnham, "Vocational preference and P–O fit: Reflections on Holland's theory of vocational choice," *Applied Psychology 50*, no. 1 (2001), pp. 5–29.

20. Anja Ghetta, Andreas Hirschi, Mo Wang, Jérôme Rossier, and Anne Herrmann, "Birds of a feather flock together: How congruence between worker and occupational personality relates to job satisfaction over time," *Journal of Vocational Behavior* (2020), p. 103412; Melanie C. Harper

and Marie F. Shoffner, "Counseling for continued career development after retirement: An application of the theory of work adjustment," *The Career Development Quarterly 52*, no. 3 (2004), pp. 272–284; Myrna Reis and Dolores Pushkar Gold, "Retirement, personality, and life satisfaction: A review and two models," *Journal of Applied Gerontology 12*, no. 2 (1993), pp. 261–282; Laura Venz and Mo Wang, "The importance of interests for understanding retirement." In Christopher D. Nye and James Rounds (eds.). *Vocational Interests in the Workplace: Rethinking Behavior at Work* (New York, NY: Routledge, 2019), pp. 165–188.

21. Edward Julius Stieglitz, *The Second Forty Years* (New York, NY: J. B. Lippincott Co., 1946).

22. David W. Smith, "Aging and the careers of symphony orchestra musicians," *Medical Problems of Performing Artists 4*, no. 2 (1989), pp. 81–85.

23. Johnnie Temple, *"Getting Old Blues"* (London, UK: Decca Records, 1939).

24. Jeanette N. Cleveland and Lynn M. Shore, "Work and employment." In James E. Birren (ed.). *Encyclopedia of Gerontology 2* (New York, NY: Academic Press, 1996).

25. New Kids on the Block, *New Kids on the Block* (New York, NY: Columbia Records Group, 1986).

26. Jean E. Kubeck, Norma D. Delp, Tammy K. Haslett, and Michael A. McDaniel, "Does job-related training performance decline with age?" *Psychology and Aging 1*, no. 11 (1996), pp. 92–107.

27. Kurt Kraiger, "Designing effective training for older workers." In *The Palgrave Handbook of Age Diversity and Work* (London, UK: Palgrave Macmillan, 2017), pp. 639–667.

28. Leo Missinne, *Reflections on Aging: A Spiritual Guide* (Liguorit, MO: Liguori Publications, 1990), p. 10.

29. Carl Rogers, *A Way of Being* (Boston, MA: Houghton Mifflin Co., 1980).

30. Daniel C. Feldman and Kenneth S. Shultz, "Career embeddedness and career crafting among older workers," *Aging and Work in the 21st Century* (New York, NY: Routledge, 2018), pp. 191–212.

31. Eugene L. Thomas, "Mid-career changes: Self-selected or externally mandated?" *Vocational Guidance Quarterly 25*, no. 4 (1977), pp. 320–328.

32. Timothy A. Judge, Daniel Heller, and Michael K. Mount, "Five-factor model of personality and job satisfaction: A meta-analysis," *Journal of Applied Psychology 87*, no. 3 (2002), pp. 530–541; Sherry E. Sullivan, "The changing nature of careers: A review and research agenda," *Journal of Management 25*, no. 3 (1999), pp. 457–484; Eugene L. Thomas, "A typology of mid-life career changers," *Journal of Vocational Behavior 16*, no. 2 (1980), pp. 173–182.

33. Jon Lorence and Jeylan T. Mortimer, "Job involvement through the life course: A panel study of three age groups," *American Sociological Review* (1985), pp. 618–638; Ulrich Orth, Richard W. Robins, and Keith F. Widaman, "Life-span development of self-esteem and its effects on important life outcomes," *Journal of Personality and Social Psychology 102*, no. 6 (2012), pp. 1271–1288.

34. Jeanette N. Cleveland and Lynn M. Shore, "Self- and supervisory perspectives on age and work attitudes and performance," *Journal of Applied Psychology 77*, no. 4 (1992), pp. 469–484; Spencer G. Niles and Gary E. Goodnough, "Life-role salience and values: A review of recent research," *The Career Development Quarterly 45*, no. 1 (1996), pp. 65–86; Christine M. Riordan and Lynn McFarlane Shore, "Demographic diversity and employee attitudes: An empirical examination of relational demography within work units," *Journal of Applied Psychology 82*, no. 3 (1997), pp. 342–358; Peter Warr, "Age and occupational well-being," *Psychology and Aging 7*, no. 1 (1992), pp. 37–45; Peter Warr, *Work, Unemployment, and Mental Health* (Oxford, UK: Oxford University Press, 1987).

35. Jean M. Twenge, "A review of the empirical evidence on generational differences in work attitudes," *Journal of Business and Psychology 25*, no. 2 (2010), pp. 201–210.

36. Salvator A. Piazza, personal communications with Dean D. VonDras, 1978–1980. Read more about Salvator A. Piazza (1917–1986) in the articles, "Stokowski Hears 12 Young Musicians in Secret Audition," *St. Louis Post-Dispatch*, May 24, 1940, p. 3. www.newspapers.com/newspage/139313577 (accessed July 15, 2020); "Big local music program (excerpts taken from the December 17, 1953, issue of *The Troy Tribune*)," *Troy Times Tribune Newspaper Archives*, December 19, 2013, p. 35. https://newspaperarchive.com/troy-times-tribune-dec-19–2013-p-35 (accessed July 15, 2020); "Employees honored by Hazelwood Schools," July 13, 1978, *St. Louis Post-Dispatch*, p. 85. www.newspapers.com/newspage/139148691 (accessed July 15, 2020).

37. Malcom Sargeant, *Age Discrimination in Employment* (New York, NY: Routledge, 2016).

38. Bill Doerrfeld, "Ageism in composer opportunities," *NewMusicBox*, June 5, 2013. https://nmbx.newmusicusa.org/ageism-in-composer-opportunities (accessed May 27, 2020); Bill Turner, "If you're gray, you're sent away," *Allegro 113*, no. 2 (2013). www.local802afm.org/allegro/articles/if-youre-gray-youre-sent-away (accessed May 27, 2020).

39. Richard A. Posthuma and Michael A. Campion, "Age stereotypes in the workplace: Common stereotypes, moderators, and future research directions," *Journal of Management 35*, no. 1 (2009), pp. 158–188.

40. Richard A. Posthuma, Maria Fernanda Wagstaff, and Michael A. Campion, "16 age stereotypes and workplace age discrimination." In J. W. Hedge and W. C. Borman (eds.). *The Oxford Handbook of Work and Aging* (Oxford, UK: Oxford University Press, 2012), pp. 298–312; Lisa M. Finkelstein, Eden B. King, and Elora C. Voyles, "Age meta-stereotyping and cross-age workplace interactions: A meta view of age stereotypes at work," *Work, Aging and Retirement 1*, no. 1 (2015), pp. 26–40.

41. Richard A. Posthuma and Michael A. Campion, "Age stereotypes in the workplace: Common stereotypes, moderators, and future research directions," *Journal of Management 35*, no. 1 (2009), pp. 158–188; Malcolm Sargeant, *Age Discrimination: Ageism in Employment and Service Provision* (New York: Routledge, 2016).

42. William J. Carnes and Nina Radojevich-Kelley, "The effects of the glass ceiling on women in the workforce: Where are they and where are they going?" *Review of Management Innovation & Creativity 4*, no. 10 (2011), pp. 70–79; Cindi Katz and Janice Monk, *Full Circles: Geographies of Women over the Life Course* (New York, NY: Routledge, 2014).

43. Sarah Damaske and Adrianne Frech, "Women's work pathways across the life course," *Demography 53*, no. 2 (2016), pp. 365–391; Geraldine Pratt and Susan Hanson, "Women and work across the life course." In C. Katz and J. Monk (eds.). *Full Circles: Geographies of Women over the Life Course* (New York, NY: Routledge, 1993), pp. 27–54; Heather E. Quick and Phyllis Moen, "Gender, employment and retirement quality: A life course approach to the differential experiences of men and women," *Journal of Occupational Health Psychology 3*, no. 1 (1998), pp. 44–64.

44. Irene Padavic and Barbara F. Reskin, *Women and Men at Work* (Thousand Oaks, CA: Pine Forge Press, 2002).

45. Geraldine Grady and Alma M. McCarthy, "Work-life integration: Experiences of mid-career professional working mothers," *Journal of Managerial Psychology 23*, no. 5 (2008), pp. 599–622.

46. Aminah Ahmad, "Job, family and individual factors as predictors of work-family conflict," *The Journal of Human Resource and Adult Learning 4*, no. 1 (2008), pp. 57–65; Anne Grönlund, "More control, less conflict? Job demand – Control, gender and work–family conflict," *Gender, Work & Organization 14*, no. 5 (2007), pp. 476–497; Jeffrey E. Hill, "Work-family facilitation and conflict, working fathers and mothers, work-family stressors and support," *Journal of Family Issues 26*, no. 6 (2005), pp. 793–819.

47. Rachel Gali Cinamon and Yisrael Rich, "Gender differences in the importance of work and family roles: Implications for work–family conflict," *Sex Roles 47*, nos. 11–12 (2002), pp. 531–541; James D. Wright, "Are working women really more satisfied? Evidence from several national surveys," *Journal of Marriage and the Family* (1978), pp. 301–313.

48. Kathleen Fuegen, Monica Biernat, Elizabeth Haines, and Kay Deaux, "Mothers and fathers in the workplace: How gender and parental status influence judgments of job-related competence," *Journal of Social Issues 60*, no. 4 (2004), pp. 737–754; Madeline E. Heilman and Tyler G. Okimoto, "Motherhood: A potential source of bias in employment decisions," *Journal of Applied Psychology 93*, no. 1 (2008), pp. 189–198.

49. Claudia Goldin and Cecilia Rouse, "Orchestrating impartiality: The impact of 'blind' auditions on female musicians," *American Economic Review 90*, no. 4 (2000), pp. 715–741; Antoinette D. Handy, *Black Women in American Bands and Orchestras* (Metuchen, NJ: Scarecrow Press, 1998); Carol J. Oja, "Everett Lee and the racial politics of orchestral conducting," *American Music Review 43*, no. 1 (2013); Barbara Steinberg, "Open to all: How the symphony of the New World made history," *Allegro 114*, no. 2 (2014). www.local802afm.org/allegro/articles/open-to-all (accessed June 6, 2020); United Nations and the Rule of Law, "Equality and discrimination," *Human Rights*. www.un.org/ruleoflaw/thematic-areas/human-rights/equality-and-non-discrimination (accessed June 6, 2020).

50. www.catalyst.org (accessed June 6, 2020).
51. Jacob S. Hacker, Gregory A. Huber, Austin Nichols, Philipp Rehm, and Stuart Craig, *Economic Insecurity across the American States* (New York, NY: The Rockefeller Foundation, 2019).
52. Alexandra Cawthorne, "Elderly poverty: The challenge before us," *Center for American Progress*, July 2008. www.americanprogress.org/wp-content/uploa ds/issues/2008/07/pdf/elderly_poverty.pdf (accessed June 7, 2020).
53. For more information about the Social Security Trust Funds, and Medicare and Medicaid Health Insurance programs, see the following: SSA.gov, "What Are Trust Funds," Social Security Press Office. www.ssa.gov/news/ press/factsheets/WhatAreTheTrust.htm (accessed December 29, 2020); Medicare.gov, "What's Medicare?" *Centers for Medicare & Medicaid Services.* www.medicare.gov/what-medicare-covers/your-medicare-cover age-choices/whats-medicare (accessed December 29, 2020); Medicaid.gov, "Medicaid," *Centers for Medicare & Medicaid Services.* www.medicaid.gov/ medicaid/index.html (accessed December 29, 2020).
54. Human Rights Orchestra. www.musiciansforhumanrights.org/vision-new (accessed June 7, 2020).
55. Black Pearl Chamber Orchestra. www.blackpearlco.org (accessed June 7, 2020); Jeri Lynne Johnson. www.jerilynnejohnson.com/epk-1 (accessed June 7, 2020).
56. OrchKids. www.bsomusic.org/education-community/young-musicians/orch kids.aspx (accessed 7, 2020); Marin Alsop. www.bsomusic.org/musicians/ musician/marin-alsop (accessed June 7, 2020).
57. Philip Gossett, "The overtures of Rossini," *19th-Century Music 3*, no. 1 (1979), pp. 3–31; Philip Gossett, William Ashbrook, Julian Budden, Friedrich Lippmann, Andrew Porter, and Mosco Carner, *The New Grove Masters of Italian Opera: Rossini, Donizetti, Bellini, Verdi, Puccini* (New York, NY: WW Norton & Company, 1997); Emanuele Senici (ed.). *The Cambridge Companion to Rossini* (Cambridge, England: Cambridge University Press, 2004).
58. Henry Sutherland Edwards, *The Life of Rossini* (London, UK: Hurst and Blackett, 1869); Richard Osborne, *Rossini: His Life and Works, 2nd ed.* (Oxford, UK: Oxford University Press, 2007); Daniel W. Schwartz, "Rossini: A psychoanalytic approach to 'the great renunciation,'" *Journal of the American Psychoanalytic Association 13*, no. 3 (1965), pp. 551–569.
59. Daniel C. Feldman and Terry A. Beehr, "A three-phase model of retirement decision making," *American Psychologist 66*, no. 3 (2011), pp. 193–203.
60. Leisa D. Sargent, Mary Dean Lee, Bill Martin, and Jelena Zikic, "Reinventing retirement: New pathways, new arrangements, new meanings," *Human Relations 66*, no. 1 (2013), pp. 3–21.
61. Lisa Greenwald, Craig Copeland, and Jack VanDerhei, "The 2017 Retirement Confidence Survey: Many workers lack retirement confidence and feel stressed about retirement preparations," *EBRI Issue Brief 431* (2017), pp. 1–29.

62. Ousmane Faye and Gilena Andrade, "The Madrid International Plan of Action on Ageing: Where do we stand fifteen years later? Experiences and lessons from selected countries in West and Central Africa," *International Journal of Ageing in Developing Countries 2*, no. 2 (2018), pp. 153–172.

63. Barry Bosworth, Gary Burtless, and Kan Zhang, "Later retirement, inequality in old age, and the growing gap in longevity between rich and poor," *Economic Studies at Brookings 87* (2016).

64. Robert C. Atchley, *The Social Forces in Later Life: An Introduction to Social Gerontology* (Belmont, CA: Wadsworth Publishing Company, 1980).

65. David E. Bloom, David Canning, and Michael Moore, *A Theory of Retirement, No. w13630* (Cambridge, MA: National Bureau of Economic Research, 2007); E. Michael Brady, *Retirement: The Challenge of Change* (Portland, ME: University of Southern Maine, 1988); Megan C. Lytle, Pamela F. Foley, and Elizabeth W. Cotter, "Career and retirement theories: Relevance for older workers across cultures," *Journal of Career Development 42*, no. 3 (2015), pp. 185–198.

66. David Allen Coe and Johnny Paycheck, *"Take This Job and Shove It"* (Nashville, TN: Warner Chappell Music, Inc., 1977).

67. Jerry Lieber, Mike Stoller, and Leslie Uggams, "Is That All There Is?" *Leslie Uggams – What's an Uggams?* (New York, NY: Atlantic Records Group, 1968), SD 8198.

68. David J. Ekerdt, Raymond Bossé, and Sue Levkoff, "An empirical test for phases of retirement: Findings from the normative aging study," *Journal of Gerontology 40*, no. 1 (1985), pp. 95–101.

69. Robert C. Atchley, *The Sociology of Retirement* (New York, NY: Schenkman, 1976).

70. Robert C. Atchley, "The process of retirement: Comparing men and women." In Maximiliane Szinovacz (ed.). *Women's Retirement: Policy Implications of Recent Research, vol. 6* (Beverly Hills, CA: Sage, 1982), pp. 153–168.

71. Georg Henning, Magnus Lindwall, and Boo Johansson, "Continuity in well-being in the transition to retirement," *Geropsych: The Journal of Gerontopsychology and Geriatric Psychiatry 29*, no. 4 (2016), pp. 225–237; G. Mein, P. Higgs, J. Ferrie, and S. A. Stansfeld, "Paradigms of retirement: The importance of health and ageing in the Whitehall II study," *Social Science & Medicine 47*, no. 4 (1998), pp. 535–545; Mo Wang, Kène Henkens, and Hanna van Solinge, "Retirement adjustment: A review of theoretical and empirical advancements," *American Psychologist 66*, no. 3 (2011), pp. 204–213.

72. Evelyne Fouquereau, Anne Fernandez, Antonio Manuel Fonseca, Maria Constança Paul, and Virpi Uotinen, "Perceptions of and satisfaction with retirement: A comparison of six European Union countries," *Psychology and Aging 20*, no. 3 (2005), pp. 524–528.

73. Ann Buchanan and Anna Rotkirch (eds.). *The Role of Grandparents in the 21st Century: Global Perspectives on Changing Roles and Consequences* (Routledge, 2020); Tamara K. Hareven, "Aging and generational relations: A historical

and life course perspective," *Annual Review of Sociology 20*, no. 1 (1994), pp. 437–461.

74. Jacquelyn Boone James, Elyssa Besen, Christina Matz-Costa, and Marcie Pitt-Catsouphes, "Engaged as we age: The end of retirement as we know it," *The Sloan Center on Aging and Work, Issue Brief 24* (2010), pp. 1–20. https://youngatheartchorus.com (accessed July 22, 2020).

75. Amanda Sonnega, Jessica D. Faul, Mary Beth Ofstedal, Kenneth M. Langa, John W. R. Phillips, and David R. Weir, "Cohort profile: The health and retirement study (HRS)," *International Journal of Epidemiology 43*, no. 2 (2014), pp. 576–585.

76. Adam Gussow, *Mister Satan's Apprentice: A Blues Memoir* (Minneapolis, MN: University of Minnesota Press, 2009).

77. V. Scott Balcerek and Ryan Suffern, *Satan and Adam*. V. Scott Balcerek (dir.) (New York, NY: Cargo Film & Releasing, 2018); Ken Jaworoski, "Satan & Adam review: Two musicians team up to play the blues," *New York Times*, April 11, 2019, p. C7. www.nytimes.com/2019/04/11/movies/satan-and-adam-review.html (accessed June 5, 2020).

78. Andy Beta, interview with Hailu Mergia, "How 5 Musicians over 70 Are Dealing with Life, Loss, and Touring in the Age of Coronavirus," *Pitchfork*, May 11, 2020. https://pitchfork.com/features/interview/how-5-musicians-over-70-are-dealing-with-life-loss-and-touring-in-the-age-of-coronavirus (accessed May 19, 2020); Lucien Johnson, "Itineraries of Modern Ethiopian Instrumental Music" (PhD. dissertation, Victoria University of Wellington, 2017); Hailu Mergia, interview with Hailu Mergia, "Ethiopian Musician Hailu Mergia: From the Nightclubs of Addis Ababa to a Cab in DC," *The World*, July 12, 2013. www.pri.org/stories/2013–07–12/ethiopian-musician-hailu-mergia-nightclubs-addis-ababa-cab-dc (accessed May 19, 2020); Chris Richards, "Hailu Mergia: A beloved Ethiopian musician of a generation ago now stays quiet in DC," *Washington Post*, June 28, 2013. www.washingtonpost.com/entertainment/music/hailu-mergia-a-beloved-ethiopian-musician-of-a-generation-ago-now-stays-quiet-in-dc/2013/06/27/c34090b8-ddd7-11e2-948c-d644453cf169_story.html (accessed May 19, 2020); Joe Tangari, "Hailu Mergia – Hailu Mergia and His Classical Instrument," *Pitchfork*, June 28, 2013. https://pitchfork.com/reviews/albums/18162-hailu-mergia-hailu-mergia-and-his-classical-instrument (accessed May 19, 2020).

79. Henri J. Nouwen and Walter J. Gaffney, *Aging: The Fulfillment of Life* (New York, NY: Doubleday, 1976).

8 Requiem: Spirituality and End-of-Life

1. This statement is akin to ideas regarding categorization and experience expressed by people such as Kant, Husserl, Foucault, William James, and Sartre, to name a few. Also, see Michel Foucault, *The Order of Things: An Archaeology of the Human Sciences* (New York, NY: Vintage Books, 1973), p. 9.

2. Carl G. Jung, "Psychology and religion," *Volume 11 of the Collected Works of C. G. Jung*, 2nd ed. (Princeton, NJ: Princeton University Press, 1969), p. 366.
3. Dean D. VonDras, "The religio-spiritual context of lifestyle practices and health behaviors." In Dean D. VonDras (ed.). *Better Health through Spiritual Practices: A Guide to Religious Behaviors and Perspectives That Benefit Mind and Body* (Santa Barbara, CA: Praeger: An Imprint of ABC-CLIO, LLC, 2017), p. 5.
4. Joshua M. Gold, "Spirituality and self-actualization: Considerations for 21st century counsellors," *Journal of Humanistic Counseling 52* (2013), pp. 223–234.
5. Robert J. Havighurst, "Successful aging," *Processes of Aging: Social and Psychological Perspectives 1* (1963), pp. 299–320.
6. Marguerite DeLiema and Vern L. Bengtson, "Activity theory, disengagement theory, and successful aging," *Encyclopedia of Geropsychology* (2017), pp. 15–20.
7. Nestor Asiamah, "Social engagement and physical activity: Commentary on why the Activity and Disengagement Theories of ageing may both be valid," *Cogent Medicine 4*, no. 1 (2017), 1289664.
8. Lars Tornstam, "Maturing into gerotranscendence," *Journal of Transpersonal Psychology 43*, no. 2 (2011), pp. 160–180.
9. James J. Dowd, "Aging as exchange: A preface to theory," *Journal of Gerontology 30*, no. 5 (1975), pp. 584–594.
10. Robert C. Atchley, "A continuity theory of normal aging," *The Gerontologist 29*, no. 2 (1989), pp. 183–190.
11. Paul J. Griffiths, *Problems of Religious Diversity* (Hoboken, NJ: John Wiley & Sons, 2015).
12. Matthew Guerrieri, "Messiaen: Finding salvation in birdsong," *Red Bull Music Academy Daily*, March 23, 2016. https://daily.redbullmusicacademy.com/2016/03/messiaen-finding-salvation-in-birdsong (accessed October 10, 2019); Raymond Head, "Holst – Astrology and modernism in 'The Planets,'" *Tempo 187* (1993), pp. 15–24; Anamaria Mădălina Hotoran, "Musical and spiritual affinities: Olivier Messiaen and Eduard Terényi," *Recent Advances in Acoustics & Music* (2010), pp. 190–195.
13. Michael Steinberg, "Holst: The Planets," program notes, San Francisco Symphony, April 2018. www.sfsymphony.org/Watch-Listen-Learn/Read-Program-Notes/Program-Notes/Holst-The-Planets.aspx (accessed October 10, 2019).
14. Timothy Koozin, "Spiritual-temporal imagery in the music of Oliver Messiaen and Toru Takemitsu," *Contemporary Music Review 7* (1993), pp. 185–202.
15. Guerrieri, "Messiaen: Finding salvation in birdsong," 2016.
16. Martin Lamonica (deputy ed.). "Sensing the dead is perfectly normal – and often helpful," *The Conversation*, July 19, 2017. https://theconversation.com/sensing-the-dead-is-perfectly-normal-and-often-helpful-81048 (accessed August 1, 2019).

17. Diedre Barrett, "Through a glass darkly: Images of the dead in dreams," *Omega 24*, no. 4 (1991–1992), pp. 97–108.

18. W. Dewi Rees, "The hallucinations of widowhood," *British Medical Journal 4* (1971), pp. 37–41.

19. Gillian Bennett, *Alas, Poor Ghost! Traditions of Belief in Story and Discourse* (Logan, UT: Utah State University Press, 1999), p. 77.

20. Mac Randall, "Given the gift of life: Interview with Frank Vignola," *JazzTimes 48* (May 2018), p. 11.

21. V. Turner, *The Ritual Process: Structure and Antistructure* (Ithaca, NY: Cornell University Press, 1969).

22. S. H. Foulkes, *Introduction to Group-Analytic Psychotherapy: Studies in the Social Integration of Individual and Groups* (London: Karnac, 1948/1991).

23. Scott F. Madey, "Epilogue: Religion, science, and health – A question of balance or the space between?" In Dean D. VonDras (ed.). *Better Health through Spiritual Practices: A Guide to Religious Behaviors and Perspectives That Benefit Mind and Body* (Santa Barbara, CA: Praeger: An Imprint of ABC-CLIO, LLC, 2017), pp. 335–357.

24. Cheryl L. Nosek et al., "End of life dreams and visions: A qualitative perspective from hospice patients," *American Journal of Hospice and Palliative Medicine 32*, no. 3 (2015), pp. 269–274.

25. Nosek et al., "End of life dreams and visions: A qualitative perspective from hospice patients," pp. 269–274.

26. Joke Bradt and Cheryl Dileo, "Music therapy for end of life care," *Cochran Database of Systematic Reviews 1* (2010), pp. 1–23.

27. Thich Nhat Hanh, *The Heart of the Buddha's Teaching: Transforming Suffering into Peace, Joy, and Liberation* (New York, NY: Broadway Books, 1998).

28. Donald S. Lopez, "Eightfold Path," May 12, 2020. https://Britannica.com/topic/Eightfold-Path.

29. Huston Smith, *The World's Religions* (York, NY: HarperOne, 1991).

30. Albert Ellis, *Humanistic Psychotherapy: The Rational-Emotive Approach* (New York, NY: McGraw-Hill Company, 1974).

31. Carl R. Rogers, *On Becoming a Person: A Therapist's View of Psychotherapy* (Boston, MA: Houghton Mifflin Company, 1961).

32. Thich Nhat Hanh, *The Heart of the Buddha's Teaching: Transforming Suffering into Peace, Joy, and Liberation*, p. 63.

33. Laury Rappaport and Debra Kalmanowitz, "Mindfulness, psychotherapy, and the arts therapies." In Laury Rappaport (ed.). *Mindfulness and the Arts Therapies: Theory and Practice* (London, UK: Jessica Kingsley Publishers, 2014), pp. 24–36.

34. S. Sahand Mohammadi Ziabari and Jan Treur, "An Adaptive Cognitive Temporal-Causal Network Model of a Mindfulness Therapy Based on Music." *Conference Paper* (2018), pp. 1–12.

35. Teresia Lesiuk, "The development of a mindfulness-based music therapy (MBMT) program for women receiving adjuvant chemotherapy for breast cancer," *Healthcare 4* (2014), pp. 1–14.

36. Ocar Lecuona de la Cruz and Raquel Rodriguez-Carvajal, "Mindfulness and music: A promising subject of an unmapped field," *International Journal of Behavioral Research & Psychology 2*, no. 3 (2014), pp. 27–35.
37. Thich Nhat Hanh, *The Heart of the Buddha's Teaching: Transforming Suffering into Peace, Joy, and Liberation*, p. 84.
38. Donald Hodges, "Why Study Music?" *Music for Music's Sake*, National Association for Music Education. https://nafme.org/advocacy/what-to-say/music-for-musics-sake (accessed July 3, 2020).
39. Smith, *The World's Religions*, p. 107.
40. Thich Nhat Hanh, *The Heart of the Buddha's Teaching: Transforming Suffering into Peace, Joy, and Liberation*, p. 101.
41. Mihaly Csikszentmihalyi, *Flow: The Psychology of Optimal Experience* (New York, NY: HarperCollins Publishers, 2008).
42. Thich Nhat Hanh, *The Heart of the Buddha's Teaching: Transforming Suffering into Peace, Joy, and Liberation*, p. 105.
43. Smith, *The World's Religions*, p. 108.
44. Judith Allen Shelly and Sharon Fish, *Spirituality Care: The Nurse's Role* (Ann Arbor, MI: InterVarsity Press, 1988).
45. David O. Moberg, *Aging and Spirituality: Spiritual Dimensions of Aging Theory, Research, Practice, and Policy* (New York, NY: Routledge, 2001), pp. 161–166.
46. Moberg, *Aging and Spirituality: Spiritual Dimensions of Aging Theory, Research, Practice, and Policy*, pp. 161–166.
47. Robert N. Butler, "The life review: An interpretation of reminiscence in the aged," *Psychiatry 26* (1963), pp. 65–76.

9 Coda: Defining, Directing, and Celebrating Life

1. Walt Whitman, "Song of Myself," *Leaves of Grass* (This work is in the public domain, 1891–1892), p. 29.
2. Thomas Gilovich and Victoria Husted Medvec, "Some counterfactual determinants of satisfaction and regret." In Neal J. Roese and James M. Olson (eds.). *What Might Have Been: The Social Psychology of Counterfactual Thinking* (Mawah, NJ: Lawrence Erlbaum Associates, Inc., 1995), pp. 259–282.
3. Jeffrey M. Lyness, "Lessons from lives of celebrated musicians: What Armstrong, Cash, Dylan, Ellington, Fitzgerald, and Sinatra can teach us about creative resilience and aging," *American Journal of Geriatric Psychiatry 25*, no. 12 (2017), pp. 1295–1299.
4. Thomas Merton, *New Seeds of Contemplation* (New York, NY: New Directions Books, 1961), p. 60.
5. Margaret Clark, "Cultural values and dependency in later life." In *Aging and Modernization* (New York: Appleton-Century-Crofts, 1972), p. 263.
6. Vinoo Alluri, Petri Toiviainen, Iiro P. Jaaskeiainen, Enrico Glerean, Mikko Sams, and Elvira Brattico, "Large-scale brain networks emerge from dynamic processing of musical timbre, key, and rhythm," *NeuroImage 59*, no. 4 (February 2012), pp. 3677–3689.

7. David J. Chalmers, "Facing Up to the Problem of Consciousness." cogprints. org/316/1/consciousness.html (accessed August 15, 2019).

8. Gayla Mills, *Making Music for Life: Rediscover Your Musical Passion* (Mineola, NY: Dover Publications, Inc., 2019), p. 114.

9. Carl G. Jung, "The stages of life," *Volume 8 of the Collected Works of C. G. Jung*, 2nd ed. (Princeton, NJ: Princeton University Press, 1969), p. 396.

10. Jung, "The stages of life," p. 396.

11. Emily Remler, *Advanced Jazz and Latin Improvisation* (DVD, 2005). Hot Licks, Music Sales of America, distributed by Hal Leonard Corporation, NY.

12. Cristina Isabel Castellano González, Ramón García, Scarlet Cheng, Judithe Hernández, and Patssi Valdez, "Judithe Hernández and Patssi Valdez: One Path Two Journeys," exh. cat. (Pomona, CA: Millard Sheets Art Center at Fairplex, 2017).

13. Mills, *Making Music for Life: Rediscover Your Musical Passion*, pp. 158–175.

14. Dean D. VonDras and Scott F. Madey, "Perceived spousal support and attainment of health goals in later-life," *International Journal of Psychological Research 8*, no. 1 (2013), pp. 1–16.

15. Marion Lampe, personal communication with Dean D. VonDras (1984). Dr. Lampe (1928–2018) was a life-long learner who began piano lessons at age four, earned degrees from Julliard School of Music and Michigan University, and continued performing in concert into her eighties.

16. Lars Tornstam, "Maturing into geotranscendence," *The Journal of Transpersonal Psychology 43*, no. 2 (2011), pp. 166–180.

17. Flora R. Levin, *Greek Reflections on the Nature of Music* (New York, NY: Cambridge University Press, 2009).

18. Jet Propulsion Laboratory, NASA. https://voyager.jpl.nasa.gov/golden-reco rd/whats-on-the-record/music (accessed September 12, 2019).

19. Carl Sagan, F. D. Drake, Ann Druyan, Timothy Ferris, Jon Lomberg, and Linda Salzman Sagan, *Murmers of Earth: The Voyager Interstellar Record* (New York, NY: Random House, 1978).

20. Carl G. Jung, "The psychology of rebirth," *Volume 9, I, of the Collected Works of C. G. Jung*, 2nd ed. (Princeton, NJ: Princeton University Press, 1969), p. 134.

21. Muriel Rukeyser, *The Speed of Darkness* (New York: Random House, 1968), p. x.

Index

Made in the USA
Las Vegas, NV
08 March 2022

45240178R00148